THE PELICAN BOOK O...

GENERAL EDITOR : KENNETH ALLOTT

A363

VOLUME IV : PROSE OF THE ROMANTIC PERIOD

EDITED BY RAYMOND WRIGHT

THE PELICAN BOOK OF ENGLISH PROSE

GENERAL EDITOR : KENNETH ALLOTT

VOLUME IV

Prose of the Romantic Period

· 1780–1830 ·

EDITED BY RAYMOND WRIGHT

PENGUIN BOOKS

Penguin Books Ltd, Harmondsworth, Middlesex

u.s.a.: Penguin Books Inc., 3300 Clipper Mill Road, Baltimore 11, Md

CANADA: Penguin Books (Canada) Ltd, 178 Norseman Street,
Toronto 18, Ontario

AUSTRALIA: Penguin Books Pty Ltd, 762 Whitehorse Road,
Mitcham, Victoria

SOUTH AFRICA: Penguin Books (S.A.) Pty Ltd, Gibraltar House,
Regent Road, Sea Point, Cape Town

—

First published 1956

Made and printed in Great Britain
by The Whitefriars Press Ltd
London and Tonbridge

CONTENTS

CONTENTS

2. THE MOVEMENT OF IDEAS:

REFLECTION, ARGUMENT, EXHORTATION, SATIRE

CONTENTS

3. THE WORLD OF IMAGINATION, FEELING AND COMIC INVENTION: FICTION, HISTORICAL AND OCCASIONAL WRITING

CONTENTS

4. THE CRITICISM OF THE ARTS

CONTENTS

GENERAL INTRODUCTION

The Pelican Book of English Prose has the aim of bringing into focus for the ordinary reader nearly three hundred and fifty years of English prose: so that he may see for himself its variety and continuity in successive ages, the many purposes for which it has been employed (including the humbler ones), the prose styles thought expressive at different times, and the ruling interests and attitudes of particular periods with their associated changes of tone in the conduct of prose. This has involved some planning. An anthology is judged practically by what we can do with it. If it is to be read intelligently or used for study, not merely dipped into idly, it needs to support the reader's interest by a certain coherence and consistency of approach: that is to say, its contents must be properly arranged and introduced. The present anthology contains about 425,000 words of text exclusive of editorial matter and includes some three hundred writers who were at work between 1550 and 1880. These initial and terminal dates are plainly convenient: before 1550 prose cannot be read easily by the general reader without a glossary (and it will not be read, one suspects, with a glossary except by the serious student); after 1880 considerations of copyright become troublesome and begin to influence an editor's choice. The preliminary disposition of the material is in five volumes in chronological sequence, as follows:

I   Elizabethan and Jacobean prose (1550–1620)
II   Seventeenth-Century prose (1620–1700)
III Eighteenth-Century prose (1700–80)
IV Prose of the Romantic Period (1780–1830)
V   Victorian prose (1830–80)

Each volume is self-contained and independently edited, but

the unity of the whole anthology is preserved by a 'horizontal' classification which cuts across the 'vertical' chronological division just described. The anthology, then, is sub-divided both chronologically and, within each volume, by an arrangement of subject-matter in accordance with the following scheme:

1. The Picture of the Age: Scene, Personality, Event
2. The Movement of Ideas: Reflection, Argument, Exhortation, Satire
3. The World of Imagination, Feeling and Comic Invention: Fiction, Historical and Occasional Writing
4. The Criticism of the Arts

The editors of the separate volumes have found this scheme, which took its final form only after several revisions, sufficiently flexible; and it is hoped that it may provide a useful framework for the reader and enable him to grasp more rapidly the distinguishing characteristics of prose in each period. It was the general editor's task to see that the agreed scheme was followed and to act as a clearing-house for the suggestions and criticisms of his colleagues. The sharing among six editors of the task of reading and selecting pieces for the five volumes of the anthology has probably been an advantage. It has meant a wider and more accurate coverage of the enormous area of English prose between 1550 and 1880; and it has allowed particular sections of prose to be undertaken by editors whose interests are centred in the periods for which they are responsible. The disunity that might have resulted from the arrangement has been carefully guarded against: both by the adoption of the agreed scheme and by other means of ensuring a common approach which have still to be described.

Some of these means were mechanical. It was decided that a substantial proportion of the passages in each volume, usually selected from the more important writers, should be long enough to furnish material for an hour's discussion if the anthology should be used as a textbook. It was also thought desirable that the introductory essays to the five volumes should be mainly concerned with the discrimination of prose styles, and that they should all contain frequent references to the authors and extracts introduced. Again, it was proposed that in each volume passages should be chosen where possible to shed light on each other, and it was agreed that the value of the whole work would partly depend on the number of the relationships of this kind it was possible to establish. A good deal of effort lies behind whatever success has been achieved. For example, a dozen passages in Volume II bear on any discussion of political and theological attitudes in the Great Rebellion, Volumes III and IV have some nicely mixed specimens of political writing and also groups of passages which touch on marriage and the position of women, Volume I gives us Nashe and Gabriel Harvey on Nashe, Volume V Dickens and Walter Bagehot on Dickens. There are also links between the volumes – it is not an accident that a passage by Carlyle in Volume V should refer to an incident in Mungo Park's African travels which is reproduced in Volume IV. Some of these correspondences lie on the surface, as in the examples chosen, but many are more esoteric and will not be apparent until the anthology is actively used. In each volume the order of the passages in the first section, 'The Picture of the Age', is chronological, but the order in the other three sections – for the sake of these correspondences – offers what F. T. Palgrave calls 'gradations of feeling or subject'. Such gradations may or may not combine with a modified chronological plan.

More important than any of these means of ensuring singleness of approach has been the community of feeling among the editors about what an anthology of prose should be called on to illustrate. *The Pelican Book of English Prose* is not a collection of the best passages of English prose, or even, exclusively, of the best passages of the authors included in it – a collection on either principle would produce an effect less representative than the one aimed at. A common objection to prose anthologies is that their editors do not choose passages typical of the authors represented because they put an undue weight on 'fine writing'. From some anthologies one would naturally conclude that historians reserved all their energies for depicting battle-scenes, or that Lyly, Sir Thomas Browne and Landor were considerably more important as writers of prose than Hooker, Dryden and Gibbon. In contradistinction our working-hypothesis has been that prose should not be too self-conscious, that the writers of the best English prose usually had more on their minds than the problems of style, and that much respectable prose in every age is unmindful of the school-master's ferula.[1] Consequently, in compiling this anthology, we have been guided by the following principles:

1. To choose passages primarily for the interest of their subject-matter (on the assumption, which has been justified, that such passages will inevitably illustrate all the prominent varieties of prose style).

2. To choose from a particular author not his most detach-able pieces of fine writing, but passages which are typical of his normal manner when he is writing well.

3. To illustrate sparingly the 'purple passages' of English prose.

4. To include some prose at a pedestrian level of achieve-ment for its documentary value (more particularly in the first section of each volume).

The editors consider that these methods of selection give a

1. The degree of self-conscious organization that is 'natural' varies, of course, from age to age, and, in any age, according to literary kind (for example, a declamatory style is more natural in a pulpit or from the hustings than in a diary or private letter).

more accurate cross-section of English prose than is obtained from most anthologies,[1] and that the loss in serious prose-artistry is negligible. Nothing that has been said should be taken to imply a settled antipathy to ornate prose, but it is fair to admit that the editors are suspicious of its self-conscious varieties after the Restoration (while recognizing with New-man that some 'verbiage' may be the natural expression of a generous 'fullness of mind').

The Text. Modernization has been rejected and passages are reproduced with the spelling and punctuation of the copy-texts (except for the silent correction of misprints and the conservative emendation of misleading punctuation). Thus Elizabethan prose retains its 'dramatic' or haphazard pointing except in special instances, and Keats's difficulties with spelling are left to appear. The only passages given in a modernized form are those first printed long after their original composition, e.g. an Elizabethan diary first published in the middle of the nineteenth century. Some un-familiar words and phrases, which are naturally more frequent in Volumes I and II, are glossed briefly in footnotes where the context seems to require it – this is a matter that has been left to the individual editor's discretion – but no attempt has been made to supply a sense for all unusual words or to explain the many allusions.

The source of each passage is given at its foot, and the abbreviation of titles has been indicated (wherever possible the extended title has been preserved if of interest). First editions have usually been employed, but many passages included in the anthology were added by their authors to editions later

---

1. *The London Book of Prose* (1932), compiled by Professor Dobrée and Sir Herbert Read, is an obvious exception. Its excellence sets a standard for this kind of work.

than the first, or were revised through several editions, so that the preferred form of a passage may be found, for example, in a fifth edition. On the other hand, the unrevised version of a passage has sometimes been preferred by an editor for its freshness and unfamiliarity. The apparent anomalies in the choice of copy-texts are mostly explicable on such grounds, but there were a few occasions when a first edition would have been used if it had been available. The use of certain copyright material is acknowledged in a note at the end of each volume.

K. A.

INTRODUCTION

I

ALMOST all the passages included in this volume of *The Pelican Book of English Prose* were written within the lifetime of Coleridge (1772–1834) and may therefore be properly described as 'prose of the Romantic period', but only a minority of the extracts can be described without qualification as Romantic prose. Romanticism, which was a discernible trend before the period opened, did not become a dominant mode in prose all at once. Although the major authors represented, with the exception of Jane Austen, were in one or other of the acceptable senses Romantics, they were not so much drawing on a tradition as creating one, and even with them one must often hold on to certain mental reservations, as with Scott, whose subject-matter was new but whose style was hardly distinguishable from that of an eighteenth-century novelist, or as with Byron, who had an un-Romantic preference for satire. The poetry written between 1780 and 1830, or at least the greater part of that which is still read, was much more revolutionary than the prose of the period, even though in many cases the poet and the prose writer were the same person. Swift's plain style and Addison's elegance were still being recommended as models of English prose in Victorian times. It is true that before 1800 gentlemen were driving about the country in search of picturesque beauty (along the new roads which made such journeys possible), that mock-Gothic building had started, and that terror novels were in vogue, but these were the symptoms of the spread of a superficial eighteenth-century Romanticism, not of the mysticism, emotionalism and later cult of 'sensations' which were among the more important characteristics of Victorian

Romanticism in prose. The revolution of 1688 had heralded a society with values so stable that they were hardly questioned before 1789 and not much shaken until after Waterloo.

The literary revolution effected by Dryden and his successors had similar results. The mature and civilizing literature which the Augustans intended to produce was to be achieved by the study of classic originals, by cultivating grace and precision, by preserving decorum and avoiding extravagance. How important the Augustan achievement was in its effect on the conduct of prose can be suggested by quoting Johnson's well-known praise of Addison in *The Lives of the Poets*,

His prose is the model of the middle style [i.e. the intermediate style between the grand and the plain]; on grave subjects not formal, on light occasions not groveling; pure without scrupulosity, and exact without apparent elaboration; always equable, and always easy, without glowing words or pointed sentences . . .Whoever wishes to attain an English style, familiar but not coarse, and elegant but not ostentatious, must give his days and nights to the volumes of Addison.

Johnson's qualified approval of Swift's plain style as compared with Addison's elegance is symptomatic of the late-Augustan preference for a consciously artistic prose:

This easy and safe conveyance of meaning it was Swift's desire to attain, and for having attained he deserves praise, though perhaps not the highest praise. For purposes merely didactick, when something is to be told that was not known before, it is the best mode, but against that inattention by which known truths are suffered to lie neglected, it makes no provision; it instructs but does not persuade.

Johnson's criticism seems reactionary to the modern reader, as if he wanted to re-introduce the devices of rhetoric in place of the directness which Swift had achieved. (There is a connexion between classical rhetoric and an 'architectural' style such as Johnson's own.) What Johnson assumes is that matter and manner are separable, and that the latter can be adjusted for particular purposes.

Johnson's style was one of the most mannered which the second half of the eighteenth century produced. In spite of, or perhaps because of, its inversions, parallelisms and balanced polysyllables, it was an admirable style for conveying his authoritative judgements, although when used by other people it could be a weighty and imposing way of saying very little. Coleridge, in the course of lectures which he delivered in 1818, cavalierly disposed of Johnson, Gibbon and eighteenth-century prose in general, in the course of a paragraph:

After the Revolution ... a style was produced which by combining triteness of thought with singularity and excess of manner of expression, was calculated at once to soothe ignorance and to flatter vanity. The thought was carefully kept down to the immediate apprehension of the commonest understanding, and the dress was as anxiously arranged for the purpose of making the thought appear something very profound. The essence of this style consisted in a mock antithesis, that is, an opposition of mere sounds, in a rage for personification, the abstract made animate, far-fetched metaphors, strange phrases, metrical scraps, in every thing, in short, but genuine prose. Style is, of course, nothing else but the art of conveying the meaning appropriately and with perspicuity, whatever that meaning may be, and one criterion of style is that it shall not be translateable without injury to the meaning. Johnson's style has pleased many from the very fault of being perpetually translateable; he creates an impression of cleverness by never saying any thing in a common way. The best specimen of this manner is in Junius, because his antithesis is less merely verbal than Johnson's. Gibbon's manner is the worst of all; it has every fault of which this peculiar style is capable.[1]

This is the equivalent for prose of Wordsworth's attack on poetic diction in the preface to *Lyrical Ballads* (1800), with far

1. Lecture XIV.

less real provocation. It not only fails to do justice to the senatorial virtues of Johnson's grand manner and to Gibbon's more elegant variety of the same style, but it also ignores all the other possibilities of eighteenth-century prose, notably its capacity for irony, pathos, and the graces of informal narrative.

Burke's version of the grand manner was excluded from Coleridge's otherwise universal condemnation. Burke occasionally used Johnsonian antitheses, and phrases and clauses in parallel, but when he was at his best he was too passionately involved in his subject for such deliberate writing. When he was setting out maxims at the beginning of a speech or consciously using rhetorical devices he was not particularly convincing, and when, at the other extreme, he was so excited that his invective became strident and his imagery absurd, he was at his worst. His principal works, whether originally speeches or not, continually recall the spoken word, and he suffers a little from the limiting effects on perceptivity and sensitiveness of the language of oratory. (This is not a serious reservation in the case of Burke who, as Goldsmith said, 'too deep for his hearers, still went on refining'.) He rings the changes on argument, admonition, satire, political theory and historical retrospect, and returns to his main point repeatedly, not only for emphasis but to penetrate his subject further. De Quincey rightly picked on this capacity for organic development as the most distinctive feature of his style:

We may take the opportunity of noticing what it is that constitutes the peculiar and characterizing circumstances in Burke's manner of composition. It is this: that under his treatment every truth, be it what it may, every thesis of a sentence, *grows* in the very act of unfolding it. Take any sentence you please from Dr Johnson, suppose, and it will be found to contain a thought, good or bad, fully preconceived. Whereas in Burke, whatever may have been the preconception, it receives a new determination or inflection at every clause of the sentence. Some collateral adjunct of the main proposition, some temperament or restraint, some oblique glance at its remote affinities, will invariably be found to attend the progress of his sentences.[1]

His prose style, like Milton's, suggests effort, urgency, and deep conviction, and he has Milton's preference for vast numbers and panoramas rather than details.[2] Burke's conception of a nation bound together by immemorial duties and loyalties, his belief in an intuitive wisdom, and his profound distrust of 'geometrical politics', place him with Wordsworth and Scott among the Romantic conservatives, but his style is the last and the most complex of those that the eighteenth century produced. Along this line no further development was possible.

The other writers of political prose are, with one exception, undistinguished; they suffer by comparison with Burke as the historians suffer by comparison with Gibbon. Burke's manner was imitated for a time and then it shaded off into mere orotundity. The nearest approach to it in this selection, and it is not a very close one, is Windham's passionate attack on the Treaty of Amiens (p. 115), where the resemblance arises from a similarity of subject matter. Sir James Mackintosh, whose *Vindiciae Gallicae* (1791) was one of the best of the replies to Burke's *Reflections on the Revolution in France* (1790), was converted to the latter's style as well as to his political views, but declined into verbosity; Lord Brougham copied Burke, to no effect, when he wanted to be elaborately impressive. It is a pleasure to turn to Sydney Smith, whose brisk and yet elegant

1. 'Essay on Rhetoric' (1828).
2. Milton's power of suggesting the vast, the obscure, and the awe-inspiring was a constant reminder to his eighteenth-century readers of the sublimity not reducible within rules that the Augustans had missed. One of Burke's first publications was *A Philosophical Enquiry into the Origin of our Ideas of the Sublime and Beautiful* (1756).

manner at least makes no attempt to disguise the common-sensical simplicity of the matter. His fanciful wit and his puns link him with Charles Lamb and even with Thomas Hood. Of the 'written' styles, Godwin's is about the best. His *Political Justice* (1793) reads like a well-sustained argument, although it is difficult to understand why it should ever have moved his readers, who were not all as youthful and inflammable as Shelley, to enthusiasm. Bentham's usual style is probably the worst in the same category, though he could write well enough when he chose; he is remarkable as an inventor of officialese (*maximize* was one of his coinages) and for his inextricable sentences. It is difficult to frame a generalization to cover these examples; all that one can say is that political prose was losing its connexion with fine writing and passing into the hands of specialists. The difference between the gentlemanly style of the first edition of Malthus' *Essay on the Principle of Population* (1798) and the stiff 'professional' documentation of the second was perhaps a sign of the times.

The exception held over from the last paragraph is Cobbett, who belongs broadly to popular literature. He had a large following among the new reading-public, as Dickens had a few years later, and his tone is often that of an absurdly dogmatic schoolmaster. (His gospel of work and his manuals of self-help are perhaps more characteristic of the early-Victorian period than of his own.) His writing is occasionally so stressed with capitals, italics and exclamation marks that it shouts, but most of it is good plain prose, and some of it is excellent. Admittedly, the best passages are not extensive; his fads and crazes and his jibes at his enemies intrude too often. In the account of his ancestry, for example (p. 14), two fine paragraphs of autobiography written with a touching simplicity are separated by sneers at Benjamin Franklin. The reader tires of the endless references to the National Debt, the sprawling 'Wen' of Greater London, tithes and the good old days when the farm labourer had his belly full of beef and beer and not of tea and potatoes. On the credit side there are not only the autobiographical fragments and the descriptions of the countryside in *Rural Rides* (1830), where comments on the turnip crop and the types of soil are not incongruous, but also the passages where he is sustained by generous indignation. Cobbett's prose was that of a self-educated man to whom the classics meant nothing; it might have been described by a contemporary as a favourable example of 'the inartificial style'.

II

The two principal forms of Romantic fiction (as distinct from fiction of the Romantic period) were the novel of terror and the historical novel, which took as their customary subject-matter experience that lay at a tangent to the central interests of the Augustans. These new literary kinds were, in effect, revivals of the romance in forms suited to the conditions of the new age. The two types of story overlap in sensibility and subject at various points, but, briefly, the terror novel expresses an interest in the 'nightside of nature' and the unusual paths of sensibility which were ignored by the men of the Enlightenment, while the historical novel seeks refreshment in whatever is unfamiliar in time – most frequently in a 'Gothick' mediaevalism (not without its Hollywood elements). The novel of terror, which is represented in Part III of this volume by extracts from Ann Radcliffe, Mary Shelley and C. R. Maturin,[1] had its brief heyday in the period 1780–1830 and left traces on the poems of Coleridge and Keats: its prototype was, of course, Horace Walpole's pseudo-historical *Castle of Otranto* (1764). The true historical novel, a more serious

1. James Hogg's *Confessions of a Justified Sinner* (1824) is a late and much modified example of the type. For a passage from it see p. 205.

affair, became popular after the turn of the century with Sir Walter Scott and others, and was still one of the favourite kinds of fiction in Victorian times. A heightened style, whether formal, sensational or archaic, was often used in both genres. The Gothic novelist was occasionally the dupe of his own intimations of the marvellous, remote and terrible, but more often he worked as deliberately to impress his readers with his moonlit ruins and spectres as Edgar Allan Poe did when he constructed 'The Raven'. Grotesque diction and syntax in the historical novel (and in novels of terror with a historical background) have some excuse in the special problems of expression created for the novelist by the attempt to recreate the past.

Besides these two well-known kinds of Romantic fiction, the literary text-books also distinguish two lesser kinds, the doctrinaire novel and the regional novel. Bage's *Hermsprong* (1796) and John Galt's *Annals of the Parish* (1821) are, respectively, examples of these sub-varieties, both of which have non-Romantic elements. In *Hermsprong* there are 'Radical' overtones of Rousseau's ideas, but it is not – except occasionally in emphasis – particularly Romantic. The satirical tone is Voltairean in the passage given on p. 151. Galt's regional novels, or Maria Edgeworth's, may have had for the metropolitan reader the romantic attraction of simple lives passed in remote places, but they were in the main realistic novels of manners except for the pointing-up of oddities of dialect and behaviour. Scott's novels are evidence that the regional and historical categories overlap.

The novel proper, that is to say the novel which deals with contemporary manners and morals in contemporary language, was to all intents and purposes the creation of Fielding, Richardson, and their immediate successors. To say that their language was contemporary is not, however, to suggest that it was all of a piece. When the typical novelist of the seventeen-seventies copied from low life the language might be colloquial, but when he – or, more often, she – was passing moral judgements the writing would be measured and grave, and the dialogue used for the emotions of high life was often both wooden and high-flown. Fanny Burney's *Evelina* (1778) may be used to illustrate these points. Basically *Evelina* is a romance with an impudent baronet and a tyrannical grand-mother persecuting a motherless heroine, but incorporated with this material there are the realistic scenes from London life and the pictures of the Branghtons, the heroine's vulgar relatives, who seem to belong to another novel. Here is a fragment of dialogue between the hero, Lord Orville, and the heroine:

'You are going, then,' cried he, taking my hand, 'and you give me not the smallest hope of your return! – will you not, then, my too lovely friend! – will you not, at least, teach me, with fortitude like your own, to support your absence?'

'My Lord,' cried I, endeavouring to disengage my hand, 'pray let me go!'

'I will,' cried he, to my inexpressible confusion, dropping on one knee, 'if you wish to leave me!'

'Oh, my Lord,' exclaimed I, 'rise, I beseech you, rise! – such a posture to me! – surely your Lordship is not so cruel as to mock me!'

'Mock you!' repeated he earnestly, 'no I revere you!'

If the reader will turn to the extract entitled 'Evelina Ashamed of her Relatives' (p. 144), which is one of the Branghton scenes, the difference between the language thought suitable for emotional heroics and that of real life should be plain.

Contemporary readers, accustomed in fiction to extravag-ance of language such as Lord Orville's and Evelina's, might well have complained that there was no heightening of senti-ment in Jane Austen's novels, even in the love scenes. When Mr Knightley proposes to Emma Woodhouse he says, 'I can-not make speeches, Emma . . . If I loved you less, I might be able to talk about it more.' Instead of allowing Emma to make a direct reply, the novelist merely writes, 'What did she say? – Just what she ought of course. A lady always does. – She said enough to show there need not be despair – and to invite him to say more himself.' Pomposity, stale metaphors and over-elaborate sentences were reserved by Jane Austen for the speech of mean and foolish characters. Her own language was correct, lucid and largely unfigurative[1]; it was formal enough to render her occasional colloquialisms effective, but sufficiently flexible to make use of every depth of ironic device. Jane Austen wrote anti-romances, and *Sense and Sensibility* (1811) and *Northanger Abbey* (1818) offer telling criticisms of heightening the sentiments and mistaking romantic illusion for reality. The considerable positive virtues of her prose were the Augustan virtues of balance, proportion and good sense, and her moral standards were those of Dr Johnson. When Sir Thomas Bertram, in *Mansfield Park* (1814), admits to himself the errors he has made in bringing up his daughters, the language is like Johnson's, particularly in the grave use which is made of abstract terms:

They had been instructed theoretically in their religion, but never required to bring it into daily practice. To be distinguished for elegance and accomplishments – the authorized object of their youth – could have had no useful influence that way, no moral effect on the mind. He had meant them to be good, but his cares had been directed to the understanding and manners, not the disposition; and of the necessity of self-denial and humility, he feared they had never heard from any lips that could profit them.

We are so schooled *not* to take statements made in the novels at their face value – that is, to consider always their dramatic significance and the possibility of the author's withdrawal behind the ironic and the dramatic – that we are surprised to

1. There is a detailed account of Jane Austen's use of figurative language in Chapter III ('Style') of M. Lascelles' *Jane Austen and her Art* (1939).

find Jane Austen so willing to acknowledge, through Sir Thomas, the moral basis of her comedy. Fortunately there is little need here to recommend her novels: they are familiar to all classes of readers and she is by common consent the most finished and economical artist among English novelists.

It was not Scott's practice, as it was Jane Austen's, to keep his manuscripts by him for years and revise them minutely. His industry in writing and publishing left him no time to bend his mind to style, and he seems not to have cared much that this should be so. His careless prose matches his ramshackle plots; what there is of positive value in the novels lies elsewhere. It is the Romantic appeal of the remote past, his skill in describing battles and tourneys, and his detailed knowledge of ceremonies, fashions and sports, that we read the non-Scottish novels for, if we read them at all. They were written because Scott feared that the public, which he courted, might tire of his local material. In the course of reading these historical romances one may cease to notice or care about the stilted manner and the archaisms, but in a short extract they are obtrusive, as in this passage from *Ivanhoe* (1819) describing the attack on Torquilstone:

At this moment the besiegers caught sight of the red flag upon the angle of the tower which Ulrica had described to Cedric. The good yeoman Locksley was the first who was aware of it, as he was hasting to the outwork, impatient to see the progress of the assault.

'Saint George!' he cried, 'Merry Saint George for England! – To the charge, bold yeomen! – why leave ye the good knight and noble Cedric to storm the pass alone? – make in, mad priest, show thou canst fight for thy rosary – make in, brave yeomen! – the castle is ours, we have friends within – See yonder flag, it is the appointed signal – Torquilstone is ours! – Think of honour, think of spoil – One effort, and the place is ours!'

Mr Robert Liddell rightly blames Scott for doing much to make the Wardour Street language of *Ivanhoe* popular; he says, 'It did incalculable damage to the English language in the nineteenth century, and it is not dead yet; it has so completely permeated English letters, from translations of the Greek and Latin classics, down to advertisements, that many people are incapable of seeing anything objectionable in it.'[1] But he also points to the close reproduction of the dialogue of a past age in Scott's Border novels as one of the three useful ways in which historical dialogue can be written, adding that of course it can only be done successfully when the age is not too far distant. This is one reason why the novels set in the recent past (notably *The Heart of Midlothian*, *The Antiquary*, *Old Mortality* and *Guy Mannering*) are so much better than Scott's other works. In writing them he was drawing on oral tradition transmitted in the vernacular, and on his own experience. It is in these novels, too, that the width and charity of his human sympathies are most amiably expressed. The sober dignity of the fisherman's funeral in *The Antiquary* (see p. 175) could only have been achieved by a writer with as little personal vanity as Scott.

The remaining novelists who are represented in the text must be neglected here in favour of two other writers of imaginative prose: Peacock and Landor. Thomas Love Peacock, it is true, wrote novels, but they are of a peculiar kind. Parties of oddities are assembled in country houses, there are various comic incidents, the young people fall in love and so on, but the plots are hardly more than settings for the imaginary conversations which are the reason for their existence. In these extravagant and high-spirited conversations Peacock satirized all the intellectual crazes and crotchets of his time from a standpoint which is both Romantic and Attic. (The phrase is inadequate, but Peacock cannot easily be forced into any single pigeon-hole. It was typical of him that he should laugh at Romanticism and be Shelley's close friend.) Much of

1. *Some Principles of Fiction* (1953), p. 91.

the subject-matter of his satire had only a temporary importance, but occasionally, as in Mr Cranium's lecture on phren-
ology (p. 172), a topical subject could be used as the starting
point for a general attack on human folly and nastiness. On
these occasions one realizes that his ironic detachment was
not complete. When he uses precise and unevocative language
for a satirical purpose Peacock can remind us of Jane Austen,
but their tempers were utterly different. She had neither his in-
fatuated enjoyment of prejudices nor his sentiment. If we have
to look for Peacock's affiliations in English literature we may
refer tentatively to *Tristram Shandy*, where – along with much
else, for Sterne has more than a satirical interest in human
quirks and foibles – we find the same riding of hobbyhorses
by amateur philosophers instead of a plot.

At its most characteristic Landor's style in *Imaginary Conversations*, the *Pentameron*, and elsewhere, has a close heaviness
and unnaturalness. The heaviness is sometimes due to the
difficulty of finding a style apt for historical dialogue,[1] and
sometimes to the laborious accumulation of epigrams, but
the basic reason is Landor's intense and exclusive devotion to
'lapidary perfection' for its own sake. It is one of the curiosi-
ties of literature that a man so unrestrained in his behaviour
and so radical in his political feelings should have been so
devoted to cultivating classical balance and restraint in his
prose. But the truth is that the classicism is only skin-deep, the
restraint hardly more than a transparent device for a thumping
emotional emphasis. Landor's admirers have claimed that he
added a new cadence to English prose, and in some sort this
is true and perhaps historically important; but his detractors,
who are rather more numerous, have replied that he had

1. The style had to be capable of being varied – or, at least, of being
tricked out to give an appearance of variety – for conversations in
different periods and places. Sophocles, Hooker and the Duchess of
Fontanges were not to be indistinguishable.

little to say and a humourless and too monotonous way of saying it. In 'dream' passages the artistic contrivance is too insistent: the effect is often as if Gibbon had suffered a sea-change and become addicted to reverie. It seems to me that Landor's reputation for new rhythms and cadences can rest only on the well-known poetic passages such as 'Boccaccio's Dream of Fiammetta' (p. 227) and those occasional stretches of prose in the dialogues where he manipulates language to squeeze out rather 'precious' essences of sublimity, pathos and nostalgia. Even with such passages we tend to say not 'How pathetic (or sublime) that is' but 'How cleverly he has gone about to suggest pathos (or sublimity) here' – see, for example, the famous conversation between Henry VIII and Anne Boleyn. The critical and witty dialogues are better, but their prose is less noticeable. Landor has his place in the develop-ment of the prose-poetry that De Quincey and others were simultaneously discovering how to write, but careful selec-tions from his work in anthologies often impose an exag-gerated idea of his quality and importance as a prose-writer.

III

The miscellaneous prose of the years 1780–1830 is neither as extensive nor as varied as that of the following period, but even so there is a considerable amount of it which is still very readable. There is not much prose of real excellence to be found in the works of the historians, theologians or scien-tists, but the letters, travel-books, diaries and essays compen-sate for these shortcomings. The best letters of the period were undoubtedly written by the poets, and among them those of Cowper, Byron and Keats are outstanding. Cowper's effort-less letters are written in the style of an eighteenth-century gentleman well-acquainted with Addison; they are for the most part playful or confiding in tone, but there are occasional melancholy passages and glimpses of despair. Byron's letters are colloquial; he assumes a variety of Byronic poses and at the same time confirms Lady Blessington's impression of him as the Regency dandy in exile who is not quite aware that manners have changed at home. His accounts of his amours in Venice are masterly examples of comic narrative. The letters of Keats are the best of all and can need no recommendation. They are disorderly, misspelt and sometimes incoherent, as he delightedly pursues one notion after another. If there is any single impression that one gets from them it is that of Keats in process of discovering his own nature and its capabilities, and preparing himself modestly yet confidently to be a better poet than he had time given him to become. Mr T. S. Eliot's remarks on Keats as a letter-writer cannot be bettered:

The letters are certainly the most notable and the most important ever written by any English poet ... His letters are what letters ought to be; the fine things come in unexpectedly, neither introduced nor shown out, but between trifle and trifle ... There is hardly one statement of Keats about poetry, which, when considered carefully and with due allowance for the difficulties of communication, will not be found to be true; and what is more, true for greater and more mature poetry than anything that Keats ever wrote.[1]

When we turn to the diaries of the time we find that some of them have more than a period interest and qualify for higher praise than 'well-written'. If the whole of Fanny Burney's diary had been up to the standard of the passages describing her life at Court, her reputation would not have to rest on *Evelina*. Dorothy Wordsworth's Alfoxden and Grasmere journals have a distinct interest apart from their connexion with the poetry of Wordsworth and Coleridge. The journal entries given under 'Meadow, Grove, and Stream' (p. 155) show something of D. H. Lawrence's gift for describ-

1. *The Use of Poetry and the Use of Criticism*, Chapter V.

ing landscape; she has his eye for colour and detail as well as his knack of suggesting that the landscape is new-minted. Of the travel-books represented in the text it seems to me that William Beckford's *Dreams, Waking Thoughts and Incidents* (1783) and Shelley's *Letters from Abroad* (first published in 1840) are the most remarkable. Beckford writes as an eighteenth-century Romantic playing with an emotion he thinks he ought to feel ('The sky was hung with storms, and a pale moon seemed to advance with difficulty amongst broken and tempestuous clouds. It was an hour to reap plants with brazen sickles, and to meditate upon revenge'); Shelley's descriptions of Swiss glaciers and the ruins of Rome are genuine Romantic 'word-painting' where the writer is emotionally involved with his subject matter. M. G. Lewis's *Journal of a West India Proprietor* (1834) can also be recommended; it is surprisingly unaffected and sincere, coming as it does from the silliest of the terror-novelists.

The essays of Charles Lamb, Hazlitt and De Quincey depend on style and on the conscious exploitation of personality (real or assumed) for some of their interest. As a prose-writer Lamb played an unconscious part in restoring the emotional overtones of English by imitating seventeenth-century models such as Sir Thomas Browne, Burton and Fuller, and as a critic he helped to restore to currency the minor Elizabethan and Jacobean dramatists. Hazlitt, in his essay 'On Familiar Style', defends Lamb's 'Elia' manner on the rather odd ground that it 'neutralizes' the peculiarity of his ideas. He says:

Mr Lamb is the only imitator of old English style I can read with pleasure; and he is so thoroughly imbued with the spirit of his authors that the idea of imitation is almost done away. There is an inward unction, a marrowy vein, both in the thought and feeling, an intuition, deep and lively, of his subject, that carries off any quaintness or awkwardness arising from an antiquated style and dress. The matter

To arrive at Coleridge is to realize how far one has travelled from Dr Johnson, and one way of describing the changes which began during this confused transitional period would have been, at the risk of absurdity, to compare the two. Many eighteenth-century writers depended on assumptions about the suitability of various prose styles for various purposes which they shared with their relatively small but sophisticated public; writers in the early part of the nineteenth century were rather more concerned with subject-matter and emotional expression than with appropriate style. They wrote for an ever-increasing audience which was less homogeneous in its interests and education than that of their predecessors. It has already been suggested that there was no revolt of the prose writers against the eighteenth century comparable to that of the poets (and their revolt is much more obvious now than it was then). The only remarkable change before 1830 was the decline of the 'grand' style and of most forms of contrived architectural prose written for what may be called public or didactic purposes. Coleridge's objection to Johnson's 'translateableness' was, however, an indication of a growing distrust of the sharp distinction between matter and manner which was made in the eighteenth century, and of a Romantic preference for spontaneity rather than formality and contrivance.

RAYMOND WRIGHT

THE PICTURE OF THE AGE:
SCENE, PERSONALITY, EVENT

A GENTLEMAN'S GENTLEMAN

(1778)

WE went by sea from Boulogne to Dover. Sir John left his French post-chaise at Boulogne, and we arrived in London the first day of January, 1778, at Mrs. Elliott's house in Brewer-street, Golden-square. Sir John was in perfect health; he stopped in London one week; and as he was desirous of seeing his relations in Scotland, and having no further occasion for me, he paid me off. He desired me to send his baggage by sea, and he went with a gentleman in a post-chaise to Allanbank, in Berwickshire, in Scotland: so we parted, and I was out of a place. I took things very easy, as it was a good time of the year to get one. I went after none but a place with a single man, as I wanted for nothing. I had my own lodging, with my own furniture, and whether I was at home or abroad, I paid my good old landlady, a widow woman; and she made of it what she could in my absence; therefore she took care of my goods. I dressed in the same manner I went abroad. Having good cloaths, with rich vests, I wore my hanger, a silk bag at my hair; and laced ruffles; but when I went after a place I dressed in the common way. If it rained, I wore my fine silk umbrella, that the people would call after me, What,

Frenchman, why do not you get a coach? In particular the hackney coachmen and hackney chairmen would call after me; but I, knowing the men well, went straight on, and took no notice.

John Macdonald
Travels in Various Parts of Europe, Asia, and Africa (1790)

PEACE WITH AMERICA AND HER ALLIES

(1783)

IT is reported among persons of the best intelligence at Olney – the barber, the schoolmaster, and the drummer of a corps quartered at this place, that the belligerent powers are at last reconciled, the articles of the treaty adjusted, and that peace is at the door. I saw this morning, at nine o'clock, a group of about twelve figures very closely engaged in a conference, as I suppose, upon the same subject. The scene of consultation was a blacksmith's shed, very comfortably screened from the wind, and directly opposed to the morning sun. Some held their hands behind them, some had them folded across their bosom, and others had thrust them into their breeches pockets. Every man's posture bespoke a pacific turn of mind; but the distance being too great for their words to reach me, nothing transpired. I am willing, however, to hope that the secret will not be a secret long, and that you and I, equally interested in the event, though not, perhaps, equally well-informed, shall soon have an opportunity to rejoice in the completion of it. The powers of Europe have clashed with each other to a fine purpose; that the Americans, at length declared independent, may keep themselves so, if they can; and that what the parties, who have thought proper to dispute upon that point, have wrested from each other in the course of the conflict, may be, in the issue of it, restored to the proper owner. Nations may be guilty of a conduct that would render an individual infamous for ever; and yet carry their heads high, talk of their glory, and despise their neighbours. Your opinions and mine, I mean our political ones, are not exactly of a piece, yet I cannot think otherwise upon this subject than I have always done. England, more, perhaps, through the fault of her generals, than her councils, has in some instances acted with a spirit of cruel animosity she was never chargeable with till now. But this is the worst that can be said. On the other hand, the Americans, who, if they had contented themselves with a struggle for lawful liberty, would have deserved applause, seem to me to have incurred the guilt of parricide, by renouncing their parent, by making her ruin their favourite object, and by associating themselves with her worst enemy, for the accomplishment of their purpose. France, and of course Spain, have acted a treacherous, a thievish part. They have stolen America from England, and whether they are able to possess themselves of that jewel or not hereafter, it was doubtless what they intended. Holland appears to me in a meaner light than any of them. They quarrelled with a friend for an enemy's sake. The French led them by the nose, and the English have thrashed them for suffering it. My views of the contest being, and having been always such, I have consequently brighter hopes for England than her situation some time since seemed to justify. She is the only injured party. America may, perhaps, call her the aggressor; but if she were so, America has not only repelled the injury, but done a greater. As to the rest, if perfidy, treachery, avarice, and ambition can prove their cause to have been a rotten one, those proofs are found upon them. I think, therefore, that whatever scourge may be prepared for England, on some future day, her ruin is not yet to be expected.

Acknowledge, now, that I am worthy of a place under the

shed I described, and that I should make no small figure among the *quidnuncs* of Olney.

William Cowper

Letter to the Rev. John Newton (26 January, 1783)
from *The Correspondence of William Cowper*, edited
by T. Wright (1904)

THE POET AS CLIENT

(1788)

WHEN I had the honor of being introduced to you at Athole-house, I did not think of putting that acquaintance so soon to the test. – When Lear, in Shakespeare, asks old Kent why he wished to be in his service, he answers, "Because you have that in your face which I could like to call Master;" for some such similar reason, Sir, do I now solicit your Patronage. – You know, I dare say, of an application I lately made to your Board, to be admitted an Officer of Excise. – I have, according to form, been examined by a Supervisor, and today I give in his Certificate with a request for an Order for instructions. – In this affair, if I succeed, I am afraid I shall but too much need a patronising Friend. – Propriety of conduct as a Man, and fidelity and attention as an Officer, I dare engage for; but with any thing like business I am totally unacquainted. – The man who till within these eighteen months was never the wealthy master of ten guineas, can be but ill-acquainted with the busy routine. – I had intended to have closed my late meteorous appearance on the stage of Life, in the country Farmer; but after discharging some filial and fraternal claims, I find I could only fight for existence in that miserable manner, which I have lived to see throw a venerable Parent in the jaws of a Jail; where, but for the Poor Man's last and often best friend, Death, he might have ended his days.—

4

I know, Sir, that to need your goodness is to have a claim on it; may I therefore beg your Patronage to forward me in this affair till I be appointed to a Division; where, by the help of rigid Economy, I shall try to support that Independence so dear to my soul, but which has too often been so distant from my situation.

Robert Burns

Letter to Robert Graham (n.d.) from *The Letters of Robert Burns*, edited by J. De L. Ferguson (1931)

An Encounter with George III

(1789)

He asked me some questions that very greatly distressed me, relating to information given him in his illness, from various motives, but which he suspected to be false, and which I knew he had reason to suspect: yet was it most dangerous to set anything right, as I was not aware what might be the views of their having been stated wrong. I was as discreet as I knew how to be, and I hope I did no mischief; but this was the worst part of the dialogue.

He next talked to me a great deal of my dear father, and made a thousand inquiries concerning his 'History of Music'. This brought him to his favourite theme, Handel; and he told me innumerable anecdotes of him, and particularly that celebrated tale of Handel's saying of himself, when a boy, "While that boy lives, my music will never want a protector." And this, he said, I might relate to my father.

Then he ran over most of his oratorios, attempting to sing the subjects of several airs and choruses, but so dreadfully hoarse that the sound was terrible.

Dr. Willis, quite alarmed at this exertion, feared he would do himself harm, and again proposed a separation. "No! no!

no!" he exclaimed, "not yet; I have something I must just mention first."

Dr. Willis, delighted to comply, even when uneasy at compliance, again gave way.

The good King then greatly affected me. He began upon my revered old friend, Mrs. Delany; and he spoke of her with such warmth – such kindness! "She was my friend!" he cried, "and I loved her as a friend! I have made a memorandum when I lost her – I will show it you."

He pulled out a pocket-book, and rummaged some time, but to no purpose.

The tears stood in his eyes – he wiped them, and Dr. Willis again became very anxious. "Come, sir," he cried, "now do you come in and let the lady go on her walk, – come, now, you have talked a long while, – so we'll go in – if your Majesty pleases."

"No, no!" he cried, "I want to ask her a few questions; – I have lived so long out of the world, I know nothing!"

This touched me to the heart. We walked on together, and he inquired after various persons, particularly Mrs. Boscawen, because she was Mrs. Delany's friend! Then, for the same reason, after Mr. Frederick Montagu, of whom he kindly said, "I know he has a great regard for me, for all he joined the opposition." Lord Grey de Wilton, Sir Watkin Wynn, the Duke of Beaufort, and various others, followed.

He then told me he was very much dissatisfied with several of his state officers, and meant to form an entire new establishment. He took a paper out of his pocket-book, and showed me his new list.

This was the wildest thing that passed; and Dr. John Willis now seriously urged our separating; but he would not consent; he had only three more words to say, he declared, and again he conquered.

He now spoke of my father, with still more kindness, and

told me he ought to have had the post of Master of the Band, and not that little poor musician Parsons, who was not fit for it: "But Lord Salisbury," he cried, "used your father very ill in that business, and so he did me! However, I have dashed out his name, and I shall put your father's in, – as soon as I get loose again!"

This again – how affecting was this!

"And what," cried he, "has your father got, at last? nothing but that poor thing at Chelsea? O fie! fie! fie! But never mind! I will take care of him! I will do it myself!"

Then presently he added, "As to Lord Salisbury, he is out already, as this memorandum will show you, and so are many more. I shall be much better served; and when once I get away, I shall rule with a rod of iron!"

This was very unlike himself, and startled the two good doctors, who could not bear to cross him, and were exulting at my seeing his great amendment, but yet grew quite uneasy at his earnestness and volubility.

Frances Burney (later Madame d'Arblay)

Diary and Letters of Madame d'Arblay, edited
by her niece (1842–6), Vol. IV

A VISIT TO ROTHERHAM

(1789)

BY a country of much beauty, hill, dale and wood, we enter'd the town of Rotherham, and went to what is call'd the best inn, the Crown, but a more dreary, blacker, tumble-down, old casemented ruin cou'd not be. In a front room, upstairs, uneven as a plough'd field, we drank tea, and then with melancholy faces survey'd our shatter'd beds, windows broken, paper hanging down, blankets, and curtains torn; and everything number'd for sale, if purchasers can be found:

for the master of the inn has got a patent (a very odd one) for making marbles for children, which he can do of all descriptions, so well, and expeditiously, that he will soon supply all the school boys of the world.

I proposed a walk; when we pass'd thro' the church yard, by the church of great size, and with a very lofty steeple, to the stone bridge, over the River Don; below which is a fine broad fall of water.

On the opposite side over the river, is a new-built, flourishing town, arising from the cannon founderies, and great iron works, established by Mr. Walker; who not only maintains the neighbourhood, but has so, honourably, enriched himself, that he and several of his sons live in magnificent villas, built on several eminences about the town; where, I said that they ought to invent signals for invitations, and announcements of all kinds.

In Mr. Walker's work-yard, we survey'd an arch of an iron bridge, just cast; and with much pleasure the surrounding population, who are render'd warm, and happy, by the coal pits, which are every where by the road side; and down which we peep'd, and flung stones: how the little children escape falling into them is miraculous! All the people employ'd in the founderies are allowed coals; the other poor may have a cart-load for 5 shillings! From the hill, at our walks end, we cou'd discover Sheffield spires, at the end of the vale; in front the sun setting; behind us the town of Nottingham; and in the valley beneath, the furnaces vomiting forth their amazing fires, which make this country in an eternal smoke. – We made our walk as long as possible, from the dread of our dreary inn; where we supp'd on some thick chops, and un-scraped asparagus.

The Honourable John Byng (later Viscount Torrington)
The Torrington Diaries, edited by
C. B. Andrews (1935), Vol. II

ROYAL PRISONERS

JANUARY 4th, 1790. After breakfast, walk in the gardens of the Thuilleries, where there is the most extraordinary sight that either French or English eyes could ever behold at Paris. The King, walking with six grenadiers of the *milice bourgeoise*, with an officer or two of his household, and a page. The doors of the gardens are kept shut in respect to him, in order to exclude every body but deputies, or those who have admission-tickets. When he entered the palace, the doors of the gardens were thrown open for all without distinction, though the Queen was still walking with a lady of her court. She also was attended so closely by the *gardes bourgeoise*, that she could not speak, but in a low voice, without being heard by them. A mob followed her, talking very loud, and paying no other apparent respect than that of taking off their hats wherever she passed, which was indeed more than I expected. Her majesty does not appear to be in health; she seems to be much affected, and shews it in her face; but the King is as plump as ease can render him. By his orders, there is a little garden railed off, for the Dauphin to amuse himself in, and a small room is built in it to retire to in case of rain; here he was at work with his little hoe and rake, but not without a guard of two grenadiers. He is a very pretty good-natured-looking boy, of five or six years old, with an agreeable countenance; wherever he goes, all hats are taken off to him, which I was glad to observe. All the family being kept thus close prisoners (for such they are in effect) afford, at first view, a shocking spectacle; and is really so, if the act were not absolutely necessary to effect the revolution; this I conceive to be impossible; but if it were necessary, no one can blame the people for taking every measure possible to secure that liberty they had seized in the violence of a revolution. At such a moment, nothing is to be condemned but what endangers the national freedom. I must, however, freely own, that I have my doubts whether this treatment of the royal family can be justly esteemed any security to liberty; or, on the contrary, whether it were not a very dangerous step, that exposes to hazard whatever had been gained. I have spoken with several persons to-day, and have started objections to the present system, stronger even than they appear to me, in order to learn their sentiments; and it is evident, they are at the present moment under an apprehension of an attempt towards a counter revolution. The danger of it very much, if not absolutely, results from the violence which has been used towards the royal family. The National Assembly was, before that period, answerable only for the permanent constitutional laws passed for the future: since that moment, it is equally answerable for the whole conduct of the government of the state, executive as well as legislative.

Arthur Young

*Travels ... Undertaken with a View of Ascertaining
the Cultivation, Wealth, Resources, and National
Prosperity of ... France (1792)*

METHODIST MEETINGS

(1791)

THE late Mr. Wesley [1] instituted amongst his people, besides the public preachings, several kinds of private meetings; and as the *prayer-meeting* is the least private of any of them, I will first take notice of that.

To the prayer-meetings they often invited people who were not of their society: an hymn was first sung, and then they all knelt, and the first person that felt a motion, made an extemporary prayer, when he had done another began, and so on, for about two hours. But it so happened sometimes,

1. John Wesley died 1791.

that one of the brethren began to pray without having *the gift* of prayer (as they call it), and then he often stuck fast, like some of the young orators at Coach-maker's Hall, &c. Prayer-meetings were held in such high esteem amongst them that they asserted, more were "*born again*," and more "*made free* from all the remains of sin," or in other words of their own, "made *perfect* as God is perfect," in these kinds of meeting, than at public preaching, &c. Thus, as Pomfret says,

"The spirits heated will strange things produce."

But 'tis impossible for you, my friend, to form any just idea of these assemblies, except you had been present at them: one wheedles and coaxes the Divine Being, in his addresses; another is amorous and luscious; and a third so rude and commanding, he will even tell the Deity that he must be *a liar* (dreadful!) if he does not grant all they ask. In this manner will they work up one another's imaginations until they may actually be said to be in a state of intoxication.

They have another kind of private meeting after the publick preaching on Sunday evenings, in which the preacher meets all the members of the society, who stay behind after the general congregation is dismissed. To this society Mr. Wesley gave such advice as he deemed better suited to a godly few than to a promiscuous multitude of "*outward court* worshippers."

Their *Love-feast* is also a private meeting of as many members of the community as please to attend; and they generally come from all parts, within several miles of the place where love-feasts are held.

When all are met they alternately sing and pray; and such amongst them as think that their *experience* (as they call it) is remarkable, stand up in their place and relate all the transactions between God, the devil, and their souls. At such seasons as this I have heard many of them declare they had just received the pardon of all their sins, while Brother such-a-one was in prayer; another would then get up and assert that he was just at that instant made perfectly free from sin; and then the Spirit is supposed to be very powerfully at work amongst them; and such a *unison* of sighing and *groaning* succeeds, that you would think they had all lost their senses.

James Lackington
Memoirs (1791)

A COUNTRY PARSON

(1791)

MAR. 6, Sunday. . . . I read Prayers, Preached, and churched a Woman this Afternoon at Weston Church. The woman being poor returned the fee to her – Mr. and Mrs. Custance at Church, as was also my Niece, it being a fine Day and good walking. A young Sow of mine had for her first Litter – 7. Piggs.

Mar. 7, Monday. . . . Washing Week at our House and a fine Day. The small-Pox spreads much in the Parish. Abigail Roberts's Husband was very bad in it in the natural way, who was supposed to have had it before and which he thought also. His Children are inoculated by Johnny Reeve, as are also Richmonds Children near me. It is a pity that all the Poor in the Parish were not inoculated also. I am entirely for it.

Mar. 8, Tuesday. . . . Gave poor Roberts one of my old Shirts to put on in the small-Pox – His, poor Fellow, being so extremely coarse and rough, that his having the small-Pox so very full, his coarse Shirt makes it very painful to him. I sent his Family a Basket of Apples and some black Currant Robb. There are many, many People in the Parish yet (who) have never had the Smallpox. Pray God all may do well that have it or shall have it. Went this Afternoon and saw poor old John Peachman Who is very lame, found him unable to walk and having no relief from the Parish gave him money. Called also at Tom Carys Shop and left some money for Roberts's Familys Use for such useful things as they might want and they have. Recd. for 4 Pints ½ Butter, at 9d. 0.3.4. Lady Durrant at Weston House.

Mar. 9, Wednesday. . . . Henry Case of this Parish who lately lost a Cow came to my House this morning with a Petition to give him something towards buying another, as he was a Parishioner and a Tenant of mine for some Glebe Land, and having also a Wife and many Children and keeping an aged Mother, I gave him towards the same 0.10.6. Had a Note this Evening from Mr. and Mrs. Custance requesting our Company to Dinner to Morrow at West House to meet Lady Durrant &c. I sent a Note back that we would wait on them. Mr. Custance's Groom with three of Lady Durrants Servant Men came with the above Note.

Mar. 10, Thursday. . . . Mr. Jeanes called here this morning and stayed about an Hour, but Nancy being dressing would not make her appearance. We dined and spent the Afternoon at Weston House with Mr. and Mrs. Custance, Lady Durrant, Old Mrs. Collyer and Mr. Press Custance. After Coffee we all got to Loo limited to half a Crown. I lost at it 0.6.0. Nancy won three Shillings. We went and returned in Mr. Custances Coach. My right Eye-lid very much swelled and inflamed having a Stiony on it, very painful all day.

Mar. 11, Friday. . . . Mem. The Stiony on my right Eye-lid still swelled and inflamed very much. As it is commonly said that the Eye-lid being rubbed by the tail of a black Cat would do it much good if not entirely cure it, and having a black Cat, a little before dinner I made a trial of it, and very soon after dinner I found my Eye-lid much abated of the swelling and almost free from Pain. I cannot therefore but conclude it to be of the greatest service to a Stiony on the Eye-lid. Any other Cats Tail may have the above effect in all prob-ability – but I did my Eye-lid with my own black Tom Cat's Tail. Recd. for 2. Pints ½ of Butter at 9d. 0.1.10½. Lady Dur-rant and old Mrs. Collyer leave Weston to day. The latter is breaking up very fast.

James Woodforde

The Diary of a Country Parson, edited by J. Beresford (1927)

COBBETT ON HIS ANCESTORS

(1796)

WITH respect to my ancestors, I shall go no further back than my grandfather, and for this plain reason, that I never heard talk of any prior to him. He was a day-labourer, and I have heard my father say, that he worked for one farmer from the day of his marriage to that of his death, upwards of forty years. He died before I was born, but I have often slept be-neath the same roof that had sheltered him, and where his widow dwelt for several years after his death. It was a little thatched cottage with a garden before the door. It had but two windows; a damson tree shaded one, and a clump of filberts the other. Here I and my brothers went every Christmas and Whitsuntide, to spend a week or two, and torment the poor old woman with our noise and dilapidations. She used to give us milk and bread for breakfast, an apple pudding for our dinner, and a piece of bread and cheese for supper. Her fire was made of turf, cut from the neighbouring heath, and her evening light was a rush dipped in grease.

How much better is it, thus to tell the naked truth, than to descend to such miserable shifts as Doctor Franklin has had recourse to, in order to persuade people, that his fore-fathers were men of wealth and consideration. Not being able to refer his reader to the herald's office for proofs of the fame and antiquity of his family, he appeals to the etymology of his name, and points out a passage in an obsolete book, whence he has the conscience to insist on our concluding, that, in the Old English language, a *Franklin* meant a man of *good reputation and of consequence.* According to Dr. Johnson, a Franklin was what we now call a gentleman's steward or land-bailiff, a personage one degree above a bum-bailiff, and that's all.

Every one will, I hope, have the goodness to believe, that my grandfather was no philosopher. Indeed he was not. He never made a lightning rod, nor bottled up a single quart of sun-shine in the whole course of his life. He was no almanack-maker, nor quack, nor chimney-doctor, nor soap-boiler, nor ambassador, nor printer's devil: neither was he a deist, and all his children were born in wedlock. The legacies he left, were, his scythe, his reap-hook, and his flail; he bequeathed no old and irrecoverable debts to an hospital: he never *cheated the poor during his life*, nor *mocked them in his death.* He has, it is true, been suffered to sleep quietly beneath the green-sord; but, if his descendants cannot point to his statue over the door of a library, they have not the mortification to hear him daily accused of having been a whore-master, a hypocrite, and an infidel.

My father, when I was born, was a farmer. The reader will easily believe, from the poverty of his parents, that he had received no very brilliant education: he was, however, learned, for a man in his rank of life. When a little boy, he drove plough for two-pence a day, and these his earnings were appropriated to the expenses of an evening school. What a village school-master could be expected to teach, he had learnt; and had besides considerably improved himself, in several branches of the mathematicks. He understood land-surveying well, and was often chosen to draw the plans of

green-sord] greensward

15

disputed territory: in short, he had the reputation of possessing experience and understanding, which never fails, in England, to give a man in a country place, some little weight with his neighbours. He was honest, industrious, and frugal; it was not, therefore, wonderful, that he should be situated in a good farm, and happy in a wife of his own rank, like him, beloved and respected.

So much for my ancestors, from whom, if I derive no honour, I derive no shame.

William Cobbett

The Life and Adventures of Peter Porcupine (1796)

THE RITES OF HOSPITALITY

(1796)

I WAITED more than two hours, without having an opportunity of crossing the river; during which time the people who had crossed, carried information to Mansong the King, that a white man was waiting for a passage, and was coming to see him. He immediately sent over one of his chief men, who informed me that the king could not possibly see me, until he knew what had brought me into his country; and that I must not presume to cross the river without the king's permission. He therefore advised me to lodge at a distant village, to which he pointed, for the night; and said that in the morning he would give me further instructions how to conduct myself. This was very discouraging. However, as there was no remedy, I set off for the village; where I found, to my great mortification, that no person would admit me into his house. I was regarded with astonishment and fear, and was obliged to sit all day without victuals, in the shade of a tree; and the night threatened to be very uncomfortable, for the wind rose, and there was great appearance of a heavy rain; and the wild beasts are so very numerous in the neighbourhood, that I should have been under the necessity of climbing up the tree, and resting amongst the branches. About sunset, however, as I was preparing to pass the night in this manner, and had turned my horse loose, that he might graze at liberty, a woman, returning from the labours of the field, stopped to observe me, and perceiving that I was weary and dejected, inquired into my situation, which I briefly explained to her; whereupon, with looks of great compassion, she took up my saddle and bridle, and told me to follow her. Having conducted me into her hut, she lighted up a lamp, spread a mat on the floor, and told me I might remain there for the night. Finding that I was very hungry, she said she would procure me something to eat. She accordingly went out, and returned in a short time with a very fine fish; which, having caused to be half broiled upon some embers, she gave me for supper. The rites of hospitality being thus performed towards a stranger in distress; my worthy benefactress (pointing to the mat, and telling me I might sleep there without apprehension) called to the female part of her family, who had stood gazing on me all the while in fixed astonishment, to resume their task of spinning cotton; in which they continued to employ themselves great part of the night. They lighted their labour by songs, one of which was composed extempore; for I was myself the subject of it. It was sung by one of the young women, the rest joining in a sort of chorus. The air was sweet and plaintive, and the words, literally translated, were these. — "The winds roared, and the rains fell. — The poor white man, faint and weary, came and sat under our tree. — He has no mother to bring him milk; no wife to grind his corn. *Chorus.* Let us pity the white man; no mother has he, &c. &c." Trifling as this recital may appear to the reader, to a person in my situation, the circumstance was affecting in the highest degree.

I was oppressed by such unexpected kindness; and sleep fled from my eyes. In the morning I presented my compassionate landlady with two of the four brass buttons which remained on my waistcoat; the only recompence I could make her.

Mungo Park
Travels in the Interior of Africa (1799)

The Petition of the Spithead Mutineers

(1797)

To the Right Honourable the Lords Commissioners of the Admiralty.

We, the Seamen of his Majesty's navy, take the liberty of addressing your Lordships in an humble petition, shewing the many hardships and oppressions we have laboured under for many years, and which we hope your Lordships will redress as soon as possible.

We flatter ourselves that your Lordships, together with the nation in general, will acknowledge our worth and good services, both in the American war and the present; for which service your Lordships' petitioners do unanimously agree in opinion, that their worth to the nation, and laborious industry in defence of their country, deserve some better encouragement than that we meet at present, or from any we have experienced. We your petitioners, do not boast of our good services for any other purpose, than that of putting you and the nation in mind of the respect due to us; nor do we ever intend to deviate from our former character; so far from any thing of that kind, or that an Englishman or men should turn their coats; we likewise agree in opinion, that we should suffer double the hardships we have hitherto experienced, before we would suffer the crown of England to be in the least imposed upon by that of any other power in the world; we therefore beg leave to inform your Lordships of the grievances which we at present labour under.

We your humble petitioners relying, that your Lordships will take into early consideration the grievances of which we complain; and do not in the least doubt but your Lordships will comply with our desires, which are every way reasonable.

The first grievance which we have to complain of is, that our wages are too low, and ought to be raised, that we might be better able to support our wives and families in a manner comfortable, and whom we are in duty bound to support as far as our wages will allow, which, we trust, will be looked into by your Lordships and the honourable House of Commons in parliament assembled.

We your petitioners beg that your Lordships will take into consideration the grievances of which we complain, and now lay before you.

First, that our provisions be raised to the weight of sixteen ounces to the pound, and of a better quality; and that our measures may be the same as those used in the commercial trade of this country.

Secondly, that your petitioners request your honours will please to observe, there should be no flour served while we are in harbour, or any port whatever under the command of the British flag; and also that there be granted a sufficient quantity of vegetables of such kind as may be the most plentiful in the ports to which we go, which we grievously complain and lie under the want of.

Thirdly, that your Lordships will be pleased seriously to look into the state of the sick on board his Majesty's ships, that they be better attended to, and that they may have the use of such necessaries as are allowed for them in time of their sickness; and that these necessaries be not on any account embezzled.

Fourthly, that your Lordships will be so kind as to look into this affair, which is no ways unreasonable; and that we may be looked upon as a number of men standing in defence of our country; and that we may in some wise have granted an opportunity to taste the sweets of liberty on shore when in any harbour; and when we have completed the duty of our ships, after our return from sea; and that no man may incroach upon his liberty, there shall be a boundary limited, and those trespassing any further, without a written order from the commanding officer, shall be punished according to the rules of the navy; which is a natural request, and congenial to the heart of man, and certainly to us, that you make the boast of being the guardians of the land.

Fifthly, that if any man is wounded in action, his pay be continued until he is cured and discharged; and if any ship has any real grievances to complain of, we hope your Lordships will readily redress them, as far as in your power, to prevent any disturbances.

It is also unanimously agreed by the fleet, that from this day no grievance shall be received, in order to convince the nation at large, that we know when to cease to ask, as well as when to begin; and that we ask nothing but what is moderate, and may be granted, without detriment to the nation, or injury to the service.

> Given on board the Queen Charlotte, by
> the Delegates of the Fleet, this 18th day
> of April, 1797.

Anon.

Text from *The Naval Chronology*,
edited by Isaac Schomberg (1815)

DISARMING THE IRISH
(1798)

BANDON, 27th May 1798. – I received orders in April to disarm the two Carberries, which is all the country which lies from Crookham along the coast to Bandon. Sir Ralph issued a notice commanding the people to deliver their arms to the different magistrates or officers commanding the troops, informing them that if they did so they should be not only unmolested, but protected; that if they did not, or persevered in committing outrages, the troops would be sent to live upon them at free quarters, and other severe measures taken to reduce them to obedience. I afterwards issued a similar notice to this for my district, fixing the 2nd May as the date on or before which, if the arms were not delivered in, the troops should act; and to convince them that I was serious, I marched five companies of Light Infantry and a detachment of Dragoons throughout the country to Skull to be ready to act. I expected that upon the appearance of the troops the people would have given in their arms, but it had no effect. I spoke to the priests, and took every pains to represent the folly of holding out and of forcing me to resort to violent measures. I directed Major Nugent, with the troops quartered in Skibbereen, to march on the 2nd May into free quarters in the parish of Coharagh, which had been much disturbed; and I placed the five Light Companies in different divisions from Ballydehob to Ballydevilin, with orders to forage the whole of the country from Crookhaven to within seven miles of Skibbereen.

My orders were to treat the people with as much harshness as possible, as far as words and manner went, and to supply themselves with whatever provisions were necessary to enable them to live well. My wish was to excite terror, and by that means obtain our end speedily. I thought this better than to act more mildly, and be obliged to continue for any time the real oppression; and, as I was present everywhere myself, I had no doubt of being able to prevent any great abuses by the troops. The second day the people, after denying that they had any arms, began to deliver them in. After four days we extracted sixty-five muskets. Major Nugent in Coharagh was obliged to burn some houses before he could get a single arm. They then delivered in a number of pikes. I then removed the troops to another part of the country, always entreating that the arms might be delivered without forcing me to ruin them. Few parishes had the good sense to do so; such as did escaped. The terror was great. The moment a red coat appeared everybody fled. I was thus constantly employed for three weeks, during which I received about 800 pikes and 3400 stand of arms, the latter very bad. The better sort of people seemed all delighted with the operation except when it touched their own tenants, by whose ruin they saw they themselves must suffer, but they were pleased that the people were humbled, and would be civil. I found only two gentlemen who acted with liberality or manliness; the rest seemed in general to be actuated by the meanest motives. The common people have been so ill-treated by them, and so often deceived, that neither attachment nor confidence any longer exists. They have yielded in this instance to force, are humbled, but irritated to a great degree, and unless the gentlemen change their conduct and manner towards them, or Government steps in with regulations for the protection of the lower from the upper order, the pike will appear again very soon.

Sir John Moore

The Diary of Sir John Moore, edited
by J. F. Maurice (1904), Vol. I

A REMINISCENCE OF BOSWELL

(3 AUG. 1798) Asked Weld at Debrett's if he knew Boswell. He had met him at coffee-houses, &c. where B— used to drink hard and sit late. It was his custom during the sessions, to dine daily with the Judges, invited or not. He obtruded himself everywhere. Lowe (mentioned by him in his life of Johnson) once gave me a humorous picture of him. Lowe had requested Johnson to write him a letter, which Johnson did, and Boswell came in, while it was writing. His attention was immediately fixed, Lowe took the letter, retired, and was followed by Boswell. "Nothing," said Lowe, "could surprise me more. Till that moment he had so entirely overlooked me, that I did not imagine he knew there was such a creature in existence; and he now accosted me with the most overstrained and insinuating compliments possible." "How do you do, Mr. Lowe? I hope you are very well, Mr. Lowe. Pardon my freedom, Mr. Lowe, but I think I saw my dear friend, Dr. Johnson, writing a letter for you" – "Yes, Sir" – "I hope you will not think me rude, but if it would not be too great a favour, you would infinitely oblige me, if you would just let me have a sight of it. Every thing from that hand, you know, is so inestimable." – "Sir, it is on my own private affairs, but" – "I would not pry into a person's affairs, my dear Mr. Lowe; by any means. I am sure you would not accuse me of such a thing, only if it were no particular secret" – "Sir, you are welcome to read the letter." – "I thank you, my dear Mr. Lowe, you are very obliging, I take it exceedingly kind." (having read) "It is nothing, I believe, Mr. Lowe, that you would be ashamed of" – "Certainly not" – "Why then, my dear Sir, if you would do me another favour, you would make the obligation eternal. If you would but step to Peele's coffee-house with me, and just suffer me to make a copy of it, I would do any thing in my power to oblige you." – "I was

overcome," said Lowe, "by this sudden familiarity and con-
descension, accompanied with bows and grimaces. I had no
power to refuse; we went to the coffee-house, my letter was
presently transcribed, and as soon as he had put his document
in his pocket, Mr. Boswell walked away, as erect and as
proud as he was half an hour before, and I ever afterwards
was unnoticed."

Thomas Holcroft

Memoirs . . . written by Himself, and continued to the Time of
his Death from his Diary, Notes, and Other Papers (1816) [1]

THE YOUNGER PITT

(1800)

As his reasonings, even so is his eloquence. One character per-
vades his whole being. Words on words, finely arranged, and
so dexterously consequent, that the whole bears the semblance
of argument, and still keeps awake a sense of surprise; but
when all is done, nothing rememberable has been said; no
one philosophical remark, no one image, not even a pointed
aphorism. Not a sentence of Mr. Pitt's has ever been quoted,
or formed the favourite phrase of the day – a thing unexampled
in any man of equal reputation. But while he speaks, the
effect varies according to the character of his auditor. The
man of no talent is swallowed up in surprise; and when the
speech is ended, he remembers his feelings, but nothing distinct of that which produced them – (how opposite an effect
to that of nature and genius, from whose works the idea still
remains, when the feeling is passed away – remains to connect
itself with the other feelings, and combined with new impressions!) The mere man of talent hears him with admira-

---

1. Continued by William Hazlitt.

tion – the mere man of genius with contempt – the philosopher neither admires nor contemns, but listens to him with a
deep and solemn interest, tracing in the effects of his eloquence
the power of words and phrases, and that peculiar constitution
of human affairs in their present state, which so eminently
favours this power.

Such appears to us to be the prime minister of Great
Britain, whether we consider him as a statesman or as an
orator. The same character betrays itself in his private life;
the same coldness to realities, and to all whose excellence
relates to reality. He has patronised no science, he has raised
no man of genius from obscurity; he counts no one prime
work of God among his friends. From the same source he
has no attachment to female society, no fondness for children,
no perceptions of beauty in natural scenery; but he is fond of
convivial indulgences, of that stimulation, which, keeping
up the glow of self-importance and the sense of internal
power, gives feelings without the mediation of ideas .

These are the elements of his mind; the accidents of his
fortune, the circumstances that enabled such a mind to acquire
and retain such a power, would form a subject of a philosophical history, and that too of no scanty size. We can
scarcely furnish the chapter of contents to a work, which
would comprise subjects so important and delicate, as the
causes of the diffusion and intensity of secret influence; the
machinery and state intrigue of marriages; the overbalance of
the commercial interest; the panic of property struck by the
late revolution; the short-sightedness of the careful; the carelessness of the far-sighted; and all those many and various
events which have given to a decorous profession of religion,
and a seemliness of private morals, such an unwonted weight
in the attainment and preservation of public power. We are
unable to determine whether it be more consolatory or
humiliating to human nature, that so many complexities

of event, situation, character, age, and country, should be necessary in order to the production of a Mr. Pitt.

Samuel Taylor Coleridge

Morning Post (19 March, 1800) from *Essays on his Own Times*, edited by S. Coleridge (1850)

A HOLIDAY IN KESWICK

(1802)

SINCE the date of my last letter, I have been a traveller. A strong desire seized me of visiting remote regions. My first impulse was to go and see Paris. It was a trivial objection to my aspiring mind, that I did not understand a word of the language, since I certainly intend some time in my life to see Paris, and equally certainly intend never to learn the language; therefore that could be no objection. However, I am very glad I did not go, because you had left Paris (I see) before I could have set out. I believe, Stoddart promising to go with me another year, prevented that plan. My next scheme (for to my restless ambitious mind London was become a bed of thorns) was to visit the far-famed peak in Derbyshire, where the Devil sits, they say, without breeches. *This* my purer mind rejected as indelicate. And my final resolve was, a tour to the lakes. I set out with Mary to Keswick, without giving Coleridge any notice, for my time, being precious, did not admit of it. He received us with all the hospitality in the world, and gave up his time to show us all the wonders of the country. He dwells upon a small hill by the side of Keswick, in a comfortable house, quite enveloped on all sides by a net of mountains: great floundering bears and monsters they seem'd, all couchant and asleep. We got in in the evening, travelling in a post chaise from Penrith, in the midst of a gorgeous sunshine, which transmuted all the mountains into colours, purple, &c. &c. We thought we had got into fairy land. But that went off (and it never came again; while we stayed we had no more fine sunsets); and we entered Coleridge's comfortable study just in the dusk, when the mountains were all dark with clouds upon their heads. Such an impression I never received from objects of sight before, nor do I suppose I can ever again. Glorious creatures, fine old fellows, Skiddaw, &c. I never shall forget ye, how ye lay about that night, like an intrenchment; gone to bed, as it seemed for the night, but promising that ye were to be seen in the morning. Coleridge had got a blazing fire in his study, which is a large, antique, ill-shaped room, with an old-fashioned organ, never play'd upon, big enough for a church, shelves of scattered folios, an Eolian harp, and an old sofa, half bed, &c. And all looking out upon the fading view of Skiddaw, and his broad-breasted brethren: what a night! Here we staid three full weeks, in which time I visited Wordsworth's cottage, where we stayed a day or two with the Clarksons (good people, and most hospitable, at whose house we tarried one day and night), and saw Lloyd. The Wordsworths were gone to Calais. They have since been in London, and past much time with us: he is now gone into Yorkshire to be married. So we have seen Keswick, Grasmere, Ambleside, Ulswater, (where the Clarksons live), and a place at the other end of Ulswater; I forget the name; to which we travelled on a very sultry day, over the middle of Helvellyn. We have clambered up to the top of Skiddaw, and I have waded up the bed of Lodore. In fine, I have satisfied myself that there is such a thing as that which tourists call *romantic*, which I very much suspected before: they make such a spluttering about it, and toss their splendid epithets around them, till they give as dim a light as at four o'clock next morning the lamps do after an illumination. Mary was excessively tired, when she got about half way up Skiddaw, but we came to a cold rill, (than which nothing can be imagined more cold, running over cold stones), and with the reinforcement of a draught of cold water, she surmounted it most manfully. O, its fine black head, and the bleak air atop of it, with a prospect of mountains all about and about, making you giddy; then Scotland afar off, and the border countries so famous in song and ballad! It was a day that will stand out, like a mountain, I am sure, in my life. But I am returned, (I have now been come home near three weeks – I was a month out), and you cannot conceive the degradation I felt at first, from being accustomed to wander free as air among mountains, and bathe in rivers without being controul'd by any one, to come home and *work*. I felt very *little*. I had been dreaming I was a very great man. But that is going off, and I find I shall conform in time to that state of life to which it has pleased God to call me. Besides, after all, Fleet Street and the Strand are better places to live in for good and all than amidst Skiddaw.

Charles Lamb

Letter to Thomas Manning (24 September, 1802) from The Letters of Charles Lamb, edited by T. N. Talfourd (1837)

BOTANY BAY

(1803)

WHY we are to erect penitentiary houses and prisons at the distance of half the diameter of the globe, and to incur the enormous expence of feeding and transporting their inhabitants to, and at such a distance, it is extremely difficult to discover. It certainly is not from any deficiency of barren islands near our own coast, nor of uncultivated wastes in the interior; and if we were sufficiently fortunate to be wanting in such species of accommodation, we might discover in Canada, or the West Indies, or on the coast of Africa, a climate malignant enough, or a soil sufficiently sterile, to revenge all the injuries which have been inflicted on society by pick-pockets, larcenists, and petty felons. – Upon the foundation of a new colony, and especially one peopled by criminals, there is a disposition in Government (where any circumstance in the commission of the crime affords the least pretence for the commutation) to convert capital punishments into transportation; and by these means to hold forth a very dangerous, though certainly a very unintentional, encouragement to offences. And when the history of the colony has been attentively perused in the parish of St. Giles, the ancient avocation of picking pockets will certainly not become more discreditable from the knowledge, that it may eventually lead to the possession of a farm of a thousand acres on the river Hawkesbury. Since the benevolent Howard attacked our prisons, incarceration has become not only healthy, but elegant; and a county-jail is precisely the place to which any pauper might wish to retire to gratify his taste for magnificence as well as for comfort. Upon the same principle, there is some risk that transportation will be considered as one of the surest roads to honour and to wealth; and that no felon will hear a verdict of '*not guilty*,' without considering himself as cut off in the fairest career of prosperity. It is foolishly believed, that the colony of Botany Bay unites our moral and commercial interests, and that we shall receive hereafter an ample equivalent, in bales of goods, for all the vices we export. Unfortunately, the expence we have incurred in founding the colony, will not retard the natural progress of its emancipation, or prevent the attacks of other nations, who will be as desirous of reaping the fruit, as if they had sown the seed. It is a colony, besides, begun under every possible disadvantage; it is too distant to be long governed, or well defended; it is undertaken, not by the voluntary association of individuals, but by Government, and by means of compulsory labour. A nation must, indeed, be redundant in capital, that will expend it where the hopes of a just return are so very small.

It may be a curious consideration, to reflect what we are to do with this colony when it comes to years of discretion. Are we to spend another hundred millions of money in discovering its strength, and to humble ourselves again before a fresh set of Washingtons and Franklins? The moment after we have suffered such serious mischief from the escape of the old tiger, we are breeding up a young cub, whom we cannot render less ferocious, or more secure. If we are gradually to manumit the colony, as it is more and more capable of protecting itself, the degrees of emancipation, and the periods at which they are to take place, will be judged of very differently by the two nations. But we confess ourselves not to be so sanguine as to suppose, that a spirited and commercial people would in spite of the example of America, ever consent to abandon their sovereignty over an important colony, without a struggle. Endless blood and treasure will be exhausted to support a tax on kangaroos' skins; faithful Commons will go on voting fresh supplies to support a *just and necessary* war; and Newgate, then become a quarter of the world, will evince a heroism, not unworthy of the great characters by whom she was originally peopled.

Sydney Smith

Review of D. Collins's *Account of the English
Colony of New South Wales* (1798–1802) from
The Edinburgh Review (April, 1803)

SHERIDAN AT BRIGHTON

(1805)

AT last Sheridan made himself so ill with drinking, that he came to us soon after breakfast one day, saying he was in a perfect fever, desiring he might have some table beer, and declaring that he would spend that day with us, and send his excuses by Bloomfield for not dining at the Pavilion. I felt his pulse, and found it going tremendously, but instead of beer, we gave him some hot white wine, of which he drank a bottle, I remember, and his pulse subsided almost instantly. . . . After dinner that day he must have drunk at least a bottle and a half of wine. In the evening we were all going to the Pavilion, where there was to be a ball, and Sheridan said he would go home, i.e., to the Pavilion (where he slept) and would go quietly to bed. He desired me to tell the Prince, if he asked me after him, that he was far from well, and was gone to bed.

So when supper was served at the Pavilion about 12 o'clock, the Prince came up to me and said:

'What the devil have you done with Sheridan to-day, Creevey? I know he has been dining with you, and I have not seen him the whole day.'

I said he was by no means well and had gone to bed; upon which the Prince laughed heartily, as if he thought it all fudge, and then, taking a bottle of claret and glass, he put them both in my hands and said:

'Now Creevey, go to his bedside and tell him I'll drink a glass of wine with him, and if he refuses, I admit he must be damned bad indeed.'

I would willingly have excused myself on the score of his being really ill, but the Prince would not believe a word of it, so go I must. When I entered Sheridan's bedroom, he was in bed, and, his great fine eyes being instantly fixed upon me, he said: –

'Come, I see this is some joke of the Prince, and I am not in a state for it.'

I excused myself as well as I could, and as he would not touch the wine, I returned without pressing it, and the Prince seemed satisfied he must be ill.

About two o'clock, however, the supper having been long over, and everybody engaged in dancing, who should I see standing at the door but Sheridan, powdered as white as snow, as smartly dressed as ever he could be from top to toe. . . . I joined him and expressed my infinite surprise at this freak of his. He said:

'Will you go with me, my dear fellow, into the kitchen, and let me see if I can find a bit of supper.'

Having arrived there, he began to play off his cajolery upon the servants, saying if he was the Prince they should have much better accommodation, &c., &c., so that he was surrounded by supper of all kinds, every one waiting upon him. He ate away and drank a bottle of claret in a minute, returned to the ballroom, and when I left it between three and four he was dancing.

Thomas Creevey

The Creevey Papers..., edited by
H. Maxwell (1903), Vol. I

NELSON AT TRAFALGAR
(1805)

HE wore that day, as usual, his admiral's frock coat, bearing on the left breast four stars, of the different orders with which he was invested. Ornaments which rendered him so conspicuous a mark for the enemy, were beheld with ominous apprehensions by his officers. It was known that there were riflemen on board the French ships; and it could not be doubted but that his life would be particularly aimed at. They communicated their fears to each other; and the surgeon, Mr. Beatty, spoke to the chaplain, Dr. Scott, and to Mr. Scott, the public secretary, desiring that some person would entreat him to change his dress, or cover the stars: but they knew that such a request would highly displease him. "In honour I gained them," he had said when such a thing had been hinted to him formerly, "and in honour I will die with them." Mr. Beatty, however, would not have been deterred by any fear of exciting his displeasure, from speaking to him himself upon a subject, in which the weal of England as well as the life of Nelson was concerned, but he was ordered from the deck before he could find an opportunity. This was a point upon which Nelson's officers knew that it was hopeless to remonstrate or reason with him; but both Blackwood, and his own captain, Hardy, represented to him how advantageous to the fleet it would be for him to keep out of action as long as possible; and he consented at last to let the Leviathan and the Téméraire, which were sailing abreast of the Victory, be ordered to pass ahead. Yet even here the last infirmity of this noble mind was indulged; for these ships could not pass ahead if the Victory continued to carry all her sail; and so far was Nelson from shortening sail, that it was evident he took pleasure in pressing on, and rendering it impossible for them to obey his own orders. A long swell was setting into the bay of Cadiz: our ships, crowding all sail, moved majestically before it, with light winds from the south-west. The sun shone on the sails of the enemy; and their well formed line, with their numerous three-deckers, made an appearance which any other assailants would have thought formidable; – but the British sailors only admired the beauty and the splendour of the spectacle; and, in full confidence of winning what they saw, remarked to each other, what a fine sight yonder ships would make at Spithead!

The French admiral, from the Bucentaure, beheld the new manner in which his enemy was advancing, Nelson and Collingwood each leading his line; and, pointing them out to his officers, he is said to have exclaimed, that such conduct could not fail to be successful. Yet Villeneuve had made his own dispositions with the utmost skill, and the fleets under his command waited for the attack with perfect coolness. Ten minutes before twelve they opened their fire. Eight or nine of the ships immediately ahead of the Victory, and across her bows, fired single guns at her, to ascertain whether she was yet within their range. As soon as Nelson perceived that their shot passed over him, he desired Blackwood, and Captain Prowse, of the Sirius, to repair to their respective frigates; and, on their way, to tell all the captains of the line of battle ships that he depended on their exertions; and that, if by the prescribed mode of attack they found it impracticable to get into action immediately, they might adopt whatever they thought best, provided it led them quickly and closely alongside an enemy. As they were standing on the front of the poop, Blackwood took him by the hand, saying, he hoped soon to return and find him in possession of twenty prizes. He replied, "God bless you, Blackwood; I shall never see you again."

Robert Southey
The Life of Nelson (1813)

CHILDREN IN THE FACTORIES

(1807)

MR. — remarked that nothing could be so beneficial to a country as manufactures. "You see these children, sir," said he. "In most parts of England poor children are a burthen to their parents and to the parish; here the parish, which would else have to support them, is rid of all expense; they get their bread almost as soon as they can run about, and by the time they are seven or eight years old bring in money. There is no idleness among us: – they come at five in the morning; we

34

allow them half an hour for breakfast, and an hour for dinner; they leave work at six, and another set relieves them for the night; the wheels never stand still." I was looking, while he spoke, at the unnatural dexterity with which the fingers of these little creatures were playing in the machinery, half giddy myself with the noise and the endless motion: and when he told me there was no rest in these walls, day nor night, I thought that if Dante had peopled one of his hells with children, here was a scene worthy to have supplied him with new images of torment.

"These children, then," said I, "have no time to receive instruction." "That, sir," he replied, "is the evil which we have found. Girls are employed here from the age you see them till they marry, and then they know nothing about domestic work, not even how to mend a stocking or boil a potatoe. But we are remedying this now, and send the children to school for an hour after they have done work." I asked if so much confinement did not injure their health. "No," he replied, "they are as healthy as any children in the world could be. To be sure, many of them as they grew up went off in consumptions, but consumption was the disease of the English." I ventured to inquire afterwards concerning the morals of the people who were trained up in this monstrous manner, and found, what was to be expected, that in consequence of herding together such numbers of both sexes, who are utterly uninstructed in the commonest principles of religion and morality, they were as debauched and profligate as human beings under the influence of such circumstances must inevitably be; the men drunken, the women dissolute; that however high the wages they earned, they were too improvident ever to lay-by for a time of need; and that, though the parish was not at the expense of maintaining them when children, it had to provide for them in diseases induced by their mode of life, and in premature debility and old age;

the poor-rates were oppressively high, and the hospitals and workhouses always full and overflowing. I inquired how many persons were employed in the manufactory, and was told, children and all about two hundred. What was the firm of the house? – There were two partners. So! thought I, – a hundred to one!

"We are well off for hands in Manchester," said Mr. —; "manufactures are favourable to population, the poor are not afraid of having a family here, the parishes therefore have always plenty to apprentice, and we take them as fast as they can supply us. In new manufacturing towns they find it difficult to get a supply. Their only method is to send people round the country to get children from their parents. Women usually undertake this business; they promise the parents to provide for the children; one party is glad to be eased of a burthen, and it answers well to the other to find the young ones in food, lodging and clothes, and receive their wages." "But if these children should be ill-used?" said I. "Sir," he replied, "it never can be the interest of the women to use them ill, nor of the manufacturers to permit it."

It would have been in vain to argue had I been disposed to it. Mr. — was a man of humane and kindly nature, who would not himself use any thing cruelly, and judged of others by his own feelings. I thought of the cities in Arabian romance, where all the inhabitants were enchanted: here Commerce is the queen witch, and I had no talisman strong enough to disenchant those who were daily drinking of the golden cup of her charms.

'Don Manuel Alvarez Espriella' (Robert Southey)
Letters from England (1807)

36

A Very Strong Constitution

(1807)

MARCH 2. – Carlisle sd. He was one of the Surgeons who attended Mr. Richardson who at the end of the last Summer was wounded in a duel with Baron Hompesch. He was shot *through the body*, the ball passing through the Liver, Lungs, & grasing some of the Vessels near the heart. – On receiving the wound, He fell, and was convulsed, & for an hour appeared to be dying, but afterwards recovered His senses, & was brought to His lodgings in Parliament street & was able to walk from the carriage to an apartment on the ground floor, & to assist in undressing Himself. – His constitution being very strong He was able to endure the vast evacuations that could alone save his life by preventing inflammation & fever, as had suppuration taken place His death wd. have been certain. – In 13 days 236 ounces of blood were taken from his *arm*, besides 3 quarts of blood from his *side*. He was reduced to the lowest state possible witht. extinguishing life. For the 5 first days He had no sustenance allowed Him, & then only a piece of toasted bread which had been steeped in water. – Some female friends at one period having observed Him to be very low, gave him ½ a pint of milk porridge, which soon raised His pulse from 76 to 120 and it became necessary to bleed Him twice to prevent the worst consequences.

At last He recovered & is now quite well & may live 30 years longer, but He is an intemperate man, and associating with Officers at Woolwich has since been twice drunk, & been as many times bled. He is a younger brother of a person of good fortune in Kent, & has an estate of His own. – He is a Boxer; and *Hompesch* is a Duellist. In the quarrel between them in a street in London he knocked *Hompesch* down once or twice, & as a blow given in *Germany*, cannot be expiated but by the death of one of the parties, *Hompesch* since Richardson's recovery has consulted military persons, "whether He ought not to challenge him again." – Hompesch behaved very ill at the Duel. His pistol when fired a second or third time only *flashed in the pan*, but the second of Richardson attending to what He considered to be the Laws of Duelling, instantly appealed to the Baron's *Second*, That He ought not to fire again before Richardson had pulled His trigger. While words were passing between them the Baron levelled His pistol & shot Richardson. He is said to be a paltry character.

Joseph Farington
The Farington Diary, edited by J. Grieg (1924), Vol. IV

Parliamentary Elections

(1807)

Any thing like election in the plain sense of the word is unknown in England. Members are never chosen for parliament as deputies were for a Cortes, because they are the fittest persons to be deputed. Some seats are private property; – that is, the right of voting belongs to a few householders, sometimes not more than half-a-dozen, and of course these votes are commanded by the owner of the estate. The fewer they are, the more easily they are managed. Great part of a borough in the west of England was consumed some years ago by fire, and the lord of the manor would not suffer the houses to be rebuilt for this reason. If such an estate be to be sold, it is publicly advertised as carrying with it the power of returning two members; sometimes that power is veiled under the modest phrase of *a valuable appendage to the estate*, or *the desirable privilege of nominating to seats in a certain assembly*. Government hold many of these boroughs, and individuals buy in at others.

The price is as well known as the value of land, or of stock, and it is not uncommon to see a seat in a certain house advertised for in the public newspapers. In this manner are a majority of the members returned. You will see then that the house of commons must necessarily be a manageable body. This is as it should be; the people have all the forms of freedom, and the crown governs them while they believe they govern themselves. Burleigh foresaw this, and said that to govern *through* a parliament was the securest method of exercising power.

In other places, where the number of voters is something greater, so as to be too many for this kind of quiet and absolute control, the business is more difficult, and sometimes more expensive. The candidate then, instead of paying a settled sum to the lord of the borough, must deal individually with the constituents, who sell themselves to the highest bidder. Remember that an oath against bribery is required! A common mode of evading the letter of the oath is to lay a wager. "I will bet so much," says the agent of the candidate, "that you do not vote for us." "Done," says the voter free-man, – goes to the hustings, gives his voice, and returns to receive the money, not as the price of his suffrage, but as the bet which he has won. As all this is in direct violation of law, though both parties use the same means, the losing one never scruples to accuse his successful opponent of bribery, if he thinks he can establish the charge; and thus the mystery of iniquity is brought to light. It is said that at Aylesbury a punch-bowl full of guineas stood upon the table in the committee-room, and the voters were helped out of it. The price of votes varies according to their number. In some places it is as low as forty shillings, in others, at Ilchester for instance, it is thirty pounds. "Thirty pounds," said the apothecary of the place on his examination, "is the price of an Ilchester voter." When he was asked how he came to know the sum so accurately, he replied, that he attended the families of the voters professionally, and his bills were paid at election times with the money. A set of such constituents once waited upon the member whom they had chosen, to request that he would vote against the minister. "D—m you!" was his answer: "What! have I not bought you? And do you think I will not sell you?"

'Don Manuel Alvarez Espriella' (Robert Southey)
Letters from England (1807)

BULL-BAITING AND BOXING

(1807)

You may well conceive of what character the popular amusements needs must be, in a country where there is nothing to soften the manners or ameliorate the condition of the poor. The practice of bull-baiting is not merely permitted, it is even enjoined by the municipal law in some places. Attempts have twice been made in the legislature to suppress this barbarous custom: they were baffled and ridiculed, and some of the most distinguished members were absurd enough and hard-hearted enough to assert, that if such sports were abolished there would be an end of the national courage. Would to Heaven that this were true! that English courage had no better foundation than brutal ferocious cruelty! We should no longer be insulted in our ports, and our ships might defy their buccaneering cruisers. Do not suppose that this bull-baiting has any the smallest resemblance to our bull-feasts. – Even these I should agree with the Conde de Noroña, and with the Church, in condemning as wicked and inhuman; but there is a splendour in the costume, a gaiety in the spectacle, a skill and a courage displayed in the action, which afford some apology for our countrymen, whereas this English sport is even more cowardly than the bull-fights of the Portugueze. The men are exposed to no danger whatever; they fasten the animal to a ring, and the amusement is to see him toss the dogs, and the dogs lacerate his nostrils, till they are weary of torturing him, and then he is led to the slaughter-house to be butchered after their clumsy and cruel method. The bear and the badger are baited with the same barbarity; and if the rabble can get nothing else, they will divert themselves by worrying cats to death.

But the great delight of the English is in boxing, or pugilism, as it is more scientifically denominated. This practice might easily be suppressed; it is against the laws; the magistrates may interfere if they please; and its frequency therefore, under such circumstances, is an irrefragable proof of national barbarity. Cudgel-playing, quarter-staff, broadsword, all of which, brutal as such gladiatorial exhibitions are, might have given to the soldiers a serviceable dexterity, have yielded to this more brutal sport, if that may be called sport which sometimes proves fatal. When a match is made between two prize-fighters, the tidings are immediately communicated to the public in the newspapers; and paragraphs occasionally appear saying the rivals are in training, what exercise they take, and what diet, for some of them feed upon raw beef as a preparative. – Meantime, the amateurs and the gamblers choose their party, and the state of the betts appears also in the public newspapers from time to time: not unfrequently the whole is a concerted scheme, that a few rogues may cheat a great many fools. – When the combat at length takes place, as regular a report is prepared for the newspapers as if it were a national victory – the particulars are recorded with a minuteness at once ridiculous and disgraceful; for every movement has its technical or slang name, and the unprecedented science of the successful combatant becomes the theme of general admiration.

'Don Manuel Alvarez Espriella' (Robert Southey)
Letters from England (1807)

SUBSTITUTES FOR FLOGGING

(1810)

THE BASKET

OCCASIONALLY boys are put in a sack, or in a basket, suspended to the roof of the school, in sight of all the pupils, who frequently smile at the birds in the cage. This punishment is one of the most terrible that can be inflicted on boys of sense and abilities. Above all, it is dreaded by the monitors; the name of it is sufficient, and therefore it is but seldom resorted to on their account.

THE CARAVAN

Frequent or old offenders are yoked together, sometimes by a piece of wood that fastens round all their necks; and thus confined, they parade the school, walking backwards – being obliged to pay very great attention to their footseps, for fear of running against any object that might cause the yoke to hurt their necks, or to keep from falling down. Four or six can be yoked together this way.

PROCLAMATION OF THE FAULTS OF AN
OFFENDER BEFORE THE SCHOOL

When a boy is disobedient to his parents, profane in his language, has committed any offence against morality, or is remarkable for slovenliness, it is usual for him to be dressed up with labels, describing his offence, and a tin or paper cap on his head. In that manner he walks round the school, two boys preceding him, and *proclaiming* his fault; varying the proclamation according to the different offences.

SLOVENLINESS

When a boy comes to school, with dirty face or hands, and it seems to be more the effect of habit than of accident, a girl is appointed to wash his face in the sight of the whole school. This usually creates much diversion, especially when (as previously directed) she gives his cheeks a few *gentle taps of correction* with her hand. *One punishment* of this kind has kept the boys' faces clean for two years.

CONFINEMENT AFTER SCHOOL HOURS

Few punishments are so effectual as confinement after school hours. It is, however, attended with one unpleasant circumstance. In order to confine the bad boys in the school-room, after school-hours, it is often needful that the master, or some proper substitute for him, should confine himself in school, to keep them in order. This inconvenience may be avoided by tying them to the desks, or putting them in logs, &c. in such a manner that they cannot loose themselves. These variations in the *modes of unavoidable punishment*, give it the continual force of novelty, whatever shape it may assume. Any single kind of punishment, continued constantly in use, becomes familiar, and loses its effect. Nothing but *variety* can continue the power of *novelty*. Happily, in my institution, there are few occasions of punishment; and this conduces much to the pleasure it affords me. The advantages of the various modes of correction, are, that they can be inflicted, so as to give much uneasiness to the delinquents, without disturbing the mind or temper of the master.

Joseph Lancaster

The British System of Education : Being a Complete Epitome
of the Improvements and Inventions Practised at the Royal Free
Schools, Borough-Road, Southwark (1810)

THE BEHAVIOUR OF THE ARMY
IN THE PENINSULA

(1810)

I AM concerned to tell you, that, notwithstanding the pains taken by the General and other officers of the army, the conduct of the soldiers is infamous. They behave well generally when with their regiments, and under the inspection of their officers, and the General officers of the army; but when detached, and coming up from hospitals, although invariably under the command of an officer, and always well fed and taken care of, and received as children of the family by the housekeeper in Portugal, they commit every description of outrage. They have never brought up a convoy of money that they have not robbed the chest; nor of shoes, or any other article that could be of use to them, or could produce money, that they do not steal something.

I have never halted the army for 2 days that I have not been obliged to assemble a General Court Martial; and a General Court Martial was assembled during the whole time the army was at Badajoz. At this moment there are 3 General Courts Martial sitting in Portugal for the trial of soldiers guilty of wanton murders, (no less than 4 people have been killed by them since we returned to Portugal,) robberies, thefts, robbing convoys under their charge, &c. &c. I assure you that the military law is not sufficiently strong to keep them in order;

and the people of this country have almost universally such an affection for the British nation, that they are unwilling to prosecute these unworthy soldiers in cold blood for the injuries they have received from them, at the distance of time which must elapse before the soldier can be brought to trial; although ready enough to complain and prosecute when smarting under the injury. Then the truth can never be got from themselves. Perjury is as common as robbery and murder; and the consequence of swearing them to tell truth before a regimental Court Martial is, that they invariably commit perjury when examined before a General Court Martial, where formerly the sanction of an oath was seldom given to falsehood. But upon the whole of this important subject, I refer you to my letter to Lord Castlereagh of the 17th June last.

I certainly think the army are improved. They are a better army than they were some months ago. But still these terrible, continued outrages give me reason to apprehend that, notwithstanding all the precautions I have taken, and shall take, they will slip through my fingers, as they did through Sir John Moore's, when I shall be involved in any nice operation with a powerful enemy in my front.

Arthur Wellesley, Duke of Wellington

Letter to Lord Liverpool (24 January, 1810) from *The Dispatches of Field Marshal The Duke of Wellington,* edited by J. Gurwood (1834–39), Vol. V

COLERIDGE AS A LECTURER

(13 *December* 1811)

As evidences of splendid talent, original thought, and rare powers of expression and fancy, they are all his *admirers* can wish; but as a discharge of his undertaking, a fulfilment of his promise to the public, they give his *friends* great uneasiness.

As you express it, "an enchanter's spell seems to be upon him," which takes from him the power of treating upon the only subject his hearers are anxious he should consider, while it leaves him infinite ability to riot and run wild on a variety of moral and religious themes. In his sixth lecture he was, by advertisement, to speak of "Romeo and Juliet" and Shakespeare's females; unhappily, some demon whispered the name of Lancaster in his ear: and we had, in one evening, an attack on the poor Quaker, a defence of boarding-school flogging, a parallel between the ages of Elizabeth and Charles, a defence of what is untruly called unpoetic language, an account of the different languages of Europe, and a vindication of Shakespeare against the imputation of grossness!!! I suspect he did discover that offence was taken at this, for his succeeding lecture on Monday was all we could wish. He confined himself to "Romeo and Juliet" for a time, treated of the inferior characters, and delivered a most eloquent discourse on love, with a promise to point out how Shakespeare had shown the same truths in the persons of the lovers. Yesterday we were to have a continuation of the theme. Alas! Coleridge began with a parallel between religion and love, which, though one of his favourite themes, he did not manage successfully. Romeo and Juliet were forgotten. And in the next lecture we are really to hear something of these lovers. Now this will be the fourth time that his hearers have been invited expressly to hear of this play. There are to be only fifteen lectures altogether (half have been delivered), and the course is to include Shakespeare and Milton, the modern poets, &c.!!! Instead of a lecture on a definite subject, we have an immethodical rhapsody, very delightful to you and me, and only offensive from the certainty that it may and ought to offend those who come with other expectations. Yet, with all this, I cannot but be charmed with these *splendida vitia*, and my chief displeasure is occasioned by my being forced to hear the strictures of persons infinitely below Coleridge, without any power of refuting or contradicting them. Yet it is lucky he has hitherto omitted no lecture. Living with the Morgans, they force him to come with them to the lecture-room, and this is a great point gained.

Henry Crabb Robinson

Letter to Mrs. Clarkson from Diary, Reminiscences, and
Correspondence, edited by T. Sadler (1869)

ENGLISHMEN ABROAD

(Athens, 14 January 1811)

MY DEAR MADAM, – I seize an occasion to write as usual, shortly, but frequently, as the arrival of letters, where there exists no regular communication, is, of course, very precarious...[1] I have lately made several small tours of some hundred or two miles about the Morea, Attica, &c., as I have finished my grand giro by the Troad, Constantinople, &c., and am returned down again to Athens. I believe I have mentioned to you more than once, that I swam (in imitation of Leander, though without his lady) across the Hellespont, from Sestos to Abydos. Of this, and all other particulars, Fletcher, whom I have sent home with papers, &c., will apprize you. I cannot find that he is any loss; being tolerably master of the Italian and modern Greek languages, which last I am also studying with a master, I can order and discourse more than enough for a reasonable man. Besides, the perpetual lamentations after beef and beer, the stupid, bigoted contempt for every thing foreign, and insurmountable incapacity of acquiring even a few words of any language, rendered him, like all other English servants, an incumbrance. I do assure you, the plague of speaking for him, the comforts he required

1. Omission by T. Moore

(more than myself by far), the pilaws (a Turkish dish of rice and meat) which he could not eat, the wines which he could not drink, the beds where he could not sleep, and the long list of calamities, such as stumbling horses, want of *tea*!!! &c., which assailed him, would have made a lasting source of laughter to a spectator, and inconvenience to a master. After all, the man is honest enough, and, in Christendom, capable enough; but in Turkey, Lord forgive me! my Albanian soldiers, my Tartars and Jannizary, worked for him and us too, as my friend Hobhouse can testify.

It is probable I may steer homewards in spring; but to enable me to do that, I must have remittances. My own funds would have lasted me very well; but I was obliged to assist a friend, who, I know, will pay me; but, in the mean time, I am out of pocket. At present, I do not care to venture a winter's voyage, even if I were otherwise tired of travelling; but I am so convinced of the advantages of looking at mankind instead of reading about them, and the bitter effects of staying at home with all the narrow prejudices of an islander, that I think there should be a law amongst us, to set our young men abroad, for a term, among the few allies our wars have left us.

Here I see and have conversed with French, Italians, Germans, Danes, Greeks, Turks, Americans, &c., &c., &c.; and without losing sight of my own, I can judge of the countries and manners of others. Where I see the superiority of England (which, by the by, we are a good deal mistaken about in many things), I am pleased, and where I find her inferior, I am at least enlightened. Now, I might have staid, smoked in your towns, or fogged in your country, a century, without being sure of this, and without acquiring any thing more useful or amusing at home. I keep no journal, nor have I any intention of scribbling my travels. I have done with authorship, and if, in my last production, I have convinced the critics or the world I was something more than they took me for, I am satisfied;

nor will I hazard *that reputation* by a future effort. It is true I have some others in manuscript, but I leave them for those who come after me; and, if deemed worth publishing, they may serve to prolong my memory when I myself shall cease to remember. I have a famous Bavarian artist taking some views of Athens, &c., &c., for me. This will be better than scribbling, a disease I hope myself cured of. I hope, on my return, to lead a quiet, recluse life, but God knows and does best for us all; at least, so they say, and I have nothing to object, as, on the whole, I have no reason to complain of my lot. I am convinced, however, that men do more harm to themselves than ever the devil could do to them. I trust this will find you well, and as happy as we can be; you will, at least, be pleased to hear I am so, and yours ever.

George Gordon, Lord Byron
Letter to his mother from T. Moore's *Letters and
Journals of Lord Byron: with Notices of His Life* (1830)

VARIOUS CELEBRITIES

(1812)

May 24th. – A very interesting day. At half-past ten joined Wordsworth in Oxford Road; we then got into the fields, and walked to Hampstead. I read to him a number of Blake's poems, with some of which he was pleased. He regarded Blake as having in him the elements of poetry much more than either Byron or Scott. We met Miss Joanna Baillie, and accompanied her home. She is small in figure, and her gait is mean and shuffling, but her manners are those of a well-bred woman. She has none of the unpleasant airs too common to literary ladies. Her conversation is sensible. She possesses apparently considerable information, is prompt without being forward,

49

and has a fixed judgment of her own, without any disposition to force it on others. Wordsworth said of her with warmth, "If I had to present any one to a foreigner as a model of an English gentlewoman, it would be Joanna Baillie."

May 26th. – Walked to the Old Bailey to see D. I. Eaton in the pillory. As I expected, his punishment of shame was his glory. The mob was not numerous, but decidedly friendly to him. His having published Paine's "Age of Reason" was not an intelligible offence to them. I heard such exclamations as the following: "Pillory a man for publishing a book—shame!" – "I wish old Sir Wicary was there, my pockets should not be empty." – "Religious liberty!" – "Liberty of conscience!" Some avowed their willingness to stand in the pillory for a dollar. "This a punishment? this is no disgrace!" As his position changed, and fresh partisans were blessed by a sight of his round, grinning face, shouts of "bravo!" arose from a new quarter. His trial was sold on the spot. The whole affair was an additional proof of the folly of the Ministers, who ought to have known that such an exhibition would be a triumph to the cause they meant to render infamous.

May 31st. – A day of great enjoyment. Walked to Hampstead. Found Wordsworth demonstrating to Hamond some of the points of his philosophical theory. Speaking of his own poems, he said he valued them principally as being *a new power* in the literary world. Hamond's friend Miller esteemed them for their pure morality. Wordsworth said he himself looked to the powers of mind they call forth, and the energies they presuppose and excite as the standard by which they should be tried. He expatiated also on his fears lest a social war should arise between the poor and the rich, the danger of which is aggravated by the vast extension of the manufacturing system.

Wordsworth defended earnestly the Church Establishment. He even said he would shed his blood for it. Nor was he disconcerted by a laugh raised against him on account of his having before confessed that he knew not when he had been in a church in his own country. "All our ministers are so vile," said he. The mischief of allowing the clergy to depend on the caprice of the multitude he thought more than outweighed all the evils of an Establishment. And in this I agreed with him.

Dined with Wordsworth at Mr. Carr's. Sir Humphry and Lady Davy there. She and Sir H. seem to have hardly finished their honeymoon. Miss Joanna Baillie said to Wordsworth the other day, "We have witnessed a picturesque happiness." Mrs. Walter Scott was spoken of rather disparagingly, and Miss Baillie gave her this good word: "When I visited her I thought I saw a great deal to like. She seemed to admire and look up to her husband. She was very kind to her guests. Her children were well-bred, and the house was in excellent order. And she had some smart roses in her cap, and I did not like her the less for that."

Henry Crabb Robinson
Diary, Reminiscences, and Correspondence,
edited by T. Sadler (1869)

THE AMERICAN MARKET

(1812)

THERE are some political facts, which we must take as facts, because they are proved to us, without being able to account for them, or to trace them to their origin, and explain their causes. But the extent, and swift and regular progress of the American market for British goods is not of this number; we can easily and clearly account for it. In the nature of things it can be no otherwise, and the reason lies on the very surface of the fact. America is an immense agricultural country, where land is plentiful and cheap; men and labour, though quickly increasing, yet still scarce and dear when compared with the boundless regions which they occupy and cultivate. In such a country, manufacturers do not naturally thrive; every exertion, if matters be left to themselves, goes into other channels. This people is connected with England by origin, language, manners, and institutions; their tastes go along with their convenience, and they come to us as a matter of course for the articles which they do not make themselves. Only take one fact as an example: The negroes in the Southern States are clothed in English made goods, and it takes forty shillings a-year thus to supply one of those unfortunate persons. This will be admitted to be the lowest sum for which any person in American can be clothed; but take it as the average, and make deduction for the expenses above prime cost – you have a sum upon the whole population of eight millions, which approaches the value of our exports to the United States. But it is not merely in clothing; go to any house in the Union, from their large and wealthy cities to the most solitary cabin or log-house in the forests – you find in every corner the furniture, tools, and ornaments of Staffordshire, of Warwickshire, and of the northern counties of England. The wonder ceases when we thus reflect for a moment, and we plainly perceive that it can be no otherwise. The whole population of the country is made up of customers, who require and who can afford to pay for our goods. This, too, is peculiar to that nation, and it is a peculiarity as happy for them as it is profitable to us. I know the real or affected contempt with which some persons in this country treat our kinsmen of the west. I fear some angry and jealous feelings have survived our former more intimate connexion with them – feelings engendered by the event of its termination, but which it would be wiser as well as more manly to forget. Nay, there are certain romantic spirits who even despise the unadorned structure of their massive democratic society. But to me I freely acknowledge the sight of one part of it brings feelings of envy, as an Englishman; I mean the happy distinction, that over the whole extent of that boundless continent, from Canada to the Gulph of Mexico, and from the Mississippi to the Atlantic Ocean, there is not one pauper to be found. Such are the customers whom America presents to us. The rapid increase of their culture and population too, doubling in twenty-five or thirty years, must necessarily augment this demand for our goods in the same proportion. Circumstanced as the two countries are, I use no figure of speech, but speak the simple fact when I say, that not an axe falls in the woods of America which does not put in motion some shuttle, or hammer, or wheel in England.

Henry, Lord Brougham
Speech in the House of Commons (16 June, 1812)
from *Speeches . . .* (1838)

WELLINGTON'S COMMENTS ON WATERLOO

(1815)

THE first thing I did, of course, was to put out my hand and congratulate him upon his victory. He made a variety of observations in his short, natural, blunt way, but with the greatest gravity all the time, and without the least approach to anything like triumph or joy. – 'It has been a damned serious business,' he said. 'Blücher and I have lost 30,000 men. It has been a damned nice thing – the nearest run thing you ever saw in your life. Blücher lost 14,000 on Friday night, and got so damnably licked I could not find him on Saturday morning; so I was obliged to fall back to keep up my communications with him.' – Then, as he walked about, he praised greatly those Guards who kept the farm (meaning

Hugomont) against the repeated attacks of the French; and then he praised all our troops, uttering repeated expressions of astonishment at our men's courage. He repeated so often its being *so nice a thing – so nearly run a thing*, that I asked him if the French had fought better than he had ever seen them do before. – 'No,' he said, 'they have always fought the same since I first saw them at Vimeiro.' Then he said: – 'By God! I don't think it would have done if I had not been there.'

When I left the Duke, I went instantly home and wrote to England by the same courier who carried his dispatch. I sent the very conversation I have just related to Bennet. I think, however, I omitted the Duke's observation that he did not think the battle would have been won had he not been there, and I remember my reason for omitting this sentence. It did not seem fair to the Duke to state it without full explanation. There was nothing like vanity in the observation in the way he made it. I considered it only as meaning that the battle was so hardly and equally fought that nothing but confidence of our army in himself as their general could have brought them thro'. Now that seven years have elapsed since that battle, and tho' the Duke has become – very foolishly, in my opinion – a politician, and has done many wrong and foolish things since that time, yet I think of his conversation and whole conduct on the 19th – the day after the battle – exactly the same as I did then: namely – that nothing could do a conqueror more honour than his gravity and seriousness at the loss of lives he had sustained, his admission of his great danger, and the justice he did his enemy.

Thomas Creevey

The Creevey Papers . . . , edited by
H. Maxwell (1903), Vol. I

A Slave-Owner in Jamaica

(1816)

THE distance was about thirty miles, and soon after nine o'clock we reached Savannah la Mar, where I found my trustee, and a whole cavalcade, waiting to conduct me to my own estate; for he had brought with him a curricle and pair for myself, a gig for my servant, two black boys upon mules and a cart with eight oxen to convey my baggage. The road was excellent, and we had not above five miles to travel; and as soon as the carriage entered my gates, the uproar and confusion which ensued sets all description at defiance. The works were instantly all abandoned; every thing that had life came flocking to the house from all quarters; and not only the men, and the women, and the children, but, "by a bland assimilation," the hogs, and the dogs, and the geese, and the fowls, and the turkeys, all came hurrying along by instinct, to see what could possibly be the matter, and seemed to be afraid of arriving too late. Whether the pleasure of the negroes was sincere may be doubted; but certainly it was the loudest that I ever witnessed: they all talked together, sang, danced, shouted, and, in the violence of their gesticulations, tumbled over each other, and rolled about upon the ground. Twenty voices at once enquired after uncles, and aunts, and grandfathers, and great-grandmothers of mine, who had been buried long before I was in existence, and whom, I verily believe, most of them only knew by tradition. One woman held up her little naked black child to me, grinning from ear to ear; "Look, Massa, look here! him nice lilly neger for Massa!" Another complained,– "So long since none come see we, Massa; good Massa, come at last." As for the old people, they were all in one and the same story: now they had lived once to see Massa, they were ready for dying to-morrow, "them no care."

The shouts, the gaiety, the wild laughter, their strange and sudden bursts of singing and dancing, and several old women, wrapped up in large cloaks, their heads bound round with different-coloured handkerchiefs, leaning on a staff, and standing motionless in the middle of the hubbub, with their eyes fixed upon the portico which I occupied, formed an exact counterpart of the festivity of the witches in Macbeth. Nothing could be more odd or more novel than the whole scene; and yet there was something in it by which I could not help being affected; perhaps it was the consciousness that all these human beings were my *slaves*; to be sure, I never saw people look more happy in my life; and I believe their condition to be much more comfortable than that of the labourers of Great Britain; and, after all, slavery, in *their* case, is but another name for servitude, now that no more negroes can be forcibly carried away from Africa, and subjected to the horrors of the voyage, and of the seasoning after their arrival: but still I had already experienced, in the morning, that Juliet was wrong in saying "What's in a name?" for soon after my reaching the lodging-house at Savannah la Mar, a remarkably clean-looking negro lad presented himself with some water and a towel: I concluded him to be one of the inn; and, on my returning the towel, as he found that I took no notice of him, he at length ventured to introduce himself, by saying, – "Massa not know me; *me your slave!*" – and really the sound made me feel a pang at the heart. The lad appeared all gaiety and good humour, and his whole countenance expressed anxiety to recommend himself to my notice; but the word "slave" seemed to imply, that, although he did feel pleasure then in serving me, if he had detested me he must have served me still. I really felt quite humiliated at the moment, and was tempted to tell him, – "Do not say that again; say that you are my negro, but do not call yourself my slave."

Altogether, they shouted and sang me into a violent headache. It is now one in the morning, and I hear them still shouting and singing. I gave them a holiday for Saturday next, and told them that I had brought them all presents from England; and so, I believe, we parted very good friends.

Matthew Gregory Lewis
Journal of a West India Proprietor (1834)

A SELF-PORTRAIT

Tuesday 27 Oct. 1818.

MY DEAR WOODHOUSE,

Your Letter gave me a great satisfaction; more on account of its friendliness, than any relish of that matter in it which is accounted so acceptable in the 'genus irritabile'. The best answer I can give you is in a clerk-like manner to make some observations on two principle points, which seem to point like indices into the midst of the whole pro and con, about genius, and views and atchievements and ambition and cœtera. 1st. As to the poetical Character itself (I mean that sort of which, if I am any thing, I am a Member; that sort distinguished from the wordsworthian or egotistical sublime; which is a thing per se and stands alone) it is not itself – it has no self – it is every thing and nothing – It has no character – it enjoys light and shade; it lives in gusto, be it foul or fair, high or low, rich or poor, mean or elevated – It has as much delight in conceiving an Iago as an Imogen. What shocks the virtuous philosopher, delights the camelion Poet. It does no harm from its relish of the dark side of things any more than from its taste for the bright one; because they both end in speculation. A Poet is the most unpoetical of any thing in existence; because he has no Identity – he is continually in for – and filling some other Body – The Sun, the Moon, the

Sea and Men and Women who are creatures of impulse are poetical and have about them an unchangeable attribute – the poet has none; no identity – he is certainly the most unpoetical of all God's Creatures. If then he has no self, and if I am a Poet, where is the Wonder that I should say I would write no more? Might I not at that very instant have been cogitating on the Characters of Saturn and Ops? It is a wretched thing to confess; but is a very fact that not one word I ever utter can be taken for granted as an opinion growing out of my identical nature – how can it, when I have no nature? When I am in a room with People if I ever am free from speculating on creations of my own brain, then not myself goes home to myself: but the identity of every one in the room begins to press upon me that I am in a very little time an[ni]hilated – not only among Men; it would be the same in a Nursery of children: I know not whether I make myself wholly understood: I hope enough so to let you see that no dependence is to be placed on what I said that day.

In the second place I will speak of my views, and of the life I purpose to myself. I am ambitious of doing the world some good: if I should be spared that may be the work of maturer years – in the interval I will assay to reach to as high a summit in Poetry as the nerve bestowed upon me will suffer. The faint conceptions I have of Poems to come brings the blood frequently into my forehead. All I hope is that I may not lose all interest in human affairs – that the solitary indifference I feel for applause even from the finest Spirits, will not blunt any acuteness of vision I may have. I do not think it will – I feel assured I should write from the mere yearning and fondness I have for the Beautiful even if my night's labours should be burnt every morning, and no eye ever shine upon them. But even now I am perhaps not speaking from myself: but from some character in whose soul I now live. I am sure however that this next sentence is from myself. I feel your anxiety, good opinion and friendliness in the highest degree, and am

Your's most sincerely

John Keats

The Letters of John Keats, edited by M. B. Forman (1935)

JAMES WATT

(1819)

WE have said that Mr. Watt was the great *Improver* of the steam-engine; but, in truth, as to all that is admirable in its structure, or vast in its utility, he should rather be described as its *Inventor*. It was by his inventions that its action was so regulated, as to make it capable of being applied to the finest and most delicate manufactures, and its power so increased, as to set weight and solidity at defiance. By his admirable contrivance, it has become a thing stupendous alike for its force and its flexibility, – for the prodigious power which it can exert, and the ease, and precision, and ductility, with which that power can be varied, distributed, and applied. The trunk of an elephant, that can pick up a pin or rend an oak, is as nothing to it. It can engrave a seal, and crush masses of obdurate metal before it – draw out, without breaking, a thread as fine as gossamer, and lift a ship of war like a bauble in the air. It can embroider muslin and forge anchors, – cut steel into ribbands, and impel loaded vessels against the fury of the winds and waves.

It would be difficult to estimate the value of the benefits which these inventions have conferred upon this country. There is no branch of industry that has not been indebted to them; and, in all the most material, they have not only widened most magnificently the field of its exertions, but multiplied a thousand-fold the amount of its productions. It was our improved Steam-engine, in short, that fought the battles of Europe, and exalted and sustained, through the late tremendous contest, the political greatness of our land. It is the same great power which now enables us to pay the interest of our debt, and to maintain the arduous struggle in which we are still engaged, with the skill and capital of countries less oppressed with taxation. But these are poor and narrow views of its importance. It has increased indefinitely the mass of human comforts and enjoyments; and rendered cheap and accessible, all over the world, the materials of wealth and prosperity. It has armed the feeble hand of man, in short, with a power to which no limits can be assigned; completed the dominion of mind over the most refractory qualities of matter; and laid a sure foundation for all those future miracles of mechanic power which are to aid and reward the labours of after generations. It is to the genius of one man, too, that all this is mainly owing! And certainly no man ever bestowed such a gift on his kind. The blessing is not only universal, but unbounded; and the fabled inventors of the plough and the loom, who were Deified by the erring gratitude of their rude cotemporaries, conferred less important benefits on mankind than the inventor of our present steam-engine.

Francis, Lord Jeffrey

The Scotsman (4 September, 1819). Text from the
author's *Contributions to the Edinburgh Review* (1844)

THE CORONATION OF GEORGE IV

(1821)

July 19th. – I only got my ticket on Wednesday at two, and dearest Mary and I drove about to get all that was wanted.

Sir George Beaumont lent me ruffles and frill, another friend a blue velvet coat, a third a sword; I bought buckles, and the rest I had. I went to bed at ten, and arose at twelve, not having slept a wink. I dressed, breakfasted, and was at the Hall door at half-past one. Three ladies were before me. The doors opened about four, and I got a front place in the Chamberlain's box, between the door and the throne, and saw the whole room distinctly. Many of the door-keepers were tipsy; quarrels took place. The sun began to light up the old Gothic windows, the peers to stroll in, and other company of all descriptions to crowd to their places. Some took seats they had not any right to occupy, and were obliged to leave them after sturdy disputes. Others lost their tickets. The Hall occasionally echoed with the hollow roar of voices at the great door, till at last the galleries were filled; the hall began to get crowded below. Every movement, as the time approached for the King's appearance, was pregnant with interest. The appearance of a monarch has something in it like the rising of a sun. There are indications which announce the luminary's approach; a streak of light – the tipping of a cloud – the singing of the lark – the brilliance of the sky, till the cloud-edges get brighter and brighter, and he rises majestically into the heavens. So with a king's advance. A whisper of mystery turns all eyes to the throne. Suddenly two or three rise; others fall back; some talk, direct, hurry, stand still, or disappear. Then three or four of high rank appear from behind the throne; an interval is left; the crowds scarce breathe. Something rustles, and a being buried in satin, feathers, and diamonds rolls gracefully into his seat. The room rises with a sort of feathered, silken thunder. Plumes wave, eyes sparkle, glasses are out, mouths smile, and one man becomes the prime object of attraction to thousands. The way in which the king bowed was really royal. As he looked towards the peeresses and foreign ambassadors, he showed like some gorgeous bird of the East.

After all the ceremonies he arose, the procession was arranged, the music played, and the line began to move. All this was exceedingly imposing. After two or three hours' waiting, during which the attempt of the Queen[1] agitated the Hall, the doors opened, and the flower-girls entered, strewing flowers. The grace of their action, their slow movement, their white dresses, were indescribably touching; their light milky colour contrasted with the dark shadow of the archway, which, though dark, was full of rich crimson dresses that gave the shadow a tone as of deep blood; the shadow again relieved by a peep of the crowd, shining in sunlight beyond the gates, and between the shoulders of the guard that crossed the platform. The distant trumpets and shouts of the people, the slow march, and at last the appearance of the King crowned and under a golden canopy, and the universal burst of the assembly at seeing him, affected everybody. As we were all huzzaing, and the King was smiling, I could not help thinking this would be too much for any human being if a drop of poison were not dropped into the cup ere you tasted it. A man would go mad if mortality did not occasionally hold up the mirror. The Queen was to him the death's-head at this stately feast.

Benjamin Robert Haydon

Life of B. R. Haydon, Historical Painter, from his Autobiography and Journals, edited and compiled by T. Taylor (1853)

ON THE DEATH OF CASTLEREAGH

(1822)

THE ruffians who continue to praise this man, tell us that the history of his life is found in the measures of the Government for the last twenty-seven years; and that is true enough; it is

1. To enter the Abbey. She was separated from the King.

found in all the various acts that have been passed to shut the Irish up in their houses from sunset to sunrise, and to transport them without trial by jury. It is found in the Power-of-imprisonment Bill of 1817. It is found in those terrible Six Acts, one of which prescribes that the printer of a newspaper shall enter into bail even before he begins to print; which prescribes that this very pamphlet in which I am now addressing you, shall be so loaded with paper and with price, as to make it difficult to effect its circulation. It is found in another of those Acts, which was intended to transport men, and which does banish men for life, for a second time uttering that which has a tendency to bring into contempt those who pass such a law. His history is in the figure of eight and eight cyphers, which represent the amount of the National Debt. It is written in those measures which have reduced the most industrious and enterprising farmers in the world to a state of beggary, and have plunged no small number of them into despair, real insanity, and self-destruction. It is written in a mass of pauperism, hitherto wholly unknown to England, and it is written in starvation to Ireland amidst over-production. As to his family and connexions, look at the immense sums which they are now receiving out of the fruit of the people's labour. And as to any compassion that we are to feel for them, we will feel it when an end to the sufferings of the Reformers and their families will leave us a particle of compassion to bestow on any body else. The mention of the anguish of Lady CASTLEREAGH only reminds me of the anguish of poor Mrs. JOHNSON, who, brought to a death-bed by long and racking anxiety on account of her husband, harassed, persecuted, thrown into a dungeon at a hundred miles from her, merely for having *been present* at a Meeting never before deemed unlawful; when I hear Lady Castlereagh's anguish mentioned I forget, for the time, the enormous sinecure of her father, but I remember that exemplary and affectionate wife, Mrs.

Johnson, who, brought to her death-bed by the means just mentioned, earnestly prayed that she might *see* her husband before she closed her eyes for ever; and I remember, that that prayer was *rejected by Castlereagh and his colleagues*, though the husband tendered bail to any amount and offered to submit to any length of imprisonment as the price of permission to receive the last sigh of his dying wife.

William Cobbett
Cobbett's Weekly Register (17 August, 1822)

DERELICT COASTAL DEFENCES
(1823)

I HAD baited my horse at NEW ROMNEY, and was coming jogging along very soberly, now looking at the sea, then looking at the cattle, then the corn, when, my eye, in swinging round, lighted upon a *great round building*, standing upon the beach. I had scarcely had time to think about what it could be, when twenty or thirty others, standing along the coast, caught my eye; and, if any one had been behind me, he might have heard me exclaim, in a voice that made my horse bound, "The MARTELLO TOWERS by – !" Oh, Lord! To think that I should be destined to behold these monuments of the wisdom of Pitt and Dundas and Perceval! Good God! Here they are, piles of bricks in a circular form about three hundred feet (*guess*) circumference at the base, about forty feet high, and about one hundred and fifty feet circumference at the top. There is a door-way, about midway up, in each, and each has two windows. Cannons were to be fired from the top of these things, in order to defend the *country against the French Jacobins!*

I think I have counted along here upwards of thirty of

these ridiculous things, which, I dare say, cost *five*, perhaps *ten*, thousand pounds each; and one of which was, I am told, *sold* on the coast of Sussex, the other day, for TWO HUNDRED POUNDS! There is, they say, a chain of these things all the way to HASTINGS! I dare say they cost MILLIONS. But, far indeed are these from being all, or half, or a quarter of the squanderings along here. Hythe is half *barracks*; the hills are covered with barracks; and barracks most expensive, most squandering, fill up the side of the hill. Here is a CANAL (I crossed it at Appledore) made for the length of thirty miles (from Hythe, in Kent, to RYE, in Sussex) to *keep out the French*; for, those armies who had so often crossed the Rhine, and the Danube, were to be kept back by a canal, made by PITT, thirty feet wide at the most! All along the coast there are works of some sort or other; incessant sinks of money; walls of immense dimensions; masses of stone brought and put into piles. Then you see some of the walls and buildings falling down; some that have never been finished. The whole thing, all taken together, looks as if a spell had been, all of a sudden, set upon the workmen; or, in the words of the Scripture, here is the "*desolation of abomination, standing in high places.*" However, all is right. These things were made with the hearty good will of those who are now coming to ruin in consequence of the Debt, contracted for the purpose of making these things! This is all *just*. The load will come, at last, upon the right shoulders.

William Cobbett
Rural Rides (1830)

THE IRON DUKE

THE next morning I received another visit from Mrs. Porter, who informed me that she had just had an interview with my new lover, and had reported to him all I had desired her to say.

Since you object to meet a stranger, continued Mrs. Porter, his grace desires me to say, he hopes you can keep a secret, and to inform you, that it is the Duke of Wellington, who, so anxiously desires to make your acquaintance.

I have heard of his grace often, said I, in a tone of deep disappointment: for I had been indulging a kind of hope about the stranger, with the great Newfoundland dog, with whose appearance I had been so unusually struck, as to have sought for him every day, and I thought of him every hour.

His grace, Mrs. Porter proceeded, only entreats to be allowed to make your acquaintance. His situation, you know, prevents the possibility of his getting regularly introduced to you.

It will never do, said I, shaking my head.

Be assured, said Mrs. Porter, he is a remarkably fine-looking man, and, if you are afraid of my house, promise to receive him, in your own, at any hour when he may be certain to find you alone.

Well, thought I, with a sigh! I suppose he must come. I do not understand economy, and am frightened to death at debts. Argyle is going to Scotland; and I shall want a steady sort of friend, of some kind, in case a bailiff should get hold of me.

What shall I say to his grace? Mrs. Porter enquired, growing impatient.

Well then, said I, since it must be so, tell his grace, that I will receive him, to-morrow, at three; but mind, only as a common acquaintance!

Away winged Wellington's Mercury, as an old woman wings it at sixty, and most punctual to my appointment, at three, on the following day, Wellington made his appearance. He bowed first, then said –

How do you do? then thanked me for having given him permission to call on me; and then wanted to take hold of my hand.

Really, said I, withdrawing my hand, for such a renowned hero you have very little to say for yourself.

Beautiful creature! uttered Wellington, where is Lorne?

Good gracious, said I, out of all patience at his stupidity, – what come you here for, duke?

Beautiful eye, yours! reiterated Wellington.

Aye man! they are greater conquerors than ever Wellington shall be; but, to be serious, I understood you came here to try to make yourself agreeable?

What child! do you think that I have nothing better to do than to make speeches to please ladies? said Wellington.

Après avoir dépeuplé la terre, vous devez faire tout pour la repeupler, I replied.

You should see me where I shine, Wellington observed, laughing.

Where's that, in God's name?

In a field of battle, answered the hero.

Battez vous, donc, et qu'un autre me fasse la cour! said I.

But love scenes, or even love quarrels, seldom tend to amuse the reader, so, to be brief, what was a mere man, even though it were the handsome duke of Argyle, to a Wellington!!!!

Harriette Wilson

Memoirs (1825). Text from the second
edition of the same year

A Meeting in Rajpootana

(1825)

January 27. – This morning we marched eight long coss to Mohunpoora. In the way I had an opportunity of seeing some part of the magnificence which Dr. Smith had described, for we passed Sir David Ochterlony and his suite on his road to Bhurtpoor. There certainly was a very considerable number of led horses, elephants, palanqueens, and covered carriages, belonging chiefly, I apprehend, (besides his own family,) to the families of his native servants. There was an escort of two companies of infantry, a troop of regular cavalry, and I should guess forty or fifty irregulars, on horse and foot, armed with spears and matchlocks of all possible forms; the string of camels was a very long one, and the whole procession was what might pass in Europe for that of an eastern prince travelling. Still, neither in numbers nor splendour did it at all equal my expectation. Sir David himself was in a carriage and four, and civilly got out to speak to me. He is a tall and pleasing-looking old man, but was so wrapped up in shawls, kincob, fur, and a Mogul furred cap, that his face was all that was visible. I was not sorry to have even this glimpse of an old officer whose exploits in India have been so distinguished. His history is a curious one. He is the son of an American gentleman who lost his estate and country by his loyalty during the war of the separation. Sir David himself came out a cadet, without friends, to India, and literally fought his way to notice. The most brilliant parts of his career were his defence of Delhi against the Mahratta army, and the conquest of Kemaoon from the Ghorkhas. He is now considerably above seventy, infirm, and has been often advised to return to England. But he has been absent from thence fifty-four years; he has there neither friend nor relation, – he has been for many years habituated to eastern habits and parade, and who can wonder that he clings to the only country in the world where he can feel himself at home? Within these few days I had been reading Coxe's Life of Marlborough, and at this moment it struck me forcibly how little it would have seemed in the compass of possibility to any of the warriors, statesmen, or divines of Queen Anne's time, that an English General and an English Bishop would ever shake hands on a desert plain in the heart of Rajpootana!

Reginald Heber

Narrative of a Journey through the
Upper Provinces of India (1828)

A CONVERSATION WITH SCOTT

(1825)

DINED at half-past five; none but himself, a young clergyman, quite deaf, who is making a catalogue of his library, Lady Scott and daughter, and a boy, the son of his lost friend Sir — Erskine. After dinner pledged him in some whisky out of a *quaigh*; that which I drank out of very curious and beautiful. Produced several others; one that belonged to Prince Charles, with a glass bottom; others of a larger size, out of which he said his great grandfather drank. Very interesting *tête-à-tête* with him after dinner. Said that the person who first set him upon trying his talent at poetry was Mat. Lewis. He had passed the early part of his life with a set of clever, rattling, drinking fellows, whose thoughts and talents lay wholly out of the region of poetry; he, therefore, had never been led to find out his turn for it, though always fond of the old ballads. In the course of the conversation he, at last (to my no small surprise and pleasure), mentioned the novels without the least reserve as his own; "I then hit upon these novels (he said), which have been a mine of wealth to me." Had begun Waverley long before, and then thrown it by, till, having occasion for some money (to help his brother, I think), he bethought himself of it, but could not find the MS.; nor was it till he came to Abbotsford that he at last stumbled upon it. By this he made 3000*l*. The conjectures and mystification at first amused him very much: wonders himself that the secret was so well kept, as about twenty persons knew it from the first. The story of Jeanie Deans founded upon an anonymous letter which he received; has never known from whom. The circumstance of the girl having refused the testimony in court, and then taking the journey to obtain her sister's pardon, is a fact. Received some hints also from Lady Louisa Stuart (grand-daughter, I believe, to Lord Bute); these the only aids afforded to him. His only critic was the printer, who was in the secret, and who now and then started objections which he generally attended to. Had always been in the habit (while wandering alone or shooting) of forming stories and following a train of adventures in his mind, and these fancies it was that formed the groundwork of most of his novels. "I find I fail in them now, however (he said); I cannot make them as good as at first."

Thomas Moore

Memoirs, Journal, and Correspondence, edited
by Lord John Russell (1853–6), Vol. IV

SIR THOMAS LAWRENCE

(1830)

Roehampton, January 9th. – Yesterday morning died Sir Thomas Lawrence after a very short illness. Few people knew he was ill before they heard he was dead. He was *longè primus* of all living painters, and has left no one fit to succeed him in the chair of the Royal Academy. Lawrence was about sixty, very like Canning in appearance, remarkably gentlemanlike, with very mild manners, though rather too *doucereux*, agreeable in society, unassuming, and not a great talker; his mind was highly cultivated, he had a taste for every kind of literature, and was enthusiastically devoted to his art; he was very industrious, and painted an enormous number of portraits, but many of his later works are still unfinished, and great complaints used to be made of his exacting either the whole or half payment when he began a picture, but that when he had got the money he could never be prevailed on to complete it. Although he is supposed to have earned enormous sums by his paintings, he has always been a distressed man, without any visible means of expense, except a magnificent collection of drawings by the ancient masters, said to be the finest in the world, and procured at great cost. He was, however, a generous patron of young artists of merit and talent. It was always said that he lost money at play, but this assertion seems to have proceeded more from the difficulty of reconciling his pecuniary embarrassments with his enormous profits than from any proof of the fact. He was a great courtier, and is said to have been so devoted to the King that he would not paint anybody who was personally obnoxious to his Majesty; but I do not believe this is true. He is an irreparable loss; since Sir Joshua there has been no painter like him; his portraits as pictures I think are not nearly so fine as Sir Joshua's, but as likenesses many of them are quite perfect. Moore's was the last portrait he painted, and Miss Kemble's his last drawing.

Charles Cavendish Fulke Greville
The Greville Memoirs: First Part (1874)

RICKBURNING

(1830)

POOR Enfield, that has been so peaceable hitherto, has caught the inflammatory fever; the tokens are upon her; and a great fire was blazing last night in the barns and haystacks of a farmer, about half a mile from us. Where will these things end? There is no doubt of its being the work of some ill-disposed rustic; but how is he to be discovered? They go to work in the dark with strange chemical preparations, unknown to our forefathers. There is not even a dark lantern, to have a chance of detecting these Guy Fauxes. We are past the iron age, and are got into the fiery age, undreamed of by Ovid. You are lucky in Clifford's Inn, where I think you have few ricks or stacks worth the burning. Pray, keep as little corn by you as you can for fear of the worst. It was never good times in England since the poor began to speculate upon their condition. Formerly they jogged on with as little reflection as horses. The whistling ploughman went cheek by jowl with his brother that neighed. Now the biped carries a box of phosphorus in his leather breeches, and in the dead of night the half-illuminated beast steals his magic potion into a cleft in a barn, and half the country is grinning with new fires. Farmer Graystock said something to the touchy rustic, that he did not relish, and he writes his distaste in flames. What a power to intoxicate his crude brains, just muddlingly awake to perceive that something is wrong in the social system, – what a hellish faculty above gunpowder! Now the rich and poor are fairly pitted. We shall see who can hang or burn fastest.

Charles Lamb

Letter to George Dyer (20 December, 1830),
from *The Letters of Charles Lamb*, edited by
T. N. Talfourd (1837)

THE MOVEMENT OF IDEAS: REFLECTION, ARGUMENT, EXHORTATION, SATIRE

THE EVIDENCE OF GOD'S DESIGN
IN NATURE

I SHALL not, I believe, be contradicted when I say, that, if one train of thinking be more desirable than another, it is that which regards the phænomena of nature with a constant reference to a supreme intelligent Author. To have made this the ruling, the habitual sentiment of our minds, is to have laid the foundation of every thing which is religious. The world from thenceforth becomes a temple, and life itself one continued act of adoration. The change is no less than this, that, whereas formerly God was seldom in our thoughts, we can now scarcely look upon any thing without perceiving its relation to him. Every organised natural body, in the provisions which it contains for its sustentation and propagation, testifies a care on the part of the Creator expressly directed to these purposes. We are on all sides surrounded by such bodies; examined in their parts, wonderfully curious; compared with one another, no less wonderfully diversified. So that the mind, as well as the eye, may either expatiate in variety and multitude, or fix itself down to the investigation of particular divisions of the science. And in either case it will rise up from its occupation, possessed by the subject, in a very different manner, and with a very different degree of influence, from what a mere assent to any verbal proposition which can be formed concerning the existence of the Deity, at least that merely complying assent with which those about us are satisfied, and with which we are too apt to satisfy ourselves, can or will produce upon the thoughts. More especially may this difference be perceived, in the degree of admiration and of awe, with which the Divinity is regarded, when represented to the understanding by its own remarks, its own reflections, and its own reasonings, compared with what is excited by any language that can be used by others. The works of nature want only to be contemplated. When contemplated, they have everything in them which can astonish by their greatness; for, of the vast scale of operation through which our discoveries carry us, at one end we see an intelligent Power arranging planetary systems, fixing, for instance, the trajectory of *Saturn*, or constructing a ring of a hundred thousand miles diameter, to surround his body, and be suspended like a magnificent arch over the heads of his inhabitants; and, at the other, bending a hooked tooth, concerting and providing an appropriate mechanism, for the clasping and reclasping of the filaments of the feather of a humming-bird. We have proof, not only of both these works proceeding from an intelligent agent, but of their proceeding from the same agent: for, in the first place, we can trace an identity of plan, a connexion of system, from Saturn to our own globe: and when arrived upon our globe, we can, in the second place, pursue the connexion through all the organised, especially the animated, bodies which it supports. We can observe marks of a common relation, as well to one another, as to the elements of which their habitation is composed. Therefore one mind hath planned, or at least hath prescribed, a general plan for all these productions. One Being has been concerned in all.

Under this stupendous Being we live. Our happiness, our existence, is in his hands. All we expect must come from him. Nor ought we to feel our situation insecure. In every nature, and in every portion of nature, which we can descry, we find attention bestowed upon even the minutest parts. The hinges in the wings of an *earwig*, and the joints of its antennae, are as highly wrought, as if the Creator had nothing else to finish. We see no signs of diminution of care by multiplicity of objects, or of distraction of thought by variety. We have no reason to fear, therefore, our being forgotten, or overlooked, or neglected.

The existence and character of the Deity, is, in every view, the most interesting of all human speculations. In none, however, is it more so, than as it facilitates the belief of the fundamental articles of *Revelation*. It is a step to have it proved, that there must be something in the world more than what we see. It is a further step to know, that, amongst the invisible things of nature, there must be an intelligent mind, concerned in its production, order, and support. These points being assured to us by Natural Theology, we may well leave to Revelation the disclosure of many particulars, which our researches cannot reach, respecting either the nature of this Being as the original cause of all things, or his character and designs as a moral governor.

William Paley

Natural Theology (1802). Text from the
second edition of the same year

DEMONSTRATIONS OF GOD

I HOLD then, it is true, that all the (so called) Demonstrations of a God either prove too little, as that from the Order and apparent Purpose in Nature; or too much, *viz.*, that the World is itself God: or they clandestinely involve the conclusion in the Premises, passing off the mere analysis or explication of an Assertion for the Proof of it, – a species of logical legerdemain not unlike that of the Jugglers at a Fair, who putting into their mouths what seems to be a walnut, draw out a score yards of Ribbon – as in the Postulate of a First Cause. And lastly, all these Demonstrations presuppose the Idea or Conception of a God without being able to authenticate it, i.e., to give an account whence they obtained it. For it is clear, that the Proof first mentioned and the most natural and convincing of all (the Cosmological I mean, or that from the Order in Nature) presupposes the Ontological – i.e. the proof of a God from the necessity and necessary *Objectivity* of the Idea. *If* the latter can assure us of a God as an existing Reality, the former will go far to prove his Power, Wisdom, and Benevolence. All this I hold. But I also hold, that this Truth, the hardest to demonstrate, is the one which of all others least needs to be demonstrated; that though there may be no conclusive demonstrations of a good, wise, living, and personal God, there are so many convincing reasons for it, within and without – a grain of sand sufficing, and a whole universe at hand to echo the decision! – that for every mind not devoid of all reason, and desperately conscience-proof, the Truth which it is the least possible to prove, it is little less than impossible not to believe! only indeed just so much short of impossible, as to leave some room for the will and the moral election, and thereby to keep it a truth of Religion, and the possible subject of a Commandment.

Samuel Taylor Coleridge
Aids to Reflection . . . (1825)

THE PROSPECTS FOR UNITARIANISM

NOTWITHSTANDING the fullness of my own persuasion, I am far from being sanguine in my expectations with respect to others, even from the strongest evidence that I can produce of the primitive Christians having been universally or very generally Unitarians. Though there do not appear to be so many learned *Arians* at present as there were thirty or forty years ago, yet I am well aware that the impression made by their writings is such, as that those persons who have now the most reputation for theological literature, (having in fact been their disciples,) are very generally of their opinion, as I myself formerly was; and therefore that there is at present, as might well be expected, a general prepossession against me among the more learned Christians with respect to this argument.

I am also not so ignorant of history or of human nature as not to be sensible that *time* is requisite to make any considerable change even in the opinions of the learned, though it certainly requires more time to produce an equal change in those of the unlearned; and with respect to most persons who are advanced in life, it is hardly to be expected from any force of argument. But in the last ten years a very great change has been made in the opinions of those who have given much attention to theological matters, and the number of Unitarians is greatly increased. A learned *Trinitarian* is almost a phenomenon in this country, and learned *Arians* are much fewer than they have been. And when the *historical arguments* in favour of proper Unitarianism, which have hitherto been very much overlooked, shall be duly attended to, especially that which arises from the consideration of the great body of the common people among Christians having thought that Christ was simply *a man inspired of God*, and their having had no knowledge of his *pre-existence*, the conclusion that such a general persuasion must have been derived from the apostles having taught no other doctrine will not easily be avoided. It will also weigh much with those who are apt to lay great stress on the usual construction of some *particular texts*, to consider, that, in those early times, the Scriptures were constantly read by persons better qualified to understand the language of them than we at this time can pretend to be, without suggesting any such notions of the divinity or the pre-existence of

Christ, as are now supposed to be clearly contained in them. When these, I say, and other similar arguments, shall have had time to operate, they will, I am confident, meet with less obstruction continually, and produce a still greater change in ten years to come.

As the doctrine of the pre-existence of Christ came in with philosophical and speculative people, and required many centuries, and those years of gross darkness, before it laid firm hold on the minds of the common people, it will certainly remain a long time with them; and a disposition to accommodate to these will likewise operate to quicken the zeal of many teachers of Christianity in its defence. This will, no doubt, protract the æra of reformation, towards which the enlightened friends of Christianity look forwards with confidence and joy, to a more distant period.

Joseph Priestley

Letters to Dr. Horsley, Part II (1784) from Theological
and Miscellaneous Works, Vol. XVIII (1831)

THE NOBLE ANIMAL MAN

I HAVE this moment received a note from Haslam in which he expects the death of his Father – who has been for some time in a state of insensibility – his mother bears up he says very well – I shall go to town tommorrow to see him. This is the world – thus we cannot expect to give way many hours to pleasure – Circumstances are like Clouds continually gathering and bursting – While we are laughing the seed of some trouble is put into the wide arable land of events – while we are laughing it sprouts it grows and suddenly bears a poison fruit which we must pluck – Even so we have leisure to reason on the misfortunes of our friends; our own touch us too nearly for words. Very few men have ever arrived at a complete disinterestedness of Mind: very few have been influenced by a pure desire of the benefit of others – in the greater part of the Benefactors to Humanity some meretricious motive has sullied their greatness – some melodramatic scenery has fa[s]cinated them – From the manner in which I feel Haslam's misfortune I perceive how far I am from any humble standard of disinterestedness – Yet this feeling ought to be carried to its highest pitch as there is no fear of its ever injuring Society – which it would do I fear pushed to an extremity – For in wild nature the Hawk would loose his Breakfast of Robins and the Robin his of Worms – the Lion must starve as well as the swallow. The greater part of Men make their way with the same instinctiveness, the same unwandering eye from their purposes, the same animal eagerness as the Hawk. The Hawk wants a Mate, so does the Man – look at them both they set about it and procure on[e] in the same manner. They want both a nest and they both set about one in the same manner – they get their food in the same manner – The noble animal Man for his amusement smokes his pipe – the Hawk balances about the Clouds – that is the only difference of their leisures. This it is that makes the Amusement of Life – to a speculative Mind. I go among the Fields and catch a glimpse of a Stoat or a fieldmouse peeping out of the withered grass – the creature hath a purpose and its eyes are bright with it. I go amongst the buildings of a city and I see a Man hurrying along – to what? the Creature has a purpose and his eyes are bright with it. But then, as Wordsworth says, "we have all one human heart" – there is an ellectric fire in human nature tending to purify – so that among these human creatures there is continu[a]lly some birth of new heroism. The pity is that we must wonder at it: as we should at finding a pearl in rubbish. I have no doubt that thousands of people never heard of have had hearts comp[l]etely disinterested: I can remember but two – Socrates and Jesus –

their Histories evince it. What I heard a little time ago, Taylor observe with respect to Socrates may be said of Jesus – That he was so great a man that though he transmitted no writing of his own to posterity, we have his Mind and his sayings and his greatness handed to us by others. It is to be lamented that the history of the latter was written and revised by Men interested in the pious frauds of Religion. Yet through all this I see his splendour. Even here though I myself am pursueing the same instinctive course as the veriest human animal you can think of – I am however young writing at random – straining at particles of light in the midst of a great darkness – without knowing the bearing of any one assertion of any one opinion. Yet may I not in this be free from sin? May there not be superior beings amused with any graceful, though instinctive attitude my mind m[a]y fall into, as I am entertained with the alertness of a Stoat or the anxiety of a Deer? Though a quarrel in the Streets is a thing to be hated, the energies displayed in it are fine; the commonest Man shows a grace in his quarrel – By a superior being our reasoning[s] may take the same tone – though erroneous they may be fine – This is the very thing in which consists poetry; and if so it is not so fine a thing as philosophy – For the same reason that an eagle is not so fine a thing as a truth.

John Keats

Letter to George and Georgiana Keats (14 February–
3 May, 1819) from *The Letters of John Keats*, edited
by M. B. Forman (1935)

COMMON SENSE

WE hear it maintained by people of more gravity than understanding, that genius and taste are strictly reducible to rules, and that there is a rule for every thing. So far is it from being true that the finest breath of fancy is a definable thing, that the plainest common sense is only what Mr. Locke would have called a *mixed mode*, subject to a particular sort of acquired and undefinable tact. It is asked, "If you do not know the rule by which a thing is done, how can you be sure of doing it a second time?" And the answer is, "If you do not know the muscles by the help of which you walk, how is it you do not fall down at every step you take?" In art, in taste, in life, in speech, you decide from feeling, and not from reason; that is, from the impression of a number of things on the mind, which impression is true and well-founded, though you may not be able to analyse or account for it in the several particulars. In a gesture you use, in a look you see, in a tone you hear, you judge of the expression, propriety, and meaning from habit, not from reason or rules; that is to say, from innumerable instances of like gestures, looks, and tones, in innumerable other circumstances, variously modified, which are too many and too refined to be all distinctly recollected, but which do not therefore operate the less powerfully upon the mind and eye of taste. Shall we say that these impressions (the immediate stamp of nature) do not operate in a given manner till they are classified and reduced to rules, or is not the rule itself grounded upon the truth and certainty of that natural operation? How then can the distinction of the understanding as to the manner in which they operate be necessary to their producing their due and uniform effect upon the mind? If certain effects did not regularly arise out of certain causes in mind as well as matter, there could be no rule given for them: nature does not follow the rule, but suggests it. Reason is the interpreter and critic of nature and genius, not their law-giver and judge. He must be a poor creature indeed whose practical convictions do not in almost all cases outrun his deliberate understanding, or who does not feel and know much more than he can give a reason for. – Hence the distinction between eloquence and wisdom, between ingenuity and common sense. A man may be dextrous and able in explaining the grounds of his opinions, and yet may be a mere sophist, because he only sees one half of a subject. Another may feel the whole weight of a question, nothing relating to it may be lost upon him, and yet he may be able to give no account of the manner in which it affects him, or to drag his reasons from their silent lurking-places. This last will be a wise man, though neither a logician nor rhetorician. Goldsmith was a fool to Dr. Johnson in argument; that is, in assigning the specific grounds of his opinions: Dr. Johnson was a fool to Goldsmith in the fine tact, the airy, intuitive faculty with which he skimmed the surfaces of things, and unconsciously formed his opinions. Common sense is the just result of the sum-total of such unconscious impressions in the ordinary occurrences of life, as they are treasured up in the memory, and called out by the occasion.

William Hazlitt
Table Talk (1821)

THE TRUTH OF IMAGINATION

I AM certain of nothing but of the holiness of the Heart's affections and the truth of Imagination – What the imagination seizes as Beauty must be truth – whether it existed before or not – for I have the same Idea of all our Passions as of Love they are all in their sublime, creative of essential Beauty. . . . The Imagination may be compared to Adam's dream – he awoke and found it truth. I am the more zealous in this affair, because I have never yet been able to perceive how any thing can be known for truth by consequitive reasoning – and yet it must be. Can it be that even the greatest Philosopher ever arrived at his goal without putting aside numerous objections. However it may be, O for a Life of Sensations rather than of

Thoughts! It is 'a Vision in the form of Youth' a Shadow of reality to come – and this consideration has further convinced me for it has come as auxiliary to another favorite Speculation of mine, that we shall enjoy ourselves here after by having what we called happiness on Earth repeated in a finer tone and so repeated. And yet such a fate can only befall those who delight in Sensation rather than hunger as you do after Truth. Adam's dream will do here and seems to be a conviction that Imagination and its empyreal reflection is the same as human Life and its Spiritual repetition. But as I was saying – the simple imaginative Mind may have its rewards in the repeti-[ti]on of its own silent Working coming continually on the Spirit with a fine Suddenness – to compare great things with small – have you never by being Surprised with an old Melody – in a delicious place – by a delicious voice, fe[l]t over again your very Speculations and Surmises at the time it first operated on your Soul – do you not remember forming to yourself the singer's face more beautiful than it was possible and yet with the elevation of the Moment you did not think so – even then you were mounted on the Wings of Imagination so high – that the Prototype must be here after – that delicious face you will see. What a time! I am continually running away from the subject – sure this cannot be exactly the case with a complex Mind – one that is imaginative and at the same time careful of its fruits – who would exist partly on Sensation partly on thought – to whom it is necessary that years should bring the philosophic Mind – such an one I consider your's and therefore it is necessary to your eternal Happiness that you not only drink this old Wine of Heaven, which I shall call the redigestion of our most ethereal Musings on Earth; but also increase in knowledge and know all things.

John Keats

Letter to Benjamin Bailey (22 November, 1817) from *The Letters of John Keats*, edited by M. B. Forman (1935)

PROVERBS OF HELL

He who desires but acts not, breeds pestilence.

The cut worm forgives the plow.

A fool sees not the same tree that a wise man sees.

Eternity is in love with the productions of time.

All wholsom food is caught without a net or a trap.

Bring out number weight & measure in a year of dearth.

If the fool would persist in his folly he would become wise.

Prisons are built with stones of Law, Brothels with bricks of Religion.

What is now proved was once only imagin'd.

The cistern contains: the fountain overflows.

One thought fills immensity.

Always be ready to speak your mind, and a base man will avoid you.

Every thing possible to be believ'd is an image of truth.

He who has suffer'd you to impose on him knows you.

The tygers of wrath are wiser than the horses of instruction.

The eyes of fire, the nostrils of air, the mouth of water, the beard of earth.

The weak in courage is strong in cunning.

If others had not been foolish, we should be so.

As the catterpiller chooses the fairest leaves to lay her eggs on, so the priest lays his curse on the fairest joys.

Damn braces: Bless relaxes.

The head Sublime, the heart Pathos, the genitals Beauty, the hands & feet Proportion.

As the air to a bird or the sea to a fish, so is contempt to the contemptible.

Sooner murder an infant in its cradle than nurse unacted desires.

Truth can never be told so as to be understood, and not
  be believ'd.

William Blake

The Marriage of Heaven and Hell (c. 1790). Text from
W. Muir's facsimile (1885) of the Quaritch copy

THE PRINCIPLES OF CONSERVATISM

WHEN the useful parts of an old establishment are kept, and
what is superadded is to be fitted to what is retained, a vigorous
mind, steady persevering attention, various powers of comparison and combination, and the resources of an understanding fruitful in expedients are to be exercised; they are to
be exercised in a continued conflict with the combined force
of opposite vices; with the obstinacy that rejects all improvement, and the levity that is fatigued and disgusted with every
thing of which it is in possession. But you may object – "A
process of this kind is slow. It is not fit for an assembly, which
glories in performing in a few months the work of ages.
Such a mode of reforming, possibly might take up many
years." Without question it might; and it ought. It is one of
the excellencies of a method in which time is amongst the
assistants, that its operation is slow, and in some cases almost
imperceptible. If circumspection and caution are a part of
wisdom, when we work only upon inanimate matter, surely
they become a part of duty too, when the subject of our
demolition and construction is not brick and timber, but
sentient beings, by the sudden alteration of whose state, condition, and habits, multitudes may be rendered miserable. But
it seems as if it were the prevalent opinion in Paris, that an
unfeeling heart, and an undoubting confidence, are the sole
qualifications for a perfect legislator. Far different are my ideas
of that high office. The true lawgiver ought to have an heart
full of sensibility. He ought to love and respect his kind, and

to fear himself. It may be allowed to his temperament to catch his ultimate object with an intuitive glance; but his movements towards it ought to be deliberate. Political arrangement, as it is a work for social ends, is to be only wrought by social means. There mind must conspire with mind. Time is required to produce that union of minds which alone can produce all the good we aim at. Our patience will atchieve more than our force. If I might venture to appeal to what is so much out of fashion in Paris, I mean to experience, I should tell you, that in my course I have known, and, according to my measure, have co-operated with great men; and I have never yet seen any plan which has not been mended by the observations of those who were much inferior in understanding to the person who took the lead in the business. By a slow but well-sustained progress, the effect of each step is watched; the good or ill success of the first, gives light to us in the second; and so, from light to light, we are conducted with safety through the whole series. We see, that the parts of the system do not clash. The evils latent in the most promising contrivances are provided for as they arise. One advantage is as little as possible sacrificed to another. We compensate, we reconcile, we balance. We are enabled to unite into a consistent whole the various anomalies and contending principles that are found in the minds and affairs of men. From hence arises, not an excellence in simplicity, but one far superior, an excellence in composition.

- Edmund Burke

Reflections on the Revolution in France . . . (1790)

AN ANSWER TO BURKE

ALL the Governments that now exist in the world, (except the United States of America) have been fortuitously formed.

They are the produce of chance, not the work of art. They have been altered, impaired, improved and destroyed by accidental circumstances, beyond the foresight or controul of wisdom. Their parts thrown up against present emergencies formed no systematic whole. It was certainly not to have been presumed, that these *fortuitous Governments* should have surpassed the works of intellect, and precluded all nearer approaches to perfection. Their origin without doubt furnishes a strong presumption of an opposite nature. It might teach us to expect in them many discordant principles, many jarring forms, much unmixed evil, and much imperfect good, many institutions which had long survived their motive, and many of which reason had never been the author, nor utility the object. Experience, *even in the best of these Governments*, accords with such expectations.

A Government of *art*, the work of legislative intellect, reared on the immutable basis of natural right and general happiness, which should combine the excellencies, and exclude the defects of the various constitutions which chance had scattered over the world, instead of being precluded by the perfection of any of those forms, was loudly demanded by the injustice and absurdity of them all. It was time that men should learn to tolerate nothing ancient that reason does not respect, and to shrink from no novelty to which reason may conduct. It was time that the human powers, so long occupied by subordinate objects, and inferior arts, should mark the commencement of a new æra in history, by giving birth to the art of improving government, and increasing the civil happiness of man. It was time, as it has been wisely and eloquently said, that Legislators, instead of that narrow and dastardly *coasting* which never ventures to lose sight of usage and precedent, should, guided by the *polarity* of reason, hazard a bolder navigation, and discover, in unexplored regions, the treasure of public felicity.

The task of the French Legislators was, however, less hazardous. The philosophers of Europe had for a century discussed all objects of public œconomy. The conviction of a great majority of enlightened men had, after many controversies, become on most questions of general politics, uniform. A degree of certainty, perhaps nearly equal to that which such topics will admit, had been attained. The National Assembly were therefore not called on to make discoveries. It was sufficient if they were not uninfluenced by the opinions, nor exempt from the spirit of their age. They were fortunate enough to live in a period when it was only necessary to affix the stamp of laws to what had been prepared by the research of philosophy.

Sir James Mackintosh
Vindiciae Gallicae (1791)

THIS METAPHOR CALLED A CROWN

BUT, after all, what is this metaphor called a crown, or rather what is monarchy? Is it a thing, or is it a name, or is it a fraud? Is it "a contrivance of human wisdom," or of human craft to obtain money from a nation under specious pretences? Is it a thing necessary to a nation? If it is, in what does that necessity consist, what services does it perform, what is its business, and what are its merits? Doth the virtue consist in the metaphor, or in the man? Doth the goldsmith that makes the crown, make the virtue also? Doth it operate like Fortunatus's wishing-cap, or Harlequin's wooden sword? Doth it make a man a conjuror? In fine, what is it? It appears to be a something going much out of fashion, falling into ridicule, and rejected in some countries both as unnecessary and expensive. In America it is considered as an absurdity, and in

France it has so far declined, that the goodness of the man, and the respect for his personal character, are the only things that preserve the appearance of its existence.

If Government be what Mr. Burke describes it, "a contrivance of human wisdom," I might ask him, if wisdom was at such a low ebb in England, that it was become necessary to import it from Holland and from Hanover? But I will do the country the justice to say, that was not the case; and even if it was, it mistook the cargo. The wisdom of every country, when properly exerted, is sufficient for all its purposes; and there could exist no more real occasion in England to have sent for a Dutch Stadtholder, or a German Elector, than there was in America to have done a similar thing. If a country does not understand its own affairs, how is a foreigner to understand them, who knows neither its laws, its manners, nor its language? If there existed a man so transcendantly wise above all others, that his wisdom was necessary to instruct a nation, some reason might be offered for monarchy; but when we cast our eyes about a country, and observe how every part understands its own affairs; and when we look around the world, and see that of all men in it, the race of kings are the most insignificant in capacity, our reason cannot fail to ask us – What are those men kept for?

If there is any thing in monarchy which we people of America do not understand, I wish Mr. Burke would be so kind as to inform us. I see in America, a government extending over a country ten times as large as England, and conducted with regularity for a fortieth part of the expence which government costs in England. If I ask a man in America, if he wants a King? he retorts, and asks me if I take him for an ideot? How is it that this difference happens? are we more or less wise than others? I see in America, the generality of people living in a stile of plenty unknown in monarchical countries; and I see that the principle of its government, which is that of the *equal Rights of Man*, is making a rapid progress in the world.

Thomas Paine

Rights of Man: Being an Answer to Mr Burke's
Attack on the French Revolution (1791)

PANTISOCRACY

Truth I pursued, as fancy sketch'd the way,
And wiser men than I went worse astray.

I WAS never myself, at any period of my life, a convert to the Jacobinical system. From my earliest manhood, it was an axiom in politics with me, that in every country where property prevailed, property must be the grand basis of the government; and that that government was the best, in which the power or political influence of the individual was in proportion to his property, provided that the free circulation of property was not impeded by any positive laws or customs, nor the tendency of wealth to accumulate in abiding masses unduly encouraged. I perceived, that if the people at large were neither ignorant nor immoral, there could be no motive for a sudden and violent change of government; and if they were, there could be no hope but of a change for the worse. The temple of despotism, like that of the Mexican God, would be rebuilt with human skulls, and more firmly, though in a different style of architecture. Thanks to the excellent education which I had received, my reason was too clear not to draw this circle of power round me, and my spirit too honest to attempt to break through it. My feelings, however, and imagination did not remain unkindled in this general conflagration; and I confess I should be more inclined to be ashamed than proud of myself, if they had. I was a sharer in the general vortex, though my little world described the path of its revolution in an orbit of its own. What I dared not

expect from constitutions of government and whole nations,
I hoped from religion and a small company of chosen individuals. I formed a plan, as harmless as it was extravagant, of
trying the experiment of human perfectibility on the banks
of the Susquehanna; where our little society, in its second
generation, was to have combined the innocence of the patri-
archal age with the knowledge and genuine refinements of
European culture; and where I dreamed that in the sober
evening of my life, I should behold the cottages of independence in the undivided dale of industry, –

> And oft, soothed sadly by some dirgeful wind,
> Muse on the sore ills I had left behind!

Strange fancies, and as vain as strange! yet to the intense
interest and impassioned zeal, which called forth and strained
every faculty of my intellect for the organization and defence
of this scheme, I owe much of whatever I at present possess,
my clearest insight into the nature of individual man, and my
most comprehensive views of his social relations, of the true
uses of trade and commerce, and how far the wealth and
relative power of nations promote or impede their welfare
and inherent strength. Nor were they less serviceable in
securing myself, and perhaps some others, from the pitfalls of
sedition: and when we at length alighted on the firm ground
of common sense from the gradually exhausted balloon of
youthful enthusiasm, though the air-built castles, which we
had been pursuing, had vanished with all their pageantry of
shifting forms and glowing colours, we were yet free from
the stains and impurities which might have remained upon
us, had we been travelling with the crowd of less imaginative
malcontents, through the dark lanes and foul by-roads of
ordinary fanaticism.

Samuel Taylor Coleridge
The Friend (1809–10). Text from
the revised third edition (1837)

Objections to a System of
National Education

REAL intellectual improvement demands that mind should as speedily as possible be advanced to the height of knowledge already existing among the enlightened members of the community, and start from thence in the pursuit of farther acquisitions. But public education has always expended its energies in the support of prejudice; it teaches its pupils, not the fortitude that shall bring every proposition to the test of examination, but the art of vindicating such tenets as may chance to be previously established. We study Aristotle or Thomas Aquinas or Bellarmine or chief justice Coke, not that we may detect their errors, but that our minds may be fully impregnated with their absurdities. This feature runs through every species of public establishment; and even in the petty institution of Sunday schools, the chief lessons that are taught, are a superstitious veneration for the church of England, and to bow to every man in a handsome coat. All this is directly contrary to the true interest of mind. All this must be unlearned, before we can begin to be wise.

It is the characteristic of mind to be capable of improvement. An individual surrenders the best attribute of man, the moment he resolves to adhere to certain fixed principles, for reasons not now present to his mind, but which formerly were. The instant in which he shuts upon himself the career of enquiry, is the instant of his intellectual decease. He is no longer a man; he is the ghost of departed man. There can be no scheme more egregiously stamped with folly, than that of separating a tenet from the evidence upon which its validity depends. If I cease from the habit of being able to recal this evidence, my belief is no longer a perception, but a prejudice; it may influence me like a prejudice; but cannot animate me like a real apprehension of truth. The difference between the man thus guided, and the man that keeps his mind perpetually alive, is the difference between cowardice and fortitude. The man who is in the best sense an intellectual being, delights to recollect the reasons that have convinced him, to repeat them to others, that they may produce conviction in them, and stand more distinct and explicit in his own mind; and he adds to this a willingness to examine objections, because he takes no pride in consistent error. The man who is not capable of this salutary exercise, to what valuable purpose can he be employed? Hence it appears that no vice can be more destructive than that which teaches us to regard any judgment as final, and not open to review. The same principle that applies to individuals applies to communities. There is no proposition, at present apprehended to be true, so valuable as to justify the introduction of an establishment for the purpose of inculcating it on mankind. Refer them to reading, to conversation, to meditation; but teach them neither creeds nor catechisms, neither moral nor political.

Secondly, the idea of national education is founded in an inattention to the nature of mind. Whatever each man does for himself is done well; whatever his neighbours or his country undertake to do for him is done ill. It is our wisdom to incite men to act for themselves, not to retain them in a state of perpetual pupillage. He that learns because he desires to learn, will listen to the instructions he receives, and apprehend their meaning. He that teaches because he desires to teach, will discharge his occupation with enthusiasm and energy. But the moment political institution undertakes to assign to every man his place, the functions of all will be discharged with supineness and indifference. Universities and expensive establishments have long been remarked for formal dulness. Civil policy has given me the power to appropriate my estate to certain theoretical purposes; but it is an idle presumption to think I can entail my views, as I can entail my fortune. Remove all those obstacles which prevent men from seeing and restrain them from pursuing their real advantage, but do not absurdly undertake to relieve them from the activity which this pursuit requires. What I earn, what I acquire only because I desire to acquire it, I estimate at its true value; but what is thrust upon me may make me indolent, but cannot make me respectable. It is extreme folly to endeavour to secure to others, independently of exertion on their part, the means of being happy. – This whole proposition of a national education, is founded upon a supposition which has been repeatedly refuted in this work, but which has recurred upon us in a thousand forms, that unpatronised truth is inadequate to the purpose of enlightening mankind.

Thirdly, the project of a national education ought uniformly to be discouraged on account of its obvious alliance with national government. This is an alliance of a more formidable nature, than the old and much contested alliance of church and state. Before we put so powerful a machine under the direction of so ambiguous an agent, it behoves us to consider well what it is that we do. Government will not fail to employ it to strengthen its hands, and perpetuate its institutions. If we could even suppose the agents of government not to propose to themselves an object, which will be apt to appear in their eyes, not merely innocent, but meritorious; the evil would not the less happen. Their views as institutors of a system of education, will not fail to be analogous to their views in their political capacity: the data upon which their conduct as statesmen is vindicated, will be the data upon which their instructions are founded. It is not true that our youth ought to be instructed to venerate the constitution, however excellent; they should be instructed to venerate truth; and the constitution only so far as it corresponded with

(yes + no)

their independent deductions of truth. Had the scheme of a national education been adopted when despotism was most triumphant, it is not to be believed that it could have for ever stifled the voice of truth. But it would have been the most formidable and profound contrivance for that purpose that imagination can suggest. Still, in the countries where liberty chiefly prevails, it is reasonably to be assumed that there are important errors, and a national education has the most direct tendency to perpetuate those errors, and to form all minds upon one model.

William Godwin

An Enquiry concerning Political Justice (1793)

THE NEGLECTED LESSONS
OF HISTORY

HENCE it is that human experience, like the stern lights of a ship at sea, illumines only the path which we have passed over. The horrors of the Peasants' War in Germany, and the direful effects of the Anabaptist tenets, which were only nominally different from those of Jacobinism by the substitution of religious for philosophical jargon, struck all Europe for a time with affright. Yet little more than a century was sufficient to obliterate all effective memory of those events: the same principles budded forth anew, and produced the same fruits from the imprisonment of Charles I. to the restoration of his son. In the succeeding generations, to the follies and vices of the European courts, and to the oppressive privileges of the nobility, were again transferred those feelings of disgust and hatred, which for a brief while the multitude had attached to the crimes and extravagances of political and religious fanaticism: and the same principles, aided by circumstances and dressed out in the ostentatious garb of a fashionable philosophy, once more rose triumphant, and effected the French revolution. That man has reflected little on human nature who does not perceive that the detestable maxims and correspondent crimes of the existing French despotism,[1] have already dimmed the recollections of the democratic phrenzy in the minds of men; by little and little, have drawn off to other objects the electric force of the feelings, which had massed and upholden those recollections; and that a favourable concurrence of occasions is alone wanting to awaken the thunder and precipitate the lightning from the opposite quarter of the political heaven. The true origin of human events is so little susceptible of that kind of evidence which can compel our belief even against our will; and so many are the disturbing forces which modify the motion given by the first projection; and every age has, or imagines it has, its own circumstances which render past experience no longer applicable to the present case; that there will never be wanting answers and explanations, and specious flatteries of hope. I well remember, that when the examples of former Jacobins, Julius Caesar, Cromwell, &c. were adduced in France and England at the commencement of the French Consulate, it was ridiculed as pedantry and pedants' ignorance, to fear a repetition of such usurpation at the close of the enlightened eighteenth century. Those who possess the *Moniteurs* of that date will find set proofs, that such results were little less than impossible, and that it was an insult to so philosophical an age, and so enlightened a nation, to dare direct the public eye towards them as lights of admonition and warning.

Samuel Taylor Coleridge
The Friend (1809–10). Text from the
revised third edition (1837)

1. Napoleon's.

PARISH RELIEF

MR. PITT's Poor-bill has the appearance of being framed with benevolent intentions, and the clamour raised against it was in many respects ill directed, and unreasonable. But it must be confessed that it possesses in a high degree the great and radical defect of all systems of the kind, that, of tending to increase population without increasing the means for its support, and thus to depress the condition of those that are not supported by parishes, and, consequently, to create more poor.

To remove the wants of the lower classes of society, is indeed an arduous task. The truth is, that the pressure of distress on this part of a community is an evil so deeply seated, that no human ingenuity can reach it. Were I to propose a palliative; and palliatives are all that the nature of the case will admit; it should be, in the first place, the total abolition of all the present parish-laws. This would at any rate give liberty and freedom of action to the peasantry of England, which they can hardly be said to possess at present. They would then be able to settle without interruption, wherever there was a prospect of a greater plenty of work, and a higher price for labour. The market of labour would then be free, and those obstacles removed, which as things are now, often for a considerable time prevent the price from rising according to the demand.

Secondly, Premiums might be given for turning up fresh land, and all possible encouragements held out to agriculture above manufactures, and to tillage above grazing. Every endeavour should be used to weaken and destroy all those institutions relating to corporations, apprenticeships, etc. which cause the labours of agriculture to be worse paid than the labours of trade and manufactures. For a country can never produce its proper quantity of food while these distinctions remain in favour of artizans. Such encouragements to agriculture would tend to furnish the market with an increasing quantity of healthy work, and at the same time, by augmenting the produce of the country, would raise the comparative price of labour, and ameliorate the condition of the labourer. Being now in better circumstances, and seeing no prospect of parish assistance, he would be more able, as well as more inclined, to enter into associations for providing against the sickness of himself or family.

Lastly, for cases of extreme distress, county workhouses might be established, supported by rates upon the whole kingdom, and free for persons of all counties, and indeed of all nations. The fare should be hard, and those that were able obliged to work. It would be desirable, that they should not be considered as comfortable asylums in all difficulties; but merely as places where severe distress might find some alleviation. A part of these houses might be separated, or others built for a most beneficial purpose, which has not been unfrequently taken notice of, that of providing a place, where any person, whether native or foreigner, might do a day's work at all times, and receive the market price for it. Many cases would undoubtedly be left for the exertion of individual benevolence.

Thomas Robert Malthus
An Essay on the Principle of Population, as it affects the
Future Improvement of Society .... (1798)

THE REPEAL OF THE COMBINATION LAWS

WE fear that the cause of savings banks may have sustained a temporary discredit from the recent conduct of workmen all over the country. The apprehension is, that, by a large united capital amongst them, they might get the upper hand of their employers altogether; that, in possession of means which could enable them to be idle, they may exercise a power most capriciously and most inconveniently for the other classes of society; that they may lay manufacturers under bondage by their impregnable combinations; and, striking work at the most critical and unexpected junctures, they may subject the whole economy of human life to jolts and sudden derangements which might be enough for its overthrow. These fears, enhanced though they have been of late by the outrages of workmen in various parts of the country, would speedily be dissipated, we believe, under the light of growing experience. The repeal of the combination laws has not even yet been adequately tried. The effervescence which has followed on that repeal, is the natural, and, we believe, the temporary effect of the anterior state of things. There was nothing more likely than that the people, when put in possession of a power which they felt to be altogether new, would take a delight in the exercise of it, and break forth into misplaced and most extravagant manifestations. But if the conduct of the one party have been extravagant, the alarm of the other party we conceive to have been equally extravagant. We trust that the alarm may have in part been dissipated, ere Government shall be induced to legislate any further upon the subject; or to trench, by any of its acts, on the great principle of every man being entitled to make the most of his own labour, and also of acting in concert with his fellows for the production of a general benefit, as great as they can possibly make out to the whole body of labourers.

The repeal of the combination laws in England has been attended with consequences which strongly remind us of the consequences that ensued, after the Revolution, from the repeal of the game laws in France. The whole population, thrown agog by their new privilege, poured forth upon the country, and, variously accoutred, made war, in grotesque and unpractised style, upon the fowls of the air and the beasts of the field. In a few months, however, the extravagance sub-sided, and the people returned to their old quiescent habits and natural occupations. We feel assured that, in like manner, this delirium of a newly awakened faculty among our British workmen will speedily pass away. They will at length become wise and temperate in the use of it. Neither party, in fact, well understand how to proceed in the unwonted relation wherein they now stand to each other. There is indefinite demand upon the one side; upon the other there are distrust, and a most sensitive dread of encroachment. They have not yet completed their trial of strength; and just because, in ignorance of each other's powers, there are yet the effort, and the excitation, and the busy rivalship, of a still undetermined conflict.

Thomas Chalmers
The Christian and Civic Economy
of Large Towns, Vol. III (1826)

FREE TRADE:
A SELF-EVIDENT PROPOSITION

NOW it is certain . . . that no commodity which can be made at home will ever be imported from a foreign country, unless it can be obtained by importation with a smaller quantity of labour, that is, cost, than it could be produced with at home. That it is desirable to have commodities produced with as small a cost of labour as possible, seems to be not only certain, but admitted. This is the object of all the improvements that are aimed at in production, by the division and distribution of labour, by refined methods of culture applied to the land, by the invention of more potent and skilful machines. It seems, indeed, to be a self-evident proposition, that whatever the quantity which a nation possesses of the means of production, the more productive they can possibly be rendered, so much the better; for this is neither more nor less than saying, that to have all the objects we desire, and to have them with little trouble, is good for mankind.

Not only is it certain, that in a state of freedom no commodity which can be made at home will ever be imported, unless it can be imported with a less quantity or cost of labour than it could be produced with at home; but whatever is the country from which it can be obtained with the smallest cost of labour, to that country recourse will be had for obtaining it, and whatever the commodity by the exportation of which it can be obtained with the smallest quantity of home labour, that is the commodity which will be exported in exchange. This results so obviously from the laws of trade, as not to require explanation. It is no more than saying, that the merchants, if left to themselves, will always buy in the cheapest market, and sell in the dearest.

It seems, therefore, to be fully established, that the business of production and exchange, if left to choose its own channels, is sure to choose those which are most advantageous to the community. It is sure to choose those channels, in which the commodities which the community desires to obtain, are obtained with the smallest cost. To obtain the commodities which it desires, and to obtain them with the smallest cost, is the whole of the good which the business of production and exchange, considered simply as such, is calculated to yield. In whatever degree, therefore, the business of production and exchange is forced out of the channels into which it would go of its own accord, in that degree the advantages arising from production and exchange are sacrificed; or, at any rate, postponed to something else. If there is any case in which they ought to be postponed to something else, that is a question of politics, and not of political economy.

James Mill
Elements of Political Economy (1821)

THE VESTED INTERESTS OF LAWYERS

THE opinions of lawyers in a question of legislation, particularly of such lawyers as are or have been practising advocates, are peculiarly liable to be tinged with falsity by the operation of sinister interest. To the interest of the community at large, that of every advocate is in a state of such direct and constant opposition (especially in civil matters), that the above assertion requires an apology to redeem it from the appearance of trifling: the apology consists in the extensively prevailing propensity to overlook and turn aside from a fact so entitled to notice. It is the people's interest that delay, vexation and expense of procedure should be as small as possible: – it is the advocate's that they should be as great as possible: viz. expense in so far as his profit is proportioned to it; factitious vexation and delay, in so far as inseparable from the profit-yielding part of the expense. As to uncertainty in the law, it is the people's interest that each man's security against wrong should be as complete as possible; that all his rights should be known to him; that all acts, which in the case of his doing them will be treated as offences, may be known to him as such, together with their eventual punishment, that he may avoid committing them, and that others may, in as few instances as possible, suffer either from the wrong or from the expensive and vexatious remedy. Hence it is their interest, that as to all these matters the rule of action, in so far as it applies to each man, should at all times be not only discoverable, but actually present to his mind. Such knowledge, which it is every man's interest to possess to the greatest, it is the lawyer's interest that he possess it to the narrowest extent possible. It is every man's interest to keep out of lawyers' hands as much as possible; it is the lawyer's interest to get him in as often, and keep him in as long, as possible: thence that any written expression of the words necessary to keep non-lawyers out of his hand may as long as possible be prevented from coming into existence, and when in existence as long as possible kept from being present to his mind, and when presented from staying there. It is the lawyer's interest, therefore, that people should continually suffer for the non-observance of laws, which, so far from having received efficient promulgation, have never yet found any authoritative expression in words. This is the perfection of oppression: yet, propose that access to knowledge of the laws be afforded by means of a code, lawyers, one and all, will join in declaring it impossible. To any effect, as occasion occurs, a judge will forge a rule of law: to that same effect, in any determinate form of words, propose to make a law, that same judge will declare it impossible. It is the judge's interest that on every occasion his declared opinion be taken for the standard of right and wrong; that whatever he declares right or wrong be universally received as such, how contrary soever such declaration be to truth and utility, or to his own declaration at other times: – hence, that within the whole field of law, men's opinions of right and wrong should be as contradictory, unsettled, and thence as obsequious to him as possible.

Jeremy Bentham
The Book of Fallacies (1824)

CONCILIATION WITH AMERICA

IN this situation, let us seriously and coolly ponder. What is it we have got by all our menaces, which have been many and ferocious? What advantage have we derived from the penal laws we have passed, and which, for the time, have been severe and numerous? What advances have we made towards our object, by the sending of a force, which, by land and sea, is no contemptible strength? Has the disorder abated? Nothing less. – When I see things in this situation, after such confident hopes, bold promises, and active exertions, I cannot, for my life, avoid a suspicion, that the plan itself is not correctly right.

If then the removal of the causes of this Spirit of American Liberty be, for the greater part, or rather entirely, impracticable; if the ideas of Criminal Process be inapplicable, or if applicable, are in the highest degree inexpedient, what way yet remains? No way is open, but the third and last – to comply with the American Spirit as necessary; or, if you please, to submit to it as a necessary Evil.

If we adopt this mode; if we mean to conciliate and concede; let us see of what nature the concession ought to be? To ascertain the nature of our concession, we must look at their complaint. The Colonies complain, that they have not the characteristic Mark and Seal of British Freedom. They complain, that they are taxed in a Parliament, in which they are not represented. If you mean to satisfy them at all, you must satisfy them with regard to this complaint. If you mean to please any people, you must give them the boon which they ask; not what you may think better for them, but of a kind totally different. Such an act may be a wise regulation, but it is no concession: whereas our present theme is the mode of giving satisfaction.

Sir, I think you must perceive, that I am resolved this day to have nothing at all to do with the question of the right of taxation. Some gentlemen startle – but it is true: I put it totally out of the question. It is less than nothing in my consideration. I do not indeed wonder, nor will you, Sir, that gentlemen of profound learning are fond of displaying it on this profound subject. But my consideration is narrow, confined, and wholly limited to the Policy of the question. I do not examine, whether the giving away a man's money be a power excepted and reserved out of the general trust of Government; and how far all mankind, in all forms of Polity, are entitled to an exercise of that Right by the Charter or Nature. Or whether, on the contrary, a Right of Taxation is necessarily involved in the general principle of Legislation, and inseparable from the ordinary Supreme Power. These are deep questions, where great names militate against each other; where reason is perplexed; and an appeal to authorities only thickens the confusion. For high and reverend authorities lift up their heads on both sides; and there is no sure footing in the middle. This point is the *great Serbonian bog, betwixt Damiata and Mount Casius old, where armies whole have sunk.* I do not intend to be overwhelmed in that bog, though in such respectable company. The question with me is, not whether you have a right to render your people miserable; but whether it is not your interest to make them happy? It is not, what a lawyer tells me, I *may* do; but what humanity, reason, and justice tell me, I ought to do. Is a politic act the worse for being a generous one? Is no concession proper, but that which is made from your want of right to keep what you grant? Or does it lessen the grace or dignity of relaxing in the exercise of an odious claim, because you have your evidence-room full of Titles, and your magazines stuffed with arms to enforce them? What signify all those titles, and all those arms? Of what avail are they, when the reason of the thing tells me, that the assertion of my title is the loss of my suit; and that I could do nothing but wound myself by the use of my own weapons?

Such is stedfastly my opinion of the absolute necessity of keeping up the concord of this empire by a Unity of Spirit, though in a diversity of operations, that, if I were sure the Colonists had, at their leaving this country, sealed a regular compact of servitude; that they had solemnly abjured all the rights of citizens; that they had made a vow to renounce all Ideas of Liberty for them and their posterity to all generations; yet I should hold myself obliged to conform to the temper I found universally prevalent in my own day, and to govern two millions of men, impatient of Servitude, on the principles of Freedom. I am not determining a point of law; I am restoring tranquillity; and the general character and situation of a people must determine what sort of government is fitted for them. That point nothing else can or ought to determine.

My idea, therefore, without considering whether we yield as a matter of right, or grant as a matter of favour, is *to admit the people of our Colonies into an interest in the constitution*; and, by recording that admission in the Journals of Parliament, to give them as strong an assurance as the nature of the thing will admit, that we mean for ever to adhere to that solemn declaration of systematic indulgence.

Edmund Burke
Speech on Conciliation with the Colonies (1775).
Text from the second edition of the same year

THE TRIAL OF LORD GEORGE GORDON

(1781)

GENTLEMEN, you have now heard, upon the solemn oaths of honest disinterested men, a faithful history of the conduct of Lord George Gordon from the day that he became a member of the Protestant Association, to the day that he was committed a prisoner to the Tower. And I have no doubt, from the attention with which I have been honoured from the beginning, that you have still kept in your minds the principles, to which I entreated you would apply it, and that you have measured it by that standard.

You have therefore only to look back to the whole of it together; – to reflect on all you have heard concerning him; – to trace him in your recollection through every part of the transaction; – and, considering it with one manly liberal view, to ask your own honest hearts, whether you can say, that this noble and unfortunate youth is a wicked and deliberate traitor, who deserves by your verdict to suffer a shameful and ignominious death, which will stain the ancient honours of his house for ever.

The crime which the Crown would have fixed upon him is, that he assembled the Protestant Association round the House of Commons, not merely *to influence and persuade Parliament by the earnestness of their supplications*, but actually to coerce it *by hostile rebellious force* – that finding himself disappointed in the success of that coercion, he afterwards incited his followers to abolish the legal indulgences to Papists, which the object of the petition was to repeal, by the burning of their houses of worship and the destruction of their property, which ended at last in a general attack on the property of all orders of men, religious and civil, – on the public treasures of the nation, – and on the very being of the Government.

To support a charge of so atrocious and unnatural a complexion, the laws of the most arbitrary nations would require the most incontrovertible proof. Either the villain must have been taken in the overt act of wickedness, or, if he worked in secret upon others, his guilt must have been brought out by the discovery of a conspiracy, or by the consistent tenour of criminality; – the very worst inquisitor that ever dealt in blood would vindicate the torture by plausibility at least, and by the semblance of truth.

What evidence, then, will a jury of Englishmen expect, from the servants of the Crown of England, before they deliver up a brother accused before them to ignominy and death? – What proof will their consciences require? – What will their plain and manly understandings accept of? – What does the immemorial custom of their fathers, and the written law of this land, warrant them in demanding? Nothing less, *in any case of blood*, than the clearest and most unequivocal conviction of guilt. . . . And what evidence, Gentlemen of the Jury, does the Crown offer to you in compliance with these sound and sacred doctrines of justice? – a few broken, interrupted, disjointed words, without context or connexion, – uttered by the speaker in agitation and heat, – heard by those who relate them to you, in the midst of tumult and confusion, – and even those words, mutilated as they are, in direct opposition to, and inconsistent with, repeated and earnest declarations, delivered at the very same time, and on the very same occasion, related to you by a much greater number of persons, and absolutely incompatible with the whole tenour of his conduct. Which of us all, Gentlemen, would be safe, standing at the bar of God or man, if we were not to be judged by the regular current of our lives and conversations, but by detached and unguarded expressions, picked out by malice, and recorded, without context or circumstances, against us? Yet such is the only evidence on which the Crown asks you to dip your hands and to stain your consciences in the innocent blood of the noble and unfortunate youth who now stands before you.

Thomas, Lord Erskine

Speeches . . . (1810)

SECRET INFLUENCE

IF, however, a change must take place, and a new ministry is to be formed and supported, not by the confidence of this House, or the public, but the sole authority of the crown, I, for one, shall not envy that honourable gentleman [1] his situation. From that moment I put in my claim for a monopoly

1. William Pitt.

of whig-principles. The glorious cause of freedom, of independence, and of the constitution, is no longer his, but mine.
In this I have lived; in this I will die. It has borne me up under
every aspersion to which my character has been subjected.
The resentments of the mean and the aversion of the great,
the rancour of the vindictive and the subtility of the base,
the dereliction of friends and the efforts of enemies, have not,
all, diverted me from that line of conduct which has always
struck me as the best. In the ardour of debate, I may have
been, like all other men, betrayed into expressions capable of
misrepresentation; but the open and broad path of the constitution has uniformly been mine. I never was the tool of
any junto. I accepted of office at the obvious inclination of
this House: I shall not hold it a moment after the least hint
from them to resume a private station.

The honourable gentleman is, however, grasping at place
on very different grounds. He is not called to it by a majority
of this House; but, in defiance of that majority stands forth
the advocate and candidate for secret influence. How will he
reconcile a conduct thus preposterous to the constitution, with
those principles for which he has pledged himself to the people
of England? By what motives can he be thus blind to a system,
which so flatly and explicitly gives the lie to all his former
professions? Will secret influence conciliate that confidence
to which his talents, connections, and principles, entitled
him; but which the aspect under which he must now appear
to an indignant and insulted public effectually bars his claim?
Will secret influence unite this House in the adoption of
measures which are not his own, and to which he only
gives the sanction of his name to save them from contempt?
Will secret influence draw along with it that affection and
cordiality from all ranks, without which the movements of
government must be absolutely at a stand? Or, is he weak and
violent enough to imagine, that his majesty's mere nomination

will singly weigh against the constitutional influence of all these considerations? For my own part, it has been always my opinion, that this country can labour under no greater misfortune than a ministry without strength and stability. The tone of government will never recover so as to establish either domestic harmony or foreign respect, without a permanent administration; and whoever knows any thing of the constitution, and the present state of parties among us, must be sensible, that this great blessing is only and substantially to be obtained and realized in connection with public confidence. It is undoubtedly the prerogative of the sovereign to chuse his own servants; but the constitution provides that these servants should not be obnoxious to his subjects by rendering all their exertions, thus circumstanced, abortive and impracticable. The honourable gentleman had, therefore, better consider how much he risks by joining an arrangement thus hostile to the interests of the people; that they will never consent to be governed by secret influence, and that all the weight of his private character, all his eloquence and popularity, will never render the midnight and despotic mandates of an interior cabinet acceptable to Englishmen.

Charles James Fox

Speech on a motion regarding the use of Court influence to prevent the passing of his East India Bill (17 December, 1783) from *Speeches . . . in the House of Commons* (1815)

WARREN HASTINGS
AND THE EAST INDIA COMPANY

AFTER having stated this complicated infamy in terms of the severest reprehension, Mr. Sheridan proceeded to observe, that he recollected to have heard it advanced by some of those admirers of Mr. Hastings, who were not so implicit as to give unqualified applause to his crimes, that they found an apology for the atrocity of them, in the greatness of his mind. To estimate the solidity of such a defence, it would be sufficient merely to consider in what consisted this prepossessing distinction, this captivating characteristic of greatness of mind. Is it not solely to be traced in great actions directed to great ends? In them, and them alone, we are to search for true estimable magnanimity. To them only can we justly affix the splendid title and honours of real greatness. There was indeed another species of greatness, which displayed itself in boldly conceiving a bad measure, and undauntedly pursuing it to its accomplishment. But had Mr. Hastings the merit of exhibiting either of these descriptions of greatness: – even of the latter? He saw nothing great – nothing magnanimous – nothing open – nothing direct in his measures, or in his mind: – on the contrary, he had too often pursued the worst objects by the worst means. His course was an eternal deviation from rectitude. He either tyrannised or deceived; and was by turns a Dionysius and a Scapin. As well might the writhing obliquity of the serpent be compared to the swift directness of the arrow, as the duplicity of Mr. Hastings's ambition to the simple steadiness of genuine magnanimity. In his mind all was shuffling, ambiguous, dark, insidious, and little: nothing simple, nothing unmixed: all affected plainness, and actual dissimulation; a heterogeneous mass of contradictory qualities; with nothing great but his crimes; and even those contrasted by the littleness of his motives, which at once denoted both his baseness and his meanness, and marked him for a traitor and a trickster. Nay, in his stile and writing, there was the same mixture of vicious contrarieties; – the most groveling ideas were conveyed in the most inflated language; giving mock consequence to low cavils, and uttering quibbles in heroics; so that his compositions disgusted the mind's taste, as much as his actions excited the soul's abhorrence. Indeed this mixture of character seemed by some unaccountable, but inherent quality, to be appropriated, though in inferior degrees, to every thing that concerned his employers. He remembered to have heard an honourable and learned gentleman (Mr. Dundas) remark, that there was something in the first frame and constitution of the company, which extended the sordid principles of their origin over all their successive operations; connecting with their civil policy, and even with their boldest achievements, the meanness of a pedlar, and the profligacy of pirates. Alike in the political and military line could be observed *auctioneering ambassadors* and *trading generals*; – and thus we saw a revolution brought about by *affidavits*; an army employed in *executing an arrest*; a town besieged on *a note of hand*; a prince dethroned for the *balance of an account*.

Richard Brinsley Sheridan

Speech in the House of Commons on the fourth charge
against Warren Hastings (7 February, 1787) from *Speeches
 . . . edited by a Constitutional Friend* (1816)

On the Attacks made upon Him and his Pension by the Duke of Bedford

I REALLY am at a loss to draw any sort of parallel between the public merits of his Grace, by which he justifies the grants he holds, and these services of mine, on the favourable construction of which I have obtained what his Grace so much disapproves. In private life, I have not at all the honour of acquaintance with the noble Duke. But I ought to presume, and it costs me nothing to do so, that he abundantly deserves the esteem and love of all who live with him. But as to public service, why truly it would not be more ridiculous for me to compare myself in rank, in fortune, in splendid descent, in youth, strength, or figure, with the Duke of Bedford, than to make a parallel between his services, and my attempts to be useful to my country. It would not be gross adulation, but uncivil irony, to say, that he has any public merit of his own to keep alive the idea of the services by which his vast landed Pensions were obtained. My merits, whatever they are, are original and personal; his are derivative. It is his ancestor, the original pensioner, that has laid up this inexhaustible fund of merit, which makes his Grace so very delicate and exceptious about the merit of all other grantees of the Crown. Had he permitted me to remain in quiet, I should have said, 'tis his estate; that's enough. It is his by law; what have I to do with it or its history? He would naturally have said on his side, 'tis this man's fortune. – He is as good now, as my ancestor was two hundred and fifty years ago. I am a young man with very old pensions; he is an old man with very young pensions, – that's all.

Why will his Grace, by attacking me, force me reluctantly to compare my little merit with that which obtained from the Crown those prodigies of profuse donation, by which he tramples on the mediocrity of humble and laborious individuals? I would willingly leave him to the Herald's College, which the philosophy of the Sans culottes (prouder by far than all the Garters, and Norroys and Clarencieux, and Rouge Dragons that ever pranced in a procession of what his friends call aristocrats and despots) will abolish with contumely and scorn. These historians, recorders, and blazoners of virtues and arms, differ wholly from that other description of historians, who never assign any act of politicians to a good motive. These gentle historians, on the contrary, dip their pens in nothing but the milk of human kindness. They seek no further for merit than the preamble of a patent, or the inscription on a tomb. With them every man created a peer is first an hero ready made. They judge of every man's capacity for office by the offices he has filled; and the more offices the more ability. Every General-officer with them is a Marlborough;

every Statesman a Burleigh; every Judge a Murray or a Yorke. They who, alive, were laughed at or pitied by all their acquaintance, make as good a figure as the best of them in the pages of Guillim, Edmondson, and Collins.

To these recorders, so full of good nature to the great and prosperous, I would willingly leave the first Baron Russel, and Earl of Bedford, and the merits of his grants. But the aulnager, the weigher, the meter of grants, will not suffer us to acquiesce in the judgment of the Prince reigning at the time when they were made. They are never good to those who earn them. Well then; since the new grantees have war made on them by the old, and that the word of the sovereign is not to be taken, let us turn our eyes to history, in which great men have always a pleasure in contemplating the heroic origin of their house.

The first peer of the name, the first purchaser of the grants, was a Mr. Russel, a person of an ancient gentleman's family raised by being a minion of Henry the Eighth. As there generally is some resemblance of character to create these relations, the favourite was in all likelihood much such another as his master. The first of these immoderate grants was not taken from the ancient demesne of the Crown, but from the recent confiscation of the ancient nobility of the land. The lion having sucked the blood of his prey, threw the offal carcass to the jackall in waiting. Having tasted once the food of confiscation, the favourites became fierce and ravenous. This worthy favourite's first grant was from the lay nobility. The second, infinitely improving on the enormity of the first, was from the plunder of the church. In truth his Grace is somewhat excusable for his dislike to a grant like mine, not only in its quantity, but in its kind so different from his own.

Mine was from a mild and benevolent sovereign; his from Henry the Eighth.

aulnager] inspector of measure and quality of woollen goods

Mine had not its fund in the murder of any innocent person of illustrious rank, or in the pillage of any body of unoffending men. His grants were from the aggregate and consolidated funds of judgments iniquitously legal, and from possessions voluntarily surrendered by the lawful proprietors with the gibbet at their door.

The merit of the grantee whom he derives from, was that of being a prompt and greedy instrument of a *levelling* tyrant, who oppressed all descriptions of his people, but who fell with particular fury on every thing that was *great and noble*. Mine has been, in endeavouring to screen every man, in every class, from oppression, and particularly in defending the high and eminent, who in the bad times of confiscating Princes, confiscating chief Governors, or confiscating Demagogues, are the most exposed to jealousy, avarice, and envy.

Edmund Burke
A Letter to a Noble Lord . . . (1796)

The Peace of Amiens

THE War depends neither upon conventions to be entered into between the two governments, nor upon acts of hostility which may be committed between the two people, by land or on the high seas; but on the existence or non-existence of that fixed, rooted, determined purpose, which France has hitherto had, and which we have no reason whatever to think she has relinquished—of accomplishing the final overthrow of this country. While that purpose exists, and shall be acted upon, we are at War, call our state by what name you please: and the only question is, whether France cannot work as effectually to her purpose in Peace; and if Peace is made in a certain way, infinitely more effectually than she can in what is professedly and declaredly War. I would really wish to ask, whether Gentlemen have never heard of a people called the Romans, a set of republicans who conquered the world in the old time; and whom the *modern Romans* take as their model in every respect, but in none more than in what relates to the overthrow of this country? Among the nations that fell under the Roman yoke, there were but few whom they were able to fetch down at a blow, – to reduce in the course of a single War. All their greater antagonists, particularly the state whose fate is chosen as a prototype of our own, were not reduced till after repeated attacks, till after several successive and alternate processes of War and Peace: a victorious War preparing the way for an advantageous Peace; and an advantageous Peace again laying the foundation of a successful War. This was at least the conduct of a great people; a people not to be put aside from their purposes by every transient blast of fortune. They had vowed the destruction of Carthage; and they never rested from their design, till they had seen it finally accomplished. The emulators of their fortune in the present day, are, in no less a degree, the emulators of their virtues; at least, of those qualities, whatever they may be, that give to man a command over his fellows. When I look at the conduct of the French Revolutionary rulers, as compared with that of their opponents; when I see the grandeur of their designs; the wisdom of their plans; the steadiness of their execution; their boldness in acting; their constancy in enduring; their contempt of all small obstacles and temporary embarrassments; their inflexible determination to perform such and such things; and the powers which they have displayed, in acting up to that determination; when I contrast these with the narrow views, the paltry interests, the occasional expedients, the desultory and wavering conduct, the want of all right feeling and just conception, that characterize so generally the governments and nations opposed to them, I confess I sink down in despondency, and am fain to admit, that if they shall have conquered the world, it will be by qualities by which they deserve to conquer it. Never were there persons, who could show a fairer title to the inheritance which they claim. The great division of mankind made by a celebrated philosopher of old, into those who were formed to govern, and those who were born only to obey, was never more strongly exemplified than by the French nation, and those who have sunk, or are sinking, under their yoke. Let us not suppose, therefore, that while these qualities, combined with these purposes, shall continue to exist, they will ever cease, by night or by day, in Peace or in War, to work their natural effect, – to gravitate towards their proper centre; or that the bold, the proud, the dignified, the determined, those who *will* great things, and will stake their existence upon the accomplishment of what they have *willed*, shall not finally prevail over those, who act upon the very opposite feelings; who will "never push their resistance beyond their convenience;" who ask for nothing but ease and safety; who look only to stave off the evil for the present day, and will take no heed of what may befal them on the morrow. We *are* therefore, in effect, at War at this moment: and the only question is, whether the War, that will henceforward proceed under the name of Peace, is likely to prove less operative and fatal, than that which has hitherto appeared in its natural and ordinary shape. That such is our state, is confessed by the authors themselves of the present Treaty, in the measures which they feel it necessary to recommend to the House. When did we ever hear before of a military establishment necessary to be kept up in time of Peace? The fact is, that we know that we are not at Peace; not such as is fit to be so called, nor that in which we might hope to sit down, for some time at least, in confidence and security, in the free and undisturbed enjoyment of the blessings which we possess. We are in that state, in which the majority, I believe, of those who hear me, are in their hearts more desirous that we should be, than, in our present prostrate and defenceless situation, they may think it prudent to avow – in a state of armed truce; and then the only questions will be, at what price we purchase this truce; what our condition will be while it lasts; and in what state it is likely to leave us, should it terminate otherwise than as we are willing to suppose.

William Windham

Speech on the Peace of Amiens (4 November, 1801)
from Speeches in Parliament of the Right Honourable
William Windham, edited by Thomas Amyot (1812)

THE DEATH PENALTY FOR
MACHINE WRECKING

IN what state of apathy have we been plunged so long, that now for the first time the house has been officially apprised of these disturbances? All this has been transacting within 130 miles of London, and yet we, "good easy men, have deemed full sure our greatness was a ripening," and have sat down to enjoy our foreign triumphs in the midst of domestic calamity. But all the cities you have taken, all the armies which have retreated before your leaders, are but paltry subjects of self-congratulation, if your land divides against itself, and your dragoons and your executioners must be let loose against your fellow-citizens. – You call these men a mob, desperate, dangerous, and ignorant; and seem to think that the only way to quiet the "*Bellua multorum capitum*" is to lop off a few of its superfluous heads. But even a mob may be better reduced to reason by a mixture of conciliation and firmness, than by additional irritation and redoubled penalties. Are we aware of our obligations to a mob? It is the mob that labour in your fields and serve in your houses, – that man your navy, and recruit your army, – that have enabled you to defy all the world, and can also defy you when neglect and calamity have driven them to despair! You may call the people a mob; but do not forget, that a mob too often speaks the sentiments of the people. And here I must remark, with what alacrity you are accustomed to fly to the succour of your distressed allies, leaving the distressed of your own country to the care of Providence or – the parish. When the Portuguese suffered under the retreat of the French, every arm was stretched out, every hand was opened, from the rich man's largess to the widow's mite, all was bestowed, to enable them to rebuild their villages and replenish their granaries. And at this moment, when thousands of misguided but most unfortunate fellow-countrymen are struggling with the extremes of hardships and hunger, as your charity began abroad it should end at home. A much less sum, a tithe of the bounty bestowed on Portugal, even if those men (which I cannot admit without enquiry) could not have been restored to their employments, would have rendered unnecessary the tender mercies of the bayonet and the gibbet. But doubtless our friends have too many foreign claims to admit a prospect of domestic relief; though never did such objects demand it. I have traversed the seat of war in the Peninsula, I have been in some of the most oppressed provinces of Turkey, but never under the most despotic of infidel governments did I behold such squalid wretchedness as I have seen since my return to the very heart of a Christian country. And what are your remedies? After months of inaction, and months of action worse than inactivity, at length comes forth the grand specific, the never-failing nostrum of all state physicians, from the days of Draco to the present time. After feeling the pulse and shaking the head over the patient, prescribing the usual course of warm water and bleeding, the warm water of your mawkish police and the lancets of your military, these convulsions must terminate in death, the sure consummation of the prescriptions of all political Sangrados.

Setting aside the palpable injustice and the certain inefficiency of the bill, are there not capital punishments sufficient in your statutes? Is there not blood enough upon your penal code, that more must be poured forth to ascend to Heaven and testify against you? How will you carry the bill into effect? Can you commit a whole county to their own prisons? Will you erect a gibbet in every field, and hang up men like scarecrows? or will you proceed (as you must to bring this measure into effect) by decimation? place the county under martial law? depopulate and lay waste all around you? and restore Sherwood Forest as an acceptable gift to the crown, in its former condition of a royal chase and an asylum for outlaws? Are these the remedies for a starving and desperate populace? Will the famished wretch who has braved your bayonets be appalled by your gibbets? When death is a relief, and the only relief it appears that you will afford him, will he be dragooned into tranquillity? Will that which could not be effected by your grenadiers, be accomplished by your executioners? If you proceed by the forms of law, where is your evidence? Those who have refused to impeach their accomplices, when transportation only was the punishment, will hardly be tempted to witness against them when death is the penalty. With all due deference to the noble lords opposite, I think a little investigation, some previous enquiry would induce even them to change their purpose. That most favourite state measure, so marvellously efficacious in many and recent instances, temporising, would not be without its advantages in this. When a proposal is made to emancipate or relieve, you hesitate, you deliberate for years, you temporise and tamper with the minds of men; but a death-bill must be passed off hand, without a thought of the consequences. Sure I am, from what I have heard, and from what I have seen, that to pass the bill under all the existing circumstances, without enquiry, without deliberation, would only be to add injustice to irritation, and barbarity to neglect.

George Gordon, Lord Byron
Maiden speech in the House of Lords (27 February, 1812)
from *The Works of Lord Byron*, Vol. VI (1832)

C.24

CATHOLIC EMANCIPATION

SOME people talk as if they were quite teazed and worried by the eternal clamours of the Catholics; but if you are eternally unjust, can you expect any thing more than to be eternally vexed by the victims of your injustice? You want all the luxury of oppression, without any of its inconvenience. I should think the Catholics very much to blame, if they ever ceased to importune the legislature for justice, so long as they could find one single member of parliament who would advocate their cause.

The putting the matter to rest by an effort of the county of York, or by any decision of parliament against them, is utterly hopeless. Every year increases the Catholic population, and the Catholic wealth, and the Catholic claims, till you are caught in one of those political attitudes to which all countries are occasionally exposed, in which you are utterly helpless, and must give way to their claims: and if you do it then, you will do it badly; you may call it an arrangement, but arrangements made at such times are much like the bargains between an highwayman and a traveller, a pistol on one side, and a purse on the other: the rapid scramble of armed vigilance, and the unqualified surrender of helpless timidity. *If you think the thing must be done at some time or another, do it when you are calm and powerful, and when you need not do it.*

There are a set of high-spirited men who are very much afraid of being afraid; who cannot brook the idea of doing any thing from fear, and whose conversation is full of fire and sword, when any apprehension of resistance is alluded to; I have a perfect confidence in the high and unyielding spirit, and in the military courage of the English; and I have no doubt, but that many of the country gentlemen, who now call out No Popery, would fearlessly put themselves at the head of their embattled yeomanry, to controul the Irish Catholics. My objection to such courage is, that it would certainly be exercised unjustly, and probably exercised in vain. I should deprecate any rising of the Catholics as the most grievous misfortune which could happen to the empire and to themselves. They had far better endure all they do endure, and a great deal worse, than try the experiment. *But if they do try it, you may depend upon it, they will do it at their own time, and not at yours.* They will not select a fortnight in the summer, during a profound peace, when corn and money abound, and when the Catholics of Europe are unconcerned spectators. If you make a resolution to be unjust, you must make another resolution to be always strong, always vigilant, and always rich; you must commit no blunders, exhibit no deficiencies, and meet with no misfortunes; you must present a square phalanx of impenetrable strength, for keen-eyed revenge is riding round your ranks; and if one heart falter, or one hand tremble, you are lost.

You may call all this threatening; I am sure I have no such absurd intention; but wish only, in sober sadness, to point out what appears to me to be the inevitable consequences of the conduct we pursue. If danger be not pointed out and insisted upon, how is it to be avoided? My firm belief is, that England will be compelled to grant ignominiously what she now refuses haughtily. Remember what happened respecting Ireland in the American war. In 1779, the Irish, whose trade was completely restricted by English laws, asked for some little relaxation, some liberty to export her own products, and to import the products of other countries; their petition was flung out of the House with the utmost disdain, and by an immense majority. In April, 1782, 70,000 Irish volunteers were under arms, the representatives of 170 armed corps met at Ulster, and the English parliament (the lords and commons both on the same day and with only one dissentient voice, the ministers moving the question) were compelled, in the most disgraceful and precipitate manner, to acknowledge the complete independence of the Irish nation, *and nothing but the good sense and moderation of Grattan prevented the separation of the two crowns.*

It is no part of my province to defend every error of the Catholic Church: I believe it has many errors, though I am sure these errors are grievously exaggerated and misrepresented. I should think it a vast accession to the happiness of mankind, if every Catholic in Europe were converted to the Protestant faith. The question is not, Whether there shall be Catholics, but the question (as they do exist and you cannot get rid of them) is, What are you to do with them? Are you to make men rebels because you cannot make them Protestants? and are you to endanger your state, because you cannot enlarge your Church? England is the ark of liberty: the English Church I believe to be one of the best establishments in the world; but what is to become of England, of its Church, its free institutions, and the beautiful political models it holds out to mankind, if Ireland should succeed in connecting itself with any other European power hostile to England? I join in the cry of No Popery, as lustily as any man in the streets, who does not know whether the Pope lives in Cumberland or Westmoreland, but I know that it is impossible to keep down European popery, and European tyranny, without the assistance, or with the opposition, of Ireland.

Sydney Smith

A Letter to the Electors upon the Catholic Question (1826)

The Pleasure Derived from Analogy

THE word *analogy*, too, as well as *induction*, is common to physics, and to pure mathematics. It is thus we speak of the analogy running through the general properties of the different conic sections, with no less propriety than of the analogy running through the anatomical structure of different tribes of animals. In some instances, these mathematical analogies are collected by a species of *induction*; in others, they are inferred as consequences from more general truths, in which they are included as particular cases. Thus, in the curves which have just been mentioned, while we content ourselves (as many elementary writers have done) with deducing their properties from mechanical descriptions on a plane, we rise experimentally from a comparison of the propositions which have been separately demonstrated with respect to each curve, to more comprehensive theorems, applicable to all of them; whereas, when we begin with considering them in their common origin, we have it in our power to trace from the source, both their generic properties, and their specific peculiarities. The satisfaction arising from this last view of the subject can be conceived by those alone who have experienced it; although I am somewhat doubtful whether it be not felt in the greatest degree by such as, after having risen from the contemplation of particular truths to other truths more general, have been at last conducted to some commanding station, where the mutual connections and affinities of the whole system are brought, at once, under the range of the eye. Even, however, before we have reached this vantage-ground, the contemplation of the analogy, considered merely as a *fact*, is pleasing to the mind; partly, from the mysterious wonder it excites, and partly from the convenient generalization of knowledge it affords. To the experienced mathematician this pleasure is farther enhanced, by the assurance which the analogy conveys, of the existence of yet undiscovered theorems, far more extensive and luminous than those which have led him, by a process so indirect, so tedious, and comparatively so unsatisfactory, to his general conclusions.

In this last respect, the pleasure derived from analogy in mathematics, resolves into the same principle with that which seems to have the chief share in rendering the analogies among the different departments of nature so interesting a subject of speculation. In both cases, a powerful and agreeable *stimulus* is applied to the curiosity, by the encouragement given to the exercise of the inventive faculties, and by the hope of future discovery, which is awakened and cherished. As the analogous properties (for instance) of the conic sections, point to some general theorems of which they are corollaries; so the analogy between the phenomena of Electricity and those of Galvanism irresistibly suggests a confident, though vague anticipation of some general physical law comprehending the phenomena of both, but differently modified in its sensible results by a diversity of circumstances. Indeed, it is by no means impossible, that the pleasure we receive even from those analogies which are the foundation of poetical metaphor and simile, may be found resolvable, in part, into the satisfaction connected with the *supposed* discovery of truth, or the *supposed* acquisition of knowledge; the faculty of imagination giving to these illusions a momentary ascendant over the sober conclusions of experience; and gratifying the understanding with a flattering consciousness of its own force, or at least with a consolatory forgetfulness of its own weakness.

Dugald Stewart

Elements of the Philosophy of the Human Mind, Vol. II (1814)

The Encroachments of Science

The sublime discoveries of Newton, and, together with these, his not less fruitful than wonderful application, of the higher mathesis to the movements of the celestial bodies, and to the laws of light, gave almost a religious sanction to the corpuscular system and mechanical theory. It became synonymous with philosophy itself. It was the sole portal at which truth was permitted to enter. The human body was treated of as an hydraulic machine, the operations of medicine were solved, and alas! even directed by reference partly to gravitation and the laws of motion, and partly by chemistry, which itself however, as far as its theory was concerned, was but a branch of mechanics working exclusively by imaginary wedges, angles, and spheres. Should the reader chance to put his hand on the 'Principles of Philosophy,' by La Forge, an immediate disciple of Descartes, he may see the phenomena of sleep solved in a copper-plate engraving, with all the figures into which the globules of the blood shaped themselves, and the results demonstrated by mathematical calculations. In short, from the time of Kepler to that of Newton, and from Newton to Hartley, not only all things in external nature, but the subtlest mysteries of life and organization, and even of the intellect and moral being, were conjured within the magic circle of mathematical formulae. And now a new light was struck by the discovery of electricity, and, in every sense of the word, both playful and serious, both for good and for evil, it may be affirmed to have electrified the whole frame of natural philosophy. Close on its heels followed the momentous discovery of the principal gases by Scheele and Priestley, the composition of water by Cavendish, and the doctrine of latent heat by Black. The scientific world was prepared for a new dynasty; accordingly, as soon as Lavoisier had reduced the infinite variety of chemical phenomena to the actions, reactions, and interchanges of a few elementary substances, or at least excited the expectation that this would speedily be effected, the hope shot up, almost instantly, into full faith, that it had been effected. Henceforward the new path, thus brilliantly opened, became the common road to all departments of knowledge: and, to this moment, it has been pursued with an eagerness and almost epidemic enthusiasm which, scarcely less than its political revolutions, characterise the spirit of the age. Many and inauspicious have been the invasions and inroads of this new conqueror into the rightful territories of other sciences; and strange alterations have been made in less harmless points than those of terminology, in homage to an art unsettled, in the very ferment of imperfect discoveries, and either without a theory, or with a theory maintained only by composition and compromise. Yet this very circumstance has favoured its encroachments, by the gratifications which its novelty affords to our curiosity, and by the keener interest and higher excitement which an unsettled and revolutionary state is sure to inspire. He who supposes that science possesses an immunity from such influences knows little of human nature. How, otherwise, could men of strong minds and sound judgments have attempted to penetrate by the clue of chemical experiment the secret recesses, the sacred adyta of organic life, without being aware that chemistry must needs be at its extreme limits, when it has approached the threshold of a higher power? Its own transgressions, however, and the failure of its enterprises will become the means of defining its absolute boundary, and we shall have to guard against the opposite error of rejecting its aid altogether as analogy, because we have repelled its ambitious claims to an identity with the vital powers.

Samuel Taylor Coleridge

Hints towards the Formation of a More Comprehensive Theory of Life (1848)

127

ANIMAL ADAPTATION
AND THE IDEA OF EVOLUTION

As air and water are supplied to animals in sufficient profusion, the three great objects of desire, which have changed the forms of many animals by their exertions to gratify them, are those of lust, hunger, and security. A great want of one part of the animal world has consisted in the desire of the exclusive possession of the females; and these have acquired weapons to combat each other for this purpose, as the very thick, shield-like, horny skin on the shoulder of the boar is a defence only against animals of his own species, who strike obliquely upwards, nor are his tushes for other purposes, except to defend himself, as he is not naturally a carnivorous animal. So the horns of the stag are sharp to offend his adversary, but are branched for the purpose of parrying or receiving the thrusts of horns similar to his own, and have therefore been formed for the purpose of combating other stags for the exclusive possession of the females; who are observed, like the ladies in the times of chivalry, to attend the car of the victor.

The birds which do not carry food to their young, and do not therefore marry, are armed with spurs for the purpose of fighting for the exclusive possession of the females, as cocks and quails. It is certain that these weapons are not provided for their defence against other adversaries, because the females of these species are without this armour. The final cause of this contest amongst the males seems to be, that the strongest and most active animal should propagate the species, which should thence become improved.

Another great want consists in the means of procuring food, which has diversified the forms of all species of animals. Thus the nose of the swine has become hard for the purpose of turning up the soil in search of insects and of roots. The trunk of the elephant is an elongation of the nose for the purpose of pulling down the branches of trees for his food, and for taking up water without bending his knees. Beasts of prey have acquired strong jaws or talons. Cattle have acquired a rough tongue and a rough palate to pull off the blades of grass, as cows and sheep. Some birds have acquired harder beaks to crack nuts, as the parrot. Others have acquired beaks adapted to break the harder seeds, as sparrows. Others for the softer seeds of flowers, or the buds of trees, as the finches. Other birds have acquired long beaks to penetrate the moister soils in search of insects or roots, as woodcocks; and others broad ones to filtrate the water of lakes, and to retain aquatic insects. All which seem to have been gradually produced during many generations by the perpetual endeavour of the creatures to supply the want of food, and to have been delivered to their posterity with constant improvement of them for the purposes required.

The third great want amongst animals is that of security, which seems much to have diversified the forms of their bodies and the colour of them: these consist in the means of escaping other animals more powerful than themselves. Hence some animals have acquired wings instead of legs, as the smaller birds, for the purpose of escape. Others great length of fin, or of membrane, as the flying fish, and the bat. Others great swiftness of foot, as the hare. Others have acquired hard or armed shells, as the tortoise and the echinus marinus.

The contrivances for the purpose of security extend even to vegetables, as is seen in the wonderful and various means of their concealing or defending their honey from insects, and their seeds from birds. On the other hand swiftness of wing has been acquired by hawks and swallows to pursue their prey; and a proboscis of admirable structure has been acquired by the bee, the moth, and the humming bird, for the purpose of plundering the nectaries of flowers. All which seem to have been formed by the original living filament, excited into action by the necessities of the creatures, which possess them, and on which their existence depends.

From thus meditating on the great similarity of the structure of the warm-blooded animals, and at the same time of the great changes they undergo both before and after their nativity; and by considering in how minute a portion of time many of the changes of animals above described have been produced; would it be too bold to imagine, that in the great length of time, since the earth began to exist, perhaps millions of ages before the commencement of the history of mankind, would it be too bold to imagine, that all warm-blooded animals have arisen from one living filament, which THE GREAT FIRST CAUSE endued with animality, with the power of acquiring new parts, attended with new propensities, directed by irritations, sensations, volitions, and associations; and thus possessing the faculty of continuing to improve by its own inherent activity, and of delivering down those improvements by generation to its posterity, world without end!

Erasmus Darwin
Zoonomia: or, The Laws of Organic Life, Vol. I (1794)

Two Theories about the Nature of Heat

Since all matter may be made to fill a smaller volume by cooling, it is evident that the particles of matter must have space between them; and since every body can communicate the power of expansion to a body of a lower temperature, that is, can give an expansive motion to its particles, it is a probable inference that its own particles are possessed of motion; but as there is no change in the position of its parts as long as its temperature is uniform, the motion, if it exist, must be a vibratory or undulatory motion, or a motion of the particles round their axes, or a motion of particles round each other.

It seems possible to account for all the phenomena of heat, if it be supposed that in solids the particles are in a constant state of vibratory motion, the particles of the hottest bodies moving with the greatest velocity, and through the greatest space; that in fluids and elastic fluids, besides the vibratory motion, which must be conceived greatest in the last, the particles have a motion round their own axes, with different velocities, the particles of elastic fluids moving with the greatest quickness; and that in etherial substances the particles move round their own axes, and separate from each other, penetrating in right lines through space. Temperature may be conceived to depend upon the velocities of the vibrations; increase of capacity on the motion being performed in greater space; and the diminution of temperature during the conversion of solids into fluids or gases, may be examined on the idea of the loss of vibratory motion, in consequence of the revolution of particles round their axes, at the moment when the body becomes fluid or aëriform, or from the loss of rapidity of vibration, in consequence of the motion of the particles through greater space.

If a specific fluid of heat be admitted, it must be supposed liable to most of the affections which the particles of common matter are assumed to possess, to account for the phenomena; such as losing its motion when combining with bodies, producing motion when transmitted from one body to another, and gaining projectile motion, when passing into free space: so that many hypotheses must be adopted to account for its mode of agency, which renders this view of the subject less simple than the other. Very delicate experiments have been made to show that bodies when heated do not increase in weight. This, as far as it goes, is an evidence against a specific subtile elastic fluid producing the calorific expansion; but it cannot be considered as decisive, on account of the imperfection of our instruments; a cubical inch of inflammable air requires a good balance to ascertain that it has any sensible weight, and a substance bearing the same relation to this, that this bears to platinum, could not, perhaps, be weighed by any methods in our possession.

Sir Humphry Davy
Elements of Chemical Philosophy (1812)
from *Collected Works* (1840)

On the First Balloon Ascents

It is certain, at least, that nothing within the reach of human ingenuity will be left unattempted to accomplish, and add all that is wanting to this last effort of philosophical contrivance. The approximating powers of the telescope, and the powers by which the thunderstorm is delivered of its contents peaceably and without mischief, were once, perhaps, in appearance more remote from discovery, and seemed less practicable, than we may now suppose it, to give direction to that which is already buoyant; especially possessed as we are of such consummate mechanical skill, already masters of principles which we have nothing to do but to apply, of which we have already availed ourselves in the similar case of navigation, and having in every fowl of the air a pattern, which now at length it may be sufficient to imitate. Wings and a tail, indeed, were of little use, while the body, so much heavier than the space of air it occupied, was sure to sink by its own weight, and could never be held in equipoise by any implements of the kind which human strength could manage. But now we float; at random, indeed, pretty much, and as the wind drives us; for want of nothing, however, but that steerage which invention, the conqueror of many equal, if not superior difficulties, may be expected to supply. – Should the point be carried, and man at last become as familiar with the air as he has long been with the ocean, will it in its consequences prove a mercy, or a judgement? I think, a judgement. First, because if a power to convey himself from place to place, like a bird, would have been good for him, his Maker would have formed him with such a capacity. But he has been a groveller upon the earth for six thousand years, and now at last, when the close of this present state of things approaches, begins to exalt himself above it. So much the worse for *him*. Like a truant school-boy, he breaks his bounds, and will have reason to repent of his presumption. – Secondly, I think it will prove a judgement, because, with the exercise of very little foresight, it is easy to prognosticate a thousand evils which the project must necessarily bring after it; amounting at last to the confusion of all order, the annihilation of all authority, with dangers both to property and person, and impunity to the offenders. Were I an absolute legislator, I would therefore make it death for a man to be convicted of flying, the moment he could be caught; and to bring him down from his altitudes by a bullet sent through his head or his carriage, should be no murder. Philosophers would call me a Vandal; the scholar would say that, had it not been for me, the fable of Dædalus would have been realized; and historians would load my memory with reproaches of phlegm, and stupidity, and oppression; but in the mean time the world would go on quietly, and if it enjoyed less liberty, would at least be more secure.

William Cowper

Letter to the Rev. John Newton (15 December, 1783) from *The Works of William Cowper*, edited by R. Southey (1835–7), Vol. II

Amiable Weakness

IT would be an endless task to trace the variety of meannesses, cares, and sorrows, into which women are plunged by the prevailing opinion, that they were created rather to feel than reason, and that all the power they obtain, must be obtained by their charms and weakness:

'Fine by defect, and amiably weak!'

And, made by this amiable weakness entirely dependent, excepting what they gain by illicit sway, on man, not only for protection, but advice, is it surprising that, neglecting the duties that reason alone points out, and shrinking from trials calculated to strengthen their minds, they only exert themselves to give their defects a graceful covering, which may serve to heighten their charms in the eye of the voluptuary, though it sink them below the scale of moral excellence?

Fragile in every sense of the word, they are obliged to look up to man for every comfort. In the most trifling dangers they cling to their support, with parasitical tenacity, piteously demanding succour; and their *natural* protector extends his arm, or lifts up his voice, to guard the lovely trembler – from what? Perhaps the frown of an old cow, or the jump of a mouse; a rat, would be a serious danger. In the name of reason, and even common sense, what can save such beings from contempt; even though they be soft and fair?

These fears, when not affected, may be very pretty; but they shew a degree of imbecility that degrades a rational creature in a way women are not aware of – for love and esteem are very distinct things.

I am fully persuaded that we should hear of none of these infantine airs, if girls were allowed to take sufficient exercise, and not confined in close rooms till their muscles are relaxed, and their powers of digestion destroyed. To carry the remark still further, if fear in girls, instead of being cherished, perhaps, created, was treated in the same manner as cowardice in boys, we should quickly see women with more dignified aspects. It is true, they could not then with equal propriety be termed the sweet flowers that smile in the walk of man; but they would be more respectable members of society, and discharge the important duties of life by the light of their own reason. 'Educate women like men,' says Rousseau, 'and the more they resemble our sex the less power will they have over us.' This is the very point I aim at. I do not wish them to have power over men; but over themselves.

Mary Wollstonecraft

A Vindication of the Rights of Woman (1792)

ADVICE TO A HUSBAND

WOMEN are a *sisterhood*. They make *common cause* in behalf of the *sex*; and, indeed, this is natural enough, when we consider the vast power that the *law* gives us over them. The law is for us, and they combine, wherever they can, to mitigate its effects. This is perfectly natural, and, to a certain extent, laudable, evincing fellow-feeling and public spirit: but when carried to the length of *"he sha'n't,"* it is despotism on the one side, and slavery on the other. Watch, therefore, the incipient steps of encroachment; and they come on so slowly, so softly, that you must be sharp-sighted if you perceive them; but the moment you *do perceive them*: your love will blind for too long a time; but the moment you do perceive them, put at once an effectual stop to their progress. Never mind the pain that it may give you: a day of pain at this time will spare you years of pain in time to come. Many a man has been miserable, and made his wife miserable too, for a score or two of years, only for want of resolution to bear one day of pain: and it is a great deal to bear; it is a great deal to do to thwart the desire of one whom you so dearly love, and whose virtues daily render her more and more dear to you. But (and this is one of the most admirable of the mother's traits) as she herself will, while the tears stream from her eyes, force the nauseous medicine down the throat of her child, whose every cry is a dagger to her heart; as she herself has the courage to do this for the sake of her child, why should you flinch from the performance of a still more important and more sacred duty towards herself, as well as towards you and your children?

Am I recommending *tyranny*? Am I recommending *disregard* of the wife's opinions and wishes? Am I recommending a *reserve* towards her that would seem to say that she was not trust-worthy, or not a party interested in her husband's affairs? By no means: on the contrary, though I would keep any thing disagreeable from her, I should not enjoy the prospect of good without making her a participator. But reason says, and God has said, that it is the duty of wives to be obedient to their husbands; and the very nature of things prescribes that there must be *a head* of every house, and an *undivided* authority. And then it is so clearly *just* that the authority should rest with him on whose head rests the whole responsibility, that a woman, when patiently reasoned with on the subject, must be a virago in her very nature not to submit with docility to the terms of her marriage vow.

There are, in almost every considerable neighbourhood, a little squadron of she-commanders, generally the youngish wives of old or weak-minded men, and generally without children. These are the tutoresses of the young wives of the vicinage; they, in virtue of their experience, not only school the wives, but scold the husbands; they teach the former how to encroach and the latter how to yield: so that if you suffer this to go quietly on, you are soon under the care of a *comité* as completely as if you were insane. You want no *comité*: reason, law, religion, the marriage vow; all these have made you head, have given you full power to rule your family, and if you give up your right, you deserve the contempt that assuredly awaits you, and also the ruin that is, in all probability, your doom.

William Cobbett
Advice to Young Men . . . (1829)

A BARRIER AGAINST MATRIMONY

NOTHWITHSTANDING your Happiness and your recommendation I hope I shall never marry. Though the most beautiful Creature were waiting for me at the end of a Journey or a Walk; though the carpet were of Silk, the Curtains of the morning Clouds; the chairs and Sofa stuffed with Cygnet's down; the food Manna, the Wine beyond Claret, the Window opening on Winander mere, I should not feel – or rather my Happiness would not be so fine, as my Solitude is sublime. Then instead of what I have described, there is a Sublimity to welcome me home. The roaring of the wind is my wife and the Stars through the window pane are my Children. The mighty abstract Idea I have of Beauty in all things stifles the more divided and minute domestic happiness – an amiable wife and sweet Children I contemplate as a part of that Beauty – but I must have a thousand of those beautiful particles to fill up my heart. I feel more and more every day, as my imagination strengthens, that I do not live in this world alone but in a thousand worlds. No sooner am I alone than shapes of epic greatness are stationed around me, and serve my Spirit the office which is equivalent to a King's body guard—then "tragedy with scepter'd pall, comes sweeping by." According to my state of mind I am with Achilles shouting in the

Trenches, or with Theocritus in the Vales of Sicily. Or I throw my whole being into Troilus, and repeating those lines, "I wander, like a lost Soul upon the stygian Banks staying for waftage", I melt into the air with a voluptuousness so delicate that I am content to be alone. These things combined with the opinion I have of the generallity of women – who appear to me as children to whom I would rather give a Sugar Plum than my time, form a barrier against Matrimony which I rejoice in. I have written this that you might see I have my share of the highest pleasures and that though I may choose to pass my days alone I shall be no Solitary.

John Keats

Letter to George and Georgiana Keats (14–31 October, 1818) from *The Letters of John Keats*, edited by M. B. Forman (1935)

THE BENEFITS OF VEGETABLE DIET

THERE is no disease, bodily or mental, which adoption of vegetable diet and pure water has not infallibly mitigated, wherever the experiment has been fairly tried. Debility is gradually converted into strength, disease into healthfulness, madness in all its hideous variety, from the ravings of the fettered maniac to the unaccountable irrationalities of ill-temper, that make a hell of domestic life, into a calm and considerate evenness of temper, that alone might offer a certain pledge of the future moral reformation of society. On a natural system of diet, old age would be our last and our only malady; the term of our existence would be protracted; we should enjoy life, and no longer preclude others from the enjoyment of it; all sensational delights would be infinitely more exquisite and perfect; the very sense of being would then be a continued pleasure, such as we now feel it in some few and favoured moments of our youth. By all that is sacred in our hopes for the human race, I conjure those who love happiness and truth to give a fair trial to the vegetable system! Reasoning is surely superfluous on a subject whose merits an experience of six months would set for ever at rest. But it is only among the enlightened and benevolent that so great a sacrifice of appetite and prejudice can be expected, even though its ultimate excellence should not admit of dispute. It is found easier, by the short-sighted victims of disease, to palliate their torments by medicine, than to prevent them by regimen. The vulgar of all ranks are invariably sensual and indocile; yet I cannot but feel myself persuaded that, when the benefits of vegetable diet are mathematically proved; when it is as clear, that those who live naturally are exempt from premature death, as that one is not nine, the most sottish of mankind will feel a preference towards a long and tranquil, contrasted with a short and painful, life. On the average, out of sixty persons, four die in three years. Hopes are entertained that, in April, 1814, a statement will be given, that sixty persons, all having lived more than three years on vegetables and pure water, are then in *perfect health*. More than two years have now elapsed; *not one of them has died*; no such example will be found in any sixty persons taken at random. Seventeen persons of all ages (the families of Dr. Lambe and Mr. Newton) have lived for seven years on this diet without a death, and almost without the slightest illness. Surely when we consider that some of these were infants, and one a martyr to asthma, now nearly subdued, we may challenge any seventeen persons taken at random in this city to exhibit a parallel case. Those, who may have been excited to question the rectitude of established habits of diet by these loose remarks, should consult Mr. Newton's luminous and eloquent essay.[1]

1. *Return to Nature, or Defence of Vegetable Regimen* (1811). [Shelley's note.]

When these proofs come fairly before the world, and are clearly seen by all who understand arithmetic, it is scarcely possible that abstinence from aliment demonstrably pernicious should not become universal. In proportion to the number of proselytes, so will be the weight of evidence; and, when a thousand persons can be produced, living on vegetables and distilled water, who have to dread no disease but old age, the world will be compelled to regard animal flesh and fermented liquors as slow but certain poisons.

Percy Bysshe Shelley

Queen Mab; a Philosophical Poem: with Notes (1813)
Text from *The Poetical Works of P. B. Shelley*, edited
by Mary Shelley (1840)

III

THE WORLD OF IMAGINATION, FEELING AND COMIC INVENTION: FICTION, HISTORICAL AND OCCASIONAL WRITING

MRS MALAPROP ON EDUCATION

*Enter to Lydia Languish Mrs. Malaprop and
Sir Anthony Absolute.*

Mrs. Mal. There, Sir Anthony, there sits the deliberate Simpleton who wants to disgrace her family, and lavish herself on a fellow not worth a shilling!

Lyd. Madam, I thought you once –

Mrs. Mal. You thought, Miss! I don't know any business you have to think at all – thought does not become a young woman; the point we would request of you is, that you will promise to forget this fellow – to illiterate him, I say, quite from your memory.

Lyd. Ah! Madam! our memories are independent of our wills. – It is not so easy to forget.

Mrs. Mal. But I say it is, Miss; there is nothing on earth so easy as to *forget*, if a person chooses to set about it. – I'm sure I have as much forgot your poor dear uncle as if he had never existed – and I thought it my duty so to do; and let me tell you, Lydia, these violent memories don't become a young woman.

Sir Anth. Why sure she won't pretend to remember what she's ordered not! – aye, this comes of her reading!

Lyd. What crime, Madam, have I committed, to be treated thus?

Mrs. Mal. Now don't attempt to extirpate yourself from the matter; you know I have proof controvertible of it. – But tell me, will you promise to do as you're bid? – Will you take a husband of your friends' choosing?

Lyd. Madam, I must tell you plainly, that had I no preference for any one else, the choice you have made would be my aversion.

Mrs. Mal. What business have you, Miss, with *preference* and *aversion*? They don't become a young woman; and you ought to know, that as both always wear off, 'tis safest in matrimony to begin with a little *aversion*. I am sure I hated your poor dear uncle before marriage as if he'd been a black-a-moor – and yet, Miss, you are sensible what a wife I made! – and when it pleased Heav'n to release me from him, 'tis unknown what tears I shed! – But suppose we were going to give you another choice, will you promise us to give up this Beverley?

Lyd. Could I belie my thoughts so far, as to give that promise, my actions would certainly as far belie my words.

Mrs. Mal. Take yourself to your room. – You are fit company for nothing but your own ill-humours.

Lyd. Willingly, Ma'am – I cannot change for the worse.

(*Exit* Lydia.)

Mrs. Mal. There's a little intricate hussy for you!

Sir Anth. It is not to be wonder'd at, Ma'am, – all this is the natural consequence of teaching girls to read. – Had I a thousand daughters, by Heavens! I'd as soon have them taught the black-art as their alphabet!

Mrs. Mal. Nay, nay, Sir Anthony, you are an absolute misanthropy.

Sir Anth. In my way hither, Mrs. Malaprop, I observed your niece's maid coming forth from a circulating library! – She had a book in each hand – they were half-bound volumes, with marbled covers! – From that moment I guess'd how full of duty I should see her mistress!

Mrs. Mal. Those are vile places, indeed!

Sir Anth. Madam, a circulating library in a town is as an evergreen tree of diabolical knowledge! – It blossoms through the year! – And depend on it, Mrs. Malaprop, that they who are so fond of handling the leaves, will long for the fruit at last.

*

Mrs. Mal. Fie, fie, Sir Anthony, you surely speak laconically!

Sir Anth. Why, Mrs. Malaprop, in moderation now, what would you have a woman know?

Mrs. Mal. Observe me, Sir Anthony. – I would by no means wish a daughter of mine to be a progeny of learning; I don't think so much learning becomes a young woman; for instance – I would never let her meddle with Greek, or Hebrew, or Algebra, or Simony, or Fluxions, or Paradoxes, or such inflammatory branches of learning – neither would it be necessary for her to handle any of your mathematical, astronomical, diabolical instruments; – But, Sir Anthony, I would send her, at nine years old, to a boarding-school, in order to learn a little ingenuity and artifice. – Then, Sir, she should have a supercilious knowledge in accounts; – and as she grew up, I would have her instructed in geometry, that she might know something of the contagious countries; – but above all, Sir Anthony, she should be mistress of orthodoxy, that she might not mis-spell, and mis-pronounce words so shamefully as girls usually do; and likewise that she might reprehend the true meaning of what she is saying. – This, Sir Anthony, is what I would have a woman know; – and I don't think there is a superstitious article in it.

Sir Anth. Well, well, Mrs. Malaprop, I will dispute the point no further with you; though I must confess that you are a truly moderate and polite arguer, for almost every third word you say is on my side of the question. – But, Mrs. Malaprop, to the more important point in debate, – you say you have no objection to my proposal?

Mrs. Mal. None, I assure you. – I am under no positive engagement with Mr. Acres, and as Lydia is so obstinate against him, perhaps your son may have better success.

Sir Anth. Well, Madam, I will write for the boy directly. – He knows not a syllable of this yet, though I have for some time had the proposal in my head. He is at present with his regiment.

Mrs. Mal. We have never seen your son, Sir Anthony; but I hope no objection on his side.

Sir Anth. Objection! – let him object if he dare! – No, no, Mrs. Malaprop, Jack knows that the least demur puts me in a frenzy directly. – My process was always very simple – in their younger days, 'twas 'Jack do this'; – if he demurred, I knock'd him down – and if he grumbled at that – I always sent him out of the room.

Mrs. Mal. Aye, and the properest way, o' my conscience! – nothing is so conciliating to young people as severity. – Well, Sir Anthony, I shall give Mr. Acres his discharge, and prepare Lydia to receive your son's invocations; – and I hope you will represent *her* to the Captain as an object not altogether illegible.

Richard Brinsley Sheridan
The Rivals (1775)

EVELINA ASHAMED OF HER RELATIVES

WHILE we were strolling round the garden, I perceived, walking with a party of ladies at some distance, Lord Orville! I instantly retreated behind Miss Branghton, and kept out of sight till we had passed him: for I dreaded being seen by him again, in a public walk, with a party of which I was ashamed.

Happily I succeeded in my design, and saw no more of him; for a sudden and violent shower of rain made us all hasten out of the gardens. We ran till we came to a small green-shop, where we begged shelter. Here we found ourselves in company with two footmen, whom the rain had driven into the shop. Their livery, I thought, I had before seen; and upon looking from the window, I perceived the same upon a coachman belonging to a carriage, which I immediately recollected to be Lord Orville's.

Fearing to be known, I whispered Miss Branghton not to speak my name. Had I considered but a moment, I should have been sensible of the inutility of such a caution, since not one of the party call me by any other appellation than that of *Cousin* or of *Miss*; but I am perpetually involved in some distress or dilemma from my own heedlessness.

This request excited very strongly her curiosity; and she attacked me with such eagerness and bluntness of enquiry, that I could not avoid telling her the reason of my making it, and, consequently, that I was known to Lord Orville: an acknowledgment which proved the most unfortunate in the world; for she would not rest till she had drawn from me the circumstances attending my first making the acquaintance. Then, calling to her sister, she said, "Lord, Polly, only think! Miss has danced with a Lord!"

"Well," cried Polly, "that's a thing I should never have thought of! And pray Miss, what did he say to you?"

This question was much sooner asked than answered; and they both became so very inquisitive and earnest, that they soon drew the attention of Madame Duval and the rest of the party, to whom, in a very short time, they repeated all they had gathered from me.

"Goodness, then," cried young Branghton, "if I was Miss, if I would not make free with his Lordship's coach to take me to town."

"Why, ay," said the father, "there would be some sense in that; that would be making some use of a Lord's acquaintance, for it would save us coach-hire."

"Lord, Miss," cried Polly, "I wish you would, for I should like of all things to ride in a coronet-coach."

"I promise you," said Madame Duval, "I'm glad you've thought of it, for I don't see no objection; – so let's have the coachman called."

"Not for the world," cried I, very much alarmed, "indeed it is utterly impossible."

"Why so?" demanded Mr. Branghton; "pray, where's the good of your knowing a Lord, if you're never the better for him?"

"*Ma foi*, child," said Madame Duval, "you don't know no more of the world than if you was a baby. Pray, Sir, (to one of the footmen), tell that coachman to draw up, for I wants to speak to him."

The man stared, but did not move. "Pray, pray, Madam," said I, "pray, Mr. Branghton, have the goodness to give up this plan; I know but very little of his Lordship, and cannot, upon any account, take so great a liberty."

"Don't say nothing about it," said Madame Duval, "for I shall have it my own way: so if *you* won't call the coachman, Sir, I'll promise you I'll call him myself."

The footman, very impertinently, laughed and turned upon his heel. Madame Duval, extremely irritated, ran out in the rain, and beckoned the coachman, who instantly obeyed her summons. Shocked beyond all expression, I flew after her, and entreated her with the utmost earnestness, to let us return in a hackney-coach: – but, oh! – she is impenetrable to persuasion! She told the man she wanted him to carry her directly to town, and that she would answer for him to Lord Orville. The man, with a sneer, thanked her, but said he should answer for himself; and was driving off, when another footman came up to him, with information that his Lord was gone into Kensington Palace, and would not want him for an hour or two.

"Why then, friend," said Mr. Branghton, (for we were followed by all the party), "where will be the great harm of your taking us to town?"

"Besides," said the son, "I'll promise you a pot of beer for my own share."

These speeches had no other answer from the coachman than a loud laugh, which was echoed by the insolent footmen. I rejoiced at their resistance; though I was certain, that if their Lord had witnessed their impertinence, they would have been instantly dismissed his service.

"*Pardi*," cried Madame Duval, "if I don't think all the footmen are the most impudentest fellows in the kingdom! But I'll promise you I'll have your master told of your airs; so you'll get no good by 'em."

"Why pray," said the coachman, rather alarmed, "did my Lord give you leave to use the coach?"

"It's no matter for that," answered she; "I'm sure if he's a gentleman, he'd let us have it sooner than we should be wet to the skin: but I'll promise you he shall know how saucy you've been, for this young lady knows him very well."

"Ay, that she does," said Miss Polly; "and she's danced with him too."

Oh how I repented my foolish mismanagement! The men bit their lips, and looked at one another in some confusion. This was perceived by our party, who, taking advantage of it, protested they would write Lord Orville word of their ill behaviour without delay. This quite startled them, and one of the footmen offered to run to the palace and ask his Lord's permission for our having the carriage.

This proposal really made me tremble; and the Branghtons all hung back upon it: but Madame Duval is never to be dissuaded from a scheme she has once formed. "Do so," cried she, "and give this child's compliments to your master, and tell him, as we ha'n't no coach here, we should be glad to go just as far as Holborn in his."

"No, no, no!" cried I; "don't go, -- I know nothing of his Lordship, – I send no message, – I have nothing to say to him!"

The men, very much perplexed, could with difficulty restrain themselves from resuming their impertinent mirth. Madame Duval scolded me very angrily, and then desired them to go directly. "Pray, then," said the coachman, "what name is to be given to my Lord?"

"Anville," answered Madame Duval, "tell him Miss Anville wants the coach; the young lady he danced with once."

I was really in an agony; but the winds could not have been more deaf to me, than those to whom I pleaded! and therefore the footman, urged by the repeated threats of Madame Duval, and perhaps recollecting the name himself, actually went to the palace with this strange message!

He returned in a few minutes, and, bowing to me with the greatest respect, said, "My Lord desires his compliments, and his carriage will be always at Miss Anville's service."

I was so much affected by this politeness, and chagrined at the whole affair, that I could scarce refrain from tears. Madame Duval and the Miss Branghtons eagerly jumped into the coach, and desired me to follow. I would rather have submitted to the severest punishment, – but all resistance was vain.

Frances Burney

Evelina, or The History of a Young Lady's Entrance into the World (1778). Text from the third edition (1779)

IN THE APENNINES

DURING three or four hours that we continued ascending, the scene increased in sterility and desolation; but, at the end of our second post, the landscape began to alter for the better: little green valleys at the base of tremendous steeps, discovered themselves; scattered over with oaks, and freshened with running waters, which the nakedness of the impending rocks set off to advantage. The sides of the cliffs in general consist of rude mis-shapen masses; but their summits are smooth and verdant, and continually browsed by herds of white goats, which were gamboling on the edge of the precipices, as we passed beneath. I joined one of these frisking assemblies, whose shadows were stretched by the setting sun, along the level herbage. There I sat a few minutes, whilst they shook their beards at me, and tried to scare me with all their horns; but I was not to be frightened, and would put up my adorations to departing day, in spite of their caperings. Being tired with skipping and butting at me in vain, the whole herd trotted away; and I after them. They led me a rare dance from crag to crag, and from thicket to thicket. It was growing dusky apace, and wreaths of smoke began to ascend from the mysterious depths of the valleys. I was ignorant what monster inhabited such retirements, so gave over my pursuit lest some Polypheme or other might make me repent it. I looked around, the carriage was out of sight; but hearing the neighing of horses at a distance, I soon came up with them, and mounted another rapid ascent, from whence an extensive tract of cliff and forest-land was discernible. The rocks here formed a spacious terrace, along which I continued surveying the distant groves, and marking the solemn approach of night. The sky was hung with storms, and a pale moon seemed to advance with difficulty amongst broken and tempestuous clouds. It was an hour to reap plants with brazen sickles, and to meditate upon revenge. A chill wind blew from the highest peak of the Apennines, inspiring evil, and making a dismal rustle amongst the woods of chesnut that hung on the mountains' side, through which we were forced to pass. I never heard such fatal murmurs; nor felt myself so gloomily disposed. I walked out of the sound of the carriage, where the glimmering moon-light prevailed, and began interpreting the language of the leaves, not greatly to my own advantage or that of any being in the universe. I was no prophet of good, but full of melan-choly bodings, and something that bordered on despair. Had I but commanded an oracle, as antient visionaries were wont, I should have thrown whole nations into dismay. How long I continued in this strange temper, I cannot pretend to say, but believe it was midnight before we emerged from the oracular forest, and saw faintly before us the huts of Lognone, where we were to sleep. This blessed hamlet is suspended on the brow of a bleak mountain, and every gust that stirs, shakes the whole village to its foundations. At our approach, two hags stalked forth with lanterns, and invited us with a grin, which I shall always remember, to a dish of mustard and crows gizzards; a dish I was more than half afraid of tasting, lest it should change me to some bird of darkness, condemned to mope eternally on the black rafters of the cottage. After repeated supplica-tions, we procured a few eggs, and some faggots to make a fire. Its blaze gave me courage to hear the hollow blasts, that whistled in the crevices; and, pitching my bed in a warm corner, I soon fell asleep; and forgot all my cares and inquietudes.

William Beckford

*Dreams, Waking Thoughts, and Incidents ; in a Series of
Letters from Various Parts of Europe* (1783)

An Attempt to Convert a Red Indian

IT appears to me, said Hermsprong, that the story I am telling you is very tedious, and totally uninteresting. The ladies, with more politeness than veracity perhaps, assured him to the contrary. I cannot, says he, make it entertaining; I must make it short.

My father was well received. The head man of the village, whose name was Lontac, and who had acquired the appellation of the Great Beaver, received him into his tent. There was a commerce of civility, but none of language. To remedy this, my father availed himself of the son's assistance, and during the winter months learned enough of their language to be able to communicate all the ideas be believed would be necessary for their mutual accommodation.

Early in spring, my father sent for stores; and having distributed presents of rum and tobacco, there was a meeting of head men from all the Nawdoessie villages, whom the Great Beaver addressed thus: — Six moons ago, a man from the American people came hither, brought by my son to strengthen peace betwixt us. He has learned our language. He loves our customs. He will reside with us a vast number of moons; perhaps till the Great Spirit calls him away. He has a wife and people. We must build him a wigwam; large, that it may be unto us a storehouse of all the good things we want from the European people. He will be our friend. When we go to war, he will aid us with his counsel. When we return from hunting, he will buy our skins. So we shall have powder and guns, cloth to warm us in winter, and rum to cheer us.

The Great Beaver's speech was well received. The wigwam was built, large and commodious. The stores were deposited. My mother and myself, for I had made my appearance in this best of worlds, arrived safe, with our European servants, our books, our music, our instruments of drawing, and every thing that could be supposed to alleviate the solitude my mother had pictured to herself.

This afflicting solitude, however, did not arrive. – The people were civil and attentive; Lontac's family obliging; and there was novelty in the scene. My father even found it difficult to procure leisure for the studies and amusements he most liked. When he could, he read, wrote, drew the rude scenes around him, and kept up a correspondence of philosophy as well as business with Mr. Germersheim.

My mother was a very good woman; not without her prejudices indeed, but a good woman, and a zealous catholic. She loved my father; she saw him in a place of safety and happy. She was happy herself, except when she thought of France, her father, and the convent. The last disturbed her most. She feared she had committed a crime; she had no confessor, and could not absolve herself. She confessed indeed to my father, who consoled her always, and would have given her absolution, had she been pleased to accept it. At length it came into her mind, that greater sins than hers might be expiated, by a conversion to Christianity of a few Nawdoessie females. How did she know but she might be the agent appointed by God, for producing this salutary change in a whole people?

Lodiquashow, the wife of Lontac, the best of squaws, the most obedient of wives, had never presumed to sit down in the presence of the Great Beaver till she had brought him six children. With her my mother determined to begin the great work, and applied herself to learn the language with an assiduity which surprised my father. Perhaps she began her pious labour before she had attained sufficient powers of explanation; for although Lodiquashow heard my mother with the most patient attention, nor once offended by interruption, contradiction, or remark; all the assent my mother was ever able to attain, was, The Great Spirit and Lontac only know.

Unable to produce any effect upon the stupid Lodiquashow,

or on the two daughters, who still remained ungiven away in marriage, she determined to try her powers on Lontac himself. Sixty moons, however, passed away before she durst venture; partly owing to a fear she had not yet acquired the full force of the Nawdoessie tongue, and partly to a sort of awe of this venerable chief, who was himself an orator, and who was much beloved, respected, and obeyed.

At length my mother asked an audience and obtained it. It appeared indeed to Lontac to be an inversion of order, that the Great Beaver should lend his ear to a woman for instruction; but there is in these people a politeness derived from education, as well as ours, which qualifies them for patient hearers to a degree I have never observed in more polished nations.

What most of all astonished my mother, was, that though Lontac, after a few lectures, seemed himself to put her on speaking and to be amused, if not instructed, she could seldom obtain an answer; and when she did, it was only to thank her for the pains she took on his account. It is true, he did not always understand; when he understood, he did not always approve; but it is only for a native American to arrive at so high a degree of politeness, as to testify disapprobation, only by a respectful silence.

Wondering that any human creature should be deaf to persuasion, and blind to the sublime truth she had now so oft explained, she began at times to be angry, and ladies are seldom angry, without a little gentle abuse. Intreated, almost commanded, to answer, Lontac spoke with all possible gravity, and the greatest respect, as follows: –

One day's journey west of this place, there is, as you have heard, a large lake called the White Bear; because white bears were numerous on its banks, and disputed the sovereignty of the adjacent lands with man. About a thousand moons ago, when the war had lasted many generations of bears and men, the two powers agreed upon a truce, and met on a certain bank of the lake, in order to have a talk. When the orators on both sides –

On both sides! exclaimed my mother.

Lontac proceeded – were preparing to speak, a figure arose from the midst of the lake, of vast dimensions; viewed on one side, it seemed to be a bear; on the other, it seemed to be a man. The white bear part of this awful figure waved its paw in the air to command silence, then said with a terrific voice –

Was ever any thing so preposterous! cries my mother. Sure it is impossible you should believe it!

Why impossible? answered Lontac; it is tradition handed down to us from our fathers. We believe because they said it.

Bears speak! again exclaimed my mother.

A serpent, answered Lontac, spake to the first woman; an ass spake to a prophet; you have said so, and therefore I believe it.

But, said my mother, they were inspired.

So was the half white bear. The Great Spirit inspires everything.

But this is so excessively absurd, said my mother.

I have not called your wonders absurd, Lontac replied; I thought it more decent to believe.

What have I told you preposterous? asked my mother.

Many things far removed from the ordinary course of nature, Lontac replied; I do not presume to call them preposterous; it is better to believe than contradict.

Such obstinacy of politeness provoked my mother, almost as much as contradiction could have done; she told my father what a stupid creature she had undertaken to instruct; and desired that he would endeavour to bring him to the light of truth. My father answered, My dear, they have had missionaries, whose holy lips have hitherto failed. Perhaps our mysteries are too refined for their gross understanding; perhaps the time appointed by Providence for their conversion is not yet come.

I despise them, said my mother, prodigiously.

Do, my dear, my father replied, as much as you can with civility for people who are always doing you services, and showing their regard. I despised them myself, till I found them my equals in knowledge of many things of which I believed them ignorant; and my superiors in the virtues of friendship, hospitality, and integrity.

I shall never be easy among them, said my mother.

You will indeed, my dear, answered my father, when you don't think of converting them.

Robert Bage
Man as He is Not; or, Hermsprong (1796)

MEADOW, GROVE, AND STREAM . . .

Alfoxden, 20th. January 1798. — The green paths down the hill-sides are channels for streams. The young wheat is streaked by silver lines of water running between the ridges, the sheep are gathered together on the slopes. After the wet dark days, the country seems more populous. It peoples itself in the sunbeams. The garden, mimic of spring, is gay with flowers. The purple-starred hepatica spreads itself in the sun, and the clustering snow-drops put forth their white heads, at first upright, ribbed with green, and like a rosebud when completely opened, hanging their heads downwards, but slowly lengthening their slender stems. The slanting woods of an unvarying brown, showing the light through the thin net-work of their upper boughs. Upon the highest ridge of that round hill covered with planted oaks, the shafts of the trees show in the light like the columns of a ruin.

23rd. – Bright sunshine. I went out at three o'clock. The sea perfectly calm blue, streaked with deeper colour by the clouds, and tongues or points of sand; on our return of a gloomy red. The sun gone down. The crescent moon, Jupiter, and Venus. The sound of the sea distinctly heard on the tops of the hills, which we could never hear in summer. We attribute this partly to the bareness of the trees, but chiefly to the absence of the singing of birds, the hum of insects, that noiseless noise which lives in the summer air. The villages marked out by beautiful beds of smoke. The turf fading into the mountain road. The scarlet flowers of the moss.

17th. *February*. – A deep snow upon the ground. William and Coleridge walked to Mr Bartelmy's, and to Stowey. William returned, and we walked through the wood into the Coombe to fetch some eggs. The sun shone bright and clear. A deep stillness in the thickest part of the wood, undisturbed except by the occasional dropping of the snow from the holly boughs; no other sound but that of the water, and the slender notes of a redbreast, which sang at intervals on the outskirts of the southern side of the wood. There the bright green moss was bare at the roots of the trees, and the little birds were upon it. The whole appearance of the wood was enchanting; and each tree, taken singly, was beautiful. The branches of the hollies pendent with their white burden, but still showing their bright red berries, and their glossy green leaves. The bare branches of the oaks thickened by the snow.

24th. – Went to the hill-top. Sat a considerable time overlooking the country towards the sea. The air blew pleasantly round us. The landscape mildly interesting. The Welsh hills capped by a huge range of tumultuous white clouds. The sea, spotted with white, of a bluish grey in general, and streaked with darker lines. The near shores clear; scattered farm houses, half-concealed by green mossy orchards, fresh straw lying at the doors; hay-stacks in the fields. Brown fallows, the springing wheat, like a shade of green over the brown earth, and the choice meadow plots, full of sheep and lambs, of a soft and vivid green; a few wreaths of blue smoke, spreading along the ground; the oaks and beeches in the hedges retaining their yellow leaves; the distant prospect on the land side, islanded with sunshine; the sea, like a basin full to the margin; the fresh-ploughed fields dark; the turnips of a lively rough green. Returned through the wood.

Dorothy Wordsworth

'Alfoxden Journal' from *The Life of William Wordsworth* by W. Knight (1889), Vol. I

The Burial of Madame Montoni

EMILY, shuddering with emotions of horror and grief, assisted by Annette, prepared the corpse for interment; and having wrapped it in cerements and covered it with a winding-sheet, they watched beside it, till past midnight, when they heard the approaching footsteps of the men, who were to lay it in its earthy bed. It was with difficulty, that Emily overcame her emotion, when, the door of the chamber being thrown open, their gloomy countenances were seen by the glare of the torch they carried, and two of them, without speaking, lifted the body on their shoulders, while the third preceding them with the light, descended through the castle towards the grave, which was in the lower vault of the chapel within the castle walls.

They had to cross two courts towards the east wing of the castle, which, adjoining the chapel, was, like it, in ruins: but the silence and gloom of these courts had now little power over Emily's mind, occupied as it was with more mournful ideas; and she scarcely heard the low and dismal hooting of the night-birds, that roosted among the ivyed battlements of the ruin, or perceived the still flittings of the bat, which frequently crossed her way. But when, having entered the chapel and passed between the mouldering pillars of the aisles, the bearers stopped at a flight of steps, that led down to a low arched door, and, their comrade having descended to unlock it, she saw imperfectly the gloomy abyss beyond; – saw the corpse of her aunt carried down these steps, and the ruffian-like figure, that stood with a torch at the bottom to receive it – all her fortitude was lost in emotions of inexpressible grief and terror. She turned to lean upon Annette, who was cold and trembling like herself, and she lingered so long on the summit of the flight, that the gleam of the torch began to die away on the pillars of the chapel, and the men were almost beyond her view. Then, the gloom around her awakening other fears, and a sense of what she considered to be her duty overcoming her reluctance, she descended to the vaults, following the echo of footsteps and the faint ray, that pierced the darkness, till the harsh grating of a distant door, that was opened to receive the corpse, again appalled her.

After the pause of a moment, she went on, and, as she entered the vaults, saw between the arches, at some distance, the men lay down the body near the edge of an open grave, where stood another of Montoni's men and a priest, whom she did not observe, till he began the burial service; then, lifting her eyes from the ground, she saw the venerable figure of the friar, and heard him in a low voice, equally solemn and affecting, perform the service for the dead. At the moment in which they let down the body into the earth, the scene was such as only the dark pencil of a Domenichino, perhaps, could have done justice to. The fierce features and wild dress of the *condottieri*, bending with their torches over the grave, into which the corpse was descending, were contrasted by the venerable figure of the monk, wrapt in long black garments, his cowl thrown back from his pale face, on which the light gleaming strongly showed the lines of affliction softened by piety, and the few grey locks, which time had spared on his temples: while, beside him, stood the softer form of Emily, who leaned for support upon Annette; her face half averted, and shaded by a thin veil, that fell over her figure; and her mild and beautiful countenance fixed in grief so solemn as admitted not of tears, while she thus saw committed untimely to the earth her last relative and friend. The gleams, thrown between the arches of the vaults, where, here and there, the broken ground marked the spots in which other bodies had been recently interred, and the general obscurity beyond were circumstances, that alone would have led on the imagination of a spectator to scenes more horrible than even that, which was pictured at the grave of the misguided and unfortunate Madame Montoni.

Ann Radcliffe
The Mysteries of Udolpho: a Romance (1794)

DR PANGLOSS

Lord Duberly, Lady Duberly, John

John. Doctor Pangloss is below, my lord.
Lord D. Odsbobs, my lady! that's the man as learns me to talk English.
Lady D. Hush! consider –

(*pointing to the servant*).

Lord D. Hum! I forgot – Curse me, my honest fellow, show him up stairs, d'ye hear.

[*Exit* JOHN]

There, was that easy?
Lady D. Tolerable.
Lord D. Well, now, get along, my lady: the doctor and I must be snug.

159

Lady D. Then I bid you a good morning, my lord. As Lady
Betty says, I wish you a *bon repos.*

[*Exit*]

Lord D. A bone repos! I don't know how it is, but the women
are more cuter at these here matters nor the men. My wife,
as every body may see, is as genteel already as if she had been
born a duchess. This Dr. Pangloss will do me a deal of good
in the way of fashioning my discourse. So – here, he is.

Enter PANGLOSS

Doctor, good morning – I wish you a bone repos! – Take a
chair, doctor.

Pang. Pardon me, my lord; I am not inclined to be sedentary;
I wish, with permission, *"erectos ad sidera tollere vultus."* –
Ovid. – Hem!

Lord D. Tollory vultures! – I suppose that that means you had
rather stand?

Pang. Fie, this is a locomotive morning with me. Just hurried,
my lord, from the Society of Arts; whence, I may say, "I
have borne my blushing honours thick upon me." – Shakespeare. – Hem!

Lord D. And what has put your honours to the blush, this
morning, doctor?

Pang. To the blush! – A ludicrous perversion of the author's
meaning. – He, he, he! – Hem! – you shall hear, my lord, –
"Lend me your ears." – Shakespeare, again. – Hem! – 'Tis
not unknown to your lordship, and the no less literary
world, that the Caledonian University of Aberdeen, long
since conferred upon me the dignity of L.L.D.; and, as I
never beheld that erudite body, I may safely say they
dubb'd me with a degree from sheer consideration of my
celebrity: –

Lord D. True.

Pang. For nothing, my lord, but my own innate modesty,
could suppose the Scotch college to be sway'd by one

pound fifteen shillings and three-pence three-farthings, paid on receiving my diploma, as a handsome compliment to the numerous and learned heads of that seminary.

Lord D. Oh, damn it, no, it wasn't for the matter of money.

Pang. I do not think it was altogether the "*auri sacra fames.*" – Virgil. – Hem! – But this very day, my lord, at eleven o'clock A.M. the Society of Arts, in consequence, as they were pleased to say, of my merits, – He, he, he! – my *merits*, my lord – have admitted me as an unworthy member; and I have, henceforward, the privilege of adding to my name the honourable title of *A double S*.

Lord D. And I make no doubt, doctor, but you have richly deserved it. I warrant a man doesn't get A double S tack'd to his name for nothing.

Pang. Decidedly not, my lord. – Yes, I am now *Artium Societatis Socius*. – My two last publications did that business. – "*Exegi monumentum aere perennius.*" – Horace. – Hem!

George Colman the Younger
The Heir at Law (1808)

ON CALAIS BEACH

August 1802. We walked by the sea-shore almost every evening with Annette and Caroline,[1] or William and I alone. I had a bad cold, and could not bathe at first, but William did. It was a pretty sight to see as we walked upon the sands when the tide was low, perhaps a hundred people bathing about a quarter of a mile distant from us. And we had delightful walks after the heat of the day was passed – seeing far off in the west the coast of England like a cloud crested with Dover castle, which was but like the summit of the cloud – the evening star and the

1. Wordsworth's former mistress and his illegitimate daughter.

glory of the sky, the reflections in the water were more beautiful than the sky itself, purple waves brighter than precious stones, for ever melting away upon the sands. The fort, a wooden building, at the entrance of the harbour at Calais, when the evening twilight was coming on, and we could not see anything of the building but its shape, which was far more distinct than in perfect daylight, seemed to be reared upon pillars of ebony, between which pillars the sea was seen in the most beautiful colours that can be conceived. Nothing in romance was ever half so beautiful. Now came in view, as the evening star sunk down, and the colours of the west faded away, the two lights of England, lighted up by Englishmen in our country to warn vessels off rocks or sands. These we used to see from the pier, when we could see no other distant objects but the clouds, the sky, and the sea itself – all was dark behind. The town of Calais seemed deserted of the light of heaven, but there was always light, and life, and joy upon the sea. One night I shall never forget – the day had been very hot, and William and I walked alone together upon the pier. The sea was gloomy, for there was a blackness over all the sky, except when it was overspread with lightning, which often revealed to us a distant vessel near, as the waves roared and broke against the pier, and they were interfused with greenish fiery light. The more distant sea always black and gloomy. It was also beautiful, on the calm hot night, to see the little boats row out of harbour with wings of fire, and the sail boats with the fiery track which they cut as they went along, and which closed up after them with a hundred thousand sparkles, and streams of glow-worm light. Caroline was delighted.

Dorothy Wordsworth

'Grasmere Journal' from *The Life of William Wordsworth* by W. Knight, (1889), Vol. I

An Elegant Irish Equipage

FROM the inn yard came a hackney chaise, in a most deplorably crazy state; the body mounted up to a prodigious height, on unbending springs, nodding forwards, one door swinging open, three blinds up, because they could not be let down, the perch tied in two places, the iron of the wheels half off, half loose, wooden pegs for linch-pins, and ropes for harness. The horses were worthy of the harness; wretched little dog-tired creatures, that looked as if they had been driven to the last gasp, and as if they had never been rubbed down in their lives; their bones starting through their skin; one lame, the other blind; one with a raw back, the other with a galled breast; one with his neck poking down over his collar, and the other with his head dragged forward by a bit of a broken bridle, held at arms' length by a man dressed like a mad beggar, in half a hat and half a wig, both awry in opposite directions; a long tattered great coat, tied round his waist by a hay-rope; the jagged rents in the skirts of this coat showing his bare legs, marbled of many colours; while something like stockings hung loose about his ankles. The noises he made, by way of threatening or encouraging his steeds, I pretend not to describe.

In an indignant voice I called to the landlord – "I hope these are not the horses – I hope this is not the chaise, intended for my servants."

The innkeeper, and the pauper who was preparing to officiate as postillion, both in the same instant exclaimed –

"*Sorrow* better chaise in the county!"

"*Sorrow!*" said I – "what do you mean by sorrow?"

"That there's no better, plase your honour, can be seen. We have two more to be sure – but one has no top, and the other no bottom. Any way there's no better can be seen than this same."

"And these horses," cried I – "why this horse is so lame he can hardly stand."

"Oh, plase your honour, tho' he can't stand, he'll *go* fast enough. He has a great deal of the rogue in him, plase your honour. He's always that way at first setting out."

"And that wretched animal with the galled breast!"

"He's all the better for it, when once he warms; it's he that will go with the speed of light, plase your honour. Sure, is not he Knockecroghery? and didn't I give fifteen guineas for him, barring the luckpenny, at the fair of Knockecroghery, and he rising four year old at the same time?"

. . . Then seizing his whip and reins in one hand, he clawed up his stockings with the other; so with one easy step he got into his place, and seated himself, coachman-like, upon a well-worn bar of wood, that served as a coach-box. "Throw me the loan of a trusty, Bartly, for a cushion," said he. A frieze coat was thrown up over the horses' heads. – Paddy caught it. "Where are you, Hosey?" cried he. "Sure I'm only rowling a wisp of straw on my leg," replied Hosey. "Throw me up," added this paragon of postillions, turning to one of the crowd of idle by-standers. "Arrah, push me up, can't ye?"

A man took hold of his knee, and threw him upon the horse; he was in his seat in a trice; then clinging by the mane of his horse, he scrambled for the bridle which was under the other horse's feet – reached it, and, well satisfied with himself, looked round at Paddy, who looked back to the chaise door at my angry servants, "secure in the last event of things." In vain the Englishman, in monotonous anger, and the Frenchman in every note of the gamut, abused Paddy; necessity and wit were on Paddy's side: he parried all that was said against his chaise, his horses, himself, and his country, with invincible comic dexterity, till at last both his adversaries, dumbfounded, clambered into the vehicle, where they were instantly shut up in straw and darkness.

Maria Edgeworth
'Ennui' from *Tales of Fashionable Life* (1809)

MR COLLINS PROPOSES

THE next day opened a new scene at Longbourn. Mr. Collins made his declaration in form. Having resolved to do it without loss of time, as his leave of absence extended only to the following Saturday, and having no feelings of diffidence to make it distressing to himself even at the moment, he set about it in a very orderly manner, with all the observances which he supposed a regular part of the business. On finding Mrs. Bennet, Elizabeth, and one of the younger girls together, soon after breakfast, he addressed the mother in these words,

"May I hope, Madam, for your interest with your fair daughter Elizabeth, when I solicit for the honour of a private audience with her in the course of this morning?"

Before Elizabeth had time for anything but a blush of surprise, Mrs. Bennet instantly answered,

"Oh, dear! – Yes – certainly. – I am sure Lizzy will be very happy – I am sure she can have no objection. – Come, Kitty, I want you upstairs." And, gathering her work together, she was hastening away, when Elizabeth called out,

"Dear Ma'am, do not go. – I beg you will not go. – Mr. Collins must excuse me. – He can have nothing to say to me that any body need not hear. I am going away myself."

"No, no, nonsense, Lizzy. – I desire you will stay where you are." – And upon Elizabeth's seeming really, with vexed and embarrassed looks, about to escape, she added, "Lizzy, I *insist* upon your staying and hearing Mr. Collins."

Elizabeth would not oppose such an injunction – and a moment's consideration making her also sensible that it would be wisest to get it over as soon and as quietly as possible, she sat down again, and tried to conceal, by incessant employment the feelings which were divided between distress and diversion. Mrs. Bennet and Kitty walked off, and as soon as they were gone Mr. Collins began.

"Believe me, my dear Miss Elizabeth, that your modesty, so far from doing you any disservice, rather adds to your other perfections. You would have been less amiable in my eyes had there *not* been this little unwillingness; but allow me to assure you that I have your respected mother's permission for this address. You can hardly doubt the purport of my discourse, however your natural delicacy may lead you to dissemble; my attentions have been too marked to be mistaken. Almost as soon as I entered the house I singled you out as the companion of my future life. But before I am run away with by my feelings on this subject, perhaps it will be advisable for me to state my reasons for marrying – and moreover for coming into Hertfordshire with the design of selecting a wife as I certainly did."

The idea of Mr. Collins, with all his solemn composure, being run away with by his feelings, made Elizabeth so near laughing that she could not use the short pause he allowed in any attempt to stop him farther, and he continued:

"My reasons for marrying are, first, that I think it a right thing for every clergyman in easy circumstances (like myself) to set the example of matrimony in his parish. Secondly, that I am convinced that it will add very greatly to my happiness; and thirdly – which perhaps I ought to have mentioned earlier, that it is the particular advice and recommendation of the very noble lady whom I have the honour of calling patroness. Twice has she condescended to give me her opinion (unasked too!) on this subject; and it was but the very Saturday night before I left Hunsford – between our pools at quadrille, while Mrs. Jenkinson was arranging Miss de Bourgh's foot-stool, that she said, 'Mr. Collins, you must marry. A clergyman like you must marry. – Chuse properly, chuse a gentlewoman for *my* sake; and for your *own*, let her be an active, useful sort of person, not brought up high, but able to make a small income go a good way. This is my advice. Find such a woman as soon as you can, bring her to Hunsford, and I will visit her.' Allow me, by the way, to observe, my fair cousin, that I do not reckon the notice and kindness of Lady Catherine de Bourgh as among the least of the advantages in my power to offer. You will find her manners beyond any thing I can describe; and your wit and vivacity I think must be acceptable to her, especially when tempered with the silence and respect which her rank will inevitably excite. Thus much for my general intention in favour of matrimony; it remains to be told why my views are directed to Longbourn instead of my own neighbourhood, where, I assure you there are many amiable young women. But the fact is, that being, as I am, to inherit this estate after the death of your honoured father, (who, however, may live many years longer,) I could not satisfy myself without resolving to chuse a wife from among his daughters, that the loss to them might be as little as possible, when the melancholy event takes place—which, however, as I have already said, may not be for several years. This has been my motive, my fair cousin, and I flatter myself it will not sink me in your esteem. And now nothing remains for me but to assure you in the most animated language of the violence of my affection. To fortune I am perfectly indifferent, and shall make no demand of that nature on your father, since I am well aware that it could not be complied with; and that one thousand pounds in the 4 per cents. which will not be yours till after your mother's decease, is all that you may ever be entitled to. On that head, therefore, I shall be uniformly silent; and you may assure yourself that no ungenerous reproach shall ever pass my lips when we are married."

It was absolutely necessary to interrupt him now.

"You are too hasty, Sir," she cried. "You forget that I have made no answer. Let me do it without farther loss of time. Accept my thanks for the compliment you are paying me. I am very sensible of the honour of your proposals, but it is impossible for me to do otherwise than decline them."

"I am not now to learn," replied Mr. Collins, with a formal wave of the hand, "that it is usual with young ladies to reject the addresses of the man whom they secretly mean to accept, when he first applies for their favour; and that sometimes the refusal is repeated a second or even a third time. I am therefore by no means discouraged by what you have just said, and shall hope to lead you to the altar ere long."

"Upon my word, Sir," cried Elizabeth, "your hope is rather an extraordinary one after my declaration. I do assure you that I am not one of those young ladies (if such young ladies there are) who are so daring as to risk their happiness on the chance of being asked a second time. I am perfectly serious in my refusal. – You could not make *me* happy, and I am convinced that I am the last woman in the world who would make *you* so. – Nay, were your friend Lady Catherine to know me, I am persuaded she would find me in every respect ill qualified for the situation."

"Were it certain that Lady Catherine would think so," said Mr. Collins very gravely – "but I cannot imagine that her ladyship would at all disapprove of you. And you may be certain that when I have the honour of seeing her again I shall speak in the highest terms of your modesty, economy, and other amiable qualifications."

"Indeed, Mr. Collins, all praise of me will be unnecessary. You must give me leave to judge for myself, and pay me the compliment of believing what I say. I wish you very happy and very rich, and by refusing your hand, do all in my power to prevent your being otherwise. In making me the offer, you must have satisfied the delicacy of your feelings with regard to my family, and may take possession of Longbourn estate whenever it falls, without any self-reproach. This matter may be considered, therefore, as finally settled." And rising as she thus spoke, she would have quitted the room, had not Mr. Collins thus addressed her,

"When I do myself the honour of speaking to you next on this subject I shall hope to receive a more favourable answer than you have now given me; though I am far from accusing you of cruelty at present, because I know it to be the established custom of your sex to reject a man on the first application, and perhaps you have even now said as much to encourage my suit as would be consistent with the true delicacy of the female character."

"Really, Mr. Collins," cried Elizabeth, with some warmth, "you puzzle me exceedingly. If what I have hitherto said can appear to you in the form of encouragement, I know not how to express my refusal in such a way as may convince you of its being one."

"You must give me leave to flatter myself, my dear cousin, that your refusal of my addresses is merely words of course. My reasons for believing it are briefly these: – It does not appear to me that my hand is unworthy your acceptance, or that the establishment I can offer would be any other than highly desirable. My situation in life, my connections with the family of De Bourgh, and my relationship to your own, are circumstances highly in my favour; and you should take it into farther consideration that in spite of your manifold attractions, it is by no means certain that another offer of marriage may ever be made you. Your portion is unhappily so small that it will in all likelihood undo the effects of your loveliness and amiable qualifications. As I must therefore conclude that you are not serious in your rejection of me, I shall chuse to attribute it to your wish of increasing my love by suspense, according to the usual practice of elegant females."

"I do assure you, Sir, that I have no pretension whatever to that kind of elegance which consists in tormenting a respectable man. I would rather be paid the compliment of being believed sincere. I thank you again and again for the honour you have done me in your proposals, but to accept them is absolutely impossible. My feelings in every respect forbid it. Can I speak plainer? Do not consider me now as an elegant female intending to plague you, but as a rational creature speaking the truth from her heart."

"You are uniformly charming!" cried he, with an air of awkward gallantry; "and I am persuaded that when sanctioned by the express authority of both your excellent parents, my proposals will not fail of being acceptable."

To such perseverance in wilful self-deception Elizabeth would make no reply, and immediately and in silence withdrew; determined that, if he persisted in considering her repeated refusals as flattering encouragement, to apply to her father, whose negative might be uttered in such a manner as must be decisive, and whose behaviour at least could not be mistaken for the affectation and coquetry of an elegant female.

Jane Austen
Pride and Prejudice (1813)

THE VALLEY OF THE ASSASSINS

AFTER many days of wandering, the Assassins pitched their tents in the valley of Bethzatanai. For ages had this fertile valley lain concealed from the adventurous search of man, among mountains of everlasting snow. The men of elder days had inhabited this spot. Piles of monumental marble and fragments of columns that in their integrity almost seemed the work of some intelligence more sportive and fantastic than the gross conceptions of mortality, lay in heaps beside the lake, and were visible beneath its transparent waves. The flowering orange-tree, the balsam, and innumerable odoriferous shrubs, grew wild in the desolated portals. The fountain tanks had overflowed, and amid the luxuriant vegetation of their margin, the yellow snake held its unmolested dwelling. Hither came the tiger and the bear to contend for those once domestic animals who had forgotten the secure servitude of their ancestors. No sound, when the famished beast of prey had retreated in despair from the awful desolation of this place, at whose completion he had assisted, but the shrill cry of the stork, and the flapping of his heavy wings from the capital of the solitary column, and the scream of the hungry vulture baffled of its only victim. The lore of ancient wisdom was sculptured in mystic characters on the rocks. The human spirit and the human hand had been busy here to accomplish its profoundest miracles. It was a temple dedicated to the god of knowledge and of truth. The palaces of the Caliphs and the Cæsars might easily surpass these ruins in magnitude and sumptuousness: but they were the design of tyrants and the work of slaves. Piercing genius and consummate prudence had planned and executed Bethzatanai. There was deep and important meaning in every lineament of its fantastic sculpture. The unintelligible legend, once so beautiful and perfect, so full of poetry and history, spoke, even in destruction, volumes of mysterious import, and obscure significance.

But in the season of its utmost prosperity and magnificence, art might not aspire to vie with nature in the valley of Bethzatanai. All that was wonderful and lovely was collected in this deep seclusion. The fluctuating elements seemed to have been rendered everlastingly permanent in forms of wonder and delight. The mountains of Lebanon had been divided to their base to form this happy valley; on every side their icy summits darted their white pinnacles into the clear blue sky, imaging, in their grotesque outline, minarets, and ruined domes, and columns worn with time. Far below, the silver clouds rolled their bright volumes in many beautiful shapes, and fed the eternal springs that, spanning the dark chasms like a thousand radiant rainbows, leaped into the quiet vale, then, lingering in many a dark glade among the groves of cypress and of palm, lost themselves in the lake. The immensity of these precipitous mountains, with their starry pyramids of snow, excluded the sun, which overtopped not, even in its meridian, their overhanging rocks. But a more heavenly and serener light was reflected from their icy mirrors, which, piercing through the many-tinted clouds, produced lights and colours of inexhaustible variety.

Percy Bysshe Shelley

'The Assassins' (*c.* 1814) from *Essays, Letters from Abroad, Translations and Fragments*, edited by Mary Shelley (1840)

A LECTURE ON PHRENOLOGY

"EVERY particular faculty of the mind has its corresponding organ in the brain. In proportion as any particular faculty or propensity acquires paramount activity in any individual, these organs develope themselves, and their developement becomes externally obvious by corresponding lumps and bumps, exuberances and protuberances, on the osseous compages of the occiput and sinciput. In all animals but man, the same organ is equally developed in every individual of the species: for instance, that of migration in the swallow – that of destruction in the tiger – that of architecture in the beaver – and that

compages] complex structure

of parental affection in the bear. The human brain, however, consists, as I have said, of a bundle or compound of all the faculties of all other animals; and from the greater develope-ment of one or more of these, in the infinite varieties of com-bination, result all the peculiarities of individual character.

"Here is the skull of a beaver; and that of Sir Christopher Wren. You observe, in both these specimens, the prodigious developement of the organ of constructiveness.

"Here is the skull of a bullfinch; and that of an eminent fiddler. You may compare the organ of music.

"Here is the skull of a tiger. You observe the organ of carnage. Here is the skull of a fox. You observe the organ of plunder. Here is the skull of a peacock. You observe the organ of vanity. Here is the skull of an illustrious robber, who, after a long and triumphant process of depredation and murder, was suddenly checked in his career by means of a certain quality inherent in preparations of hemp, which, for the sake of perspicuity, I shall call *suspensiveness*. Here is the skull of a conqueror, who, after over-running several kingdoms, burn-ing a number of cities, and causing the deaths of two or three millions of men, women, and children, was entombed with all the pageantry of public lamentation, and figured as the hero of several thousand odes and a round dozen of epics; while the poor highwayman was twice executed –

> 'At the gallows first, and after in a ballad,
> 'Sung to a villainous tune.'

You observe in both these skulls, the combined developement of the organs of carnage, plunder, and vanity, which I have separately pointed out in the tiger, the fox, and the peacock. The greater enlargement of the organ of vanity in the hero, is the only criterion by which I can distinguish them from each other. Born with the same faculties and the same propensities, these two men were formed by nature to run the same career:

the different combinations of external circumstances decided the difference of their destinies.

"Here is the skull of a Newfoundland dog. You observe the organ of benevolence, and that of attachment. Here is a human skull, in which you may observe a very striking negation of both these organs; and an equally striking developement of those of destruction, cunning, avarice, and self-love. This was one of the most illustrious statesmen that ever flourished in the page of history.

"Here is the skull of a turnspit, which, after a wretched life of *dirty work*, was turned out of doors to die on a dunghill. I have been induced to preserve it, in consequence of a remarkable similarity to this, which belonged to a courtly poet, who, having grown grey in flattering the great, was cast off in the same manner to perish by the same catastrophe."

After these and several other illustrations, during which the skulls were handed round for the inspection of the company, Mr. Cranium proceeded thus: –

"It is obvious, from what I have said, that no man can hope for worldly honour or advancement, who is not placed in such a relation to external circumstances, as may be consentaneous to his peculiar cerebral organs; and I would advise every parent, who has the welfare of his son at heart, to procure as extensive a collection as possible of the skulls of animals, and, before determining on the choice of a profession, to compare with the utmost nicety their bumps and protuberances with those of the skull of his son. If the developement of the organ of destruction point out a similarity between the youth and the tiger, let him be brought to some profession (whether that of a butcher, a soldier, or a physician, may be regulated by circumstances), in which he may be furnished with a license to kill: as, without such license, the indulgence of his natural propensity may lead to the untimely rescission of his vital thread, 'with edge of penny cord and vile reproach.' If he trace an analogy with the jackall, let all possible influence be used to procure him a place at court, where he will infallibly thrive. If his skull bear a marked resemblance to that of a magpie, it cannot be doubted that he will prove an admirable lawyer; and if with this advantageous conformation be combined any similitude to that of an owl, very confident hopes may be formed of his becoming a judge."

A furious flourish of music was now heard from the ball-room, the Squire having secretly dispatched the little butler to order it to strike up, by way of a hint to Mr. Cranium to finish his harangue. The company took the hint and adjourned tumultuously, having just understood so much of the lecture as furnished them with amusement for the ensuing twelve-month, in feeling all the skulls of all their acquaintance.

Thomas Love Peacock
Headlong Hall (1816)

A FISHERMAN'S FUNERAL

MR BLATTERGOWL had no sooner entered the hut, and received the mute and melancholy salutations of the company whom it contained, than he edged himself towards the unfortunate father, and seemed to endeavour to slide in a few words of condolence or of consolation. But the old man was incapable as yet of receiving either; he nodded, however, gruffly, and shook the clergyman's hand in acknowledgment of his good intentions, but was either unable or unwilling to make any verbal reply.

The minister next passed to the mother, moving along the floor as slowly, silently, and gradually, as if he had been afraid that the ground would, like unsafe ice, break beneath his feet, or that the first echo of a footstep was to dissolve some magic spell, and plunge the hut, with all its inmates, into a subterranean abyss. The tenor of what he said to the poor woman could only be judged by her answers, as, half-stifled by sobs ill-repressed, and by the covering which she still kept over her countenance, she faintly answered at each pause in his speech – "Yes, sir, yes! – Ye're very gude – ye're very gude! – Nae doubt, nae doubt! – It's our duty to submit! – But, O dear, my poor Steenie, the pride o' my very heart, that was sae handsome and comely, and a help to his family, and a comfort to us a', and a pleasure to a' that lookit on him! – O my bairn, my bairn, my bairn! what for is thou lying there! – and eh! what for am I left to greet for ye!"

There was no contending with this burst of sorrow and natural affection. Oldbuck had repeated recourse to his snuffbox to conceal the tears which, despite his shrewd and caustic temper, were apt to start on such occasions. The female assistants whimpered, the men held their bonnets to their faces and spoke apart with each other. The clergyman meantime addressed his ghostly consolation to the aged grandmother. At first she listened, or seemed to listen, to what he said, with the apathy of her usual unconsciousness. But as, in pressing this theme, he approached so near to her ear, that the sense of his words became distinctly intelligible to her, though unheard by those who stood more distant, her countenance at once assumed that stern and expressive cast which characterized her intervals of intelligence. She drew up her head and body, shook her head in a manner that showed at least impatience, if not scorn of his counsel, and waved her hand slightly, but with a gesture so expressive, as to indicate to all who witnessed it a marked and disdainful rejection of the ghostly consolation proffered to her. The minister stepped back as if repulsed, and, by lifting gently and dropping his hand, seemed to show at once wonder, sorrow, and compassion for her dreadful state of mind. The rest of the company sympathized, and a stifled whisper went through them, to express how much her desperate and determined manner impressed them with awe, and even horror.

In the mean time the funeral company was completed, by the arrival of one or two persons who had been expected from Fairport. The wine and spirits again circulated, and the dumb show of greeting was anew interchanged. The grandame a second time took a glass in her hand, drank its contents, and exclaimed, with a sort of laugh, "Ha! ha! I hae tasted wine twice in ae day – Whan did I that before, think ye, cummers? – Never since" –

And the transient glow vanishing from her countenance, she set the glass down, and sunk upon the settle from whence she had risen to snatch at it.

As the general amazement subsided, Mr. Oldbuck, whose heart bled to witness what he considered as the errings of the enfeebled intellect struggling with the torpid chill of age and of sorrow, observèd to the clergyman that it was time to proceed to the ceremony. The father was incapable of giving directions, but the nearest relation of the family made a sign to the carpenter, who in such cases goes through the duty of the undertaker, to proceed in his office. The creak of the screw-nails presently announced that the lid of the last mansion of mortality was in the act of being secured above its tenant. The last act which separates us for ever, even from the mortal reliques of the person we assemble to mourn, has usually its effect upon the most indifferent, selfish, and hardhearted. With a spirit of contradiction, which we may be pardoned for esteeming narrow-minded, the fathers of the Scottish kirk rejected, even on this most solemn occasion, the form of an address to the Divinity, lest they should be thought to give countenance to the rituals of Rome or of England. With much better and more liberal judgment, it is the present practice of most of the Scottish clergymen to seize this opportunity of offering a prayer, and exhortation, suitable to make an impression upon the living, while they are yet in the very presence of the reliques of him, whom they have but lately seen such as they themselves, and who now is such as they must in their time become. But this decent and praiseworthy practice was not adopted at the time of which I am treating, or, at least, Mr. Blattergowl did not act upon it, and the ceremony proceeded without any devotional exercise.

The coffin, covered with a pall, and supported upon handspikes by the nearest relatives, now only waited the father to support the head, as is customary. Two or three of these privileged persons spoke to him, but he only answered by shaking his hand and his head in token of refusal. With better intention than judgment, the friends, who considered this as an act of duty on the part of the living, and of decency towards the deceased, would have proceeded to enforce their request, had not Oldbuck interfered between the distressed father and his well-meaning tormentors, and informed them, that he himself, as landlord and master to the deceased, "would carry his head to the grave." In spite of the sorrowful occasion, the hearts of the relatives swelled within them at so marked a distinction on the part of the Laird; and old Alison Breck, who was present among other fish-women, swore almost aloud, "His honour Monkbarns should never want sax warp of oysters in the season (of which fish he was understood to be fond,) if she should gang to sea and dredge for them hersel, in the foulest wind that ever blew." And such is the temper of the Scottish common people, that, by this instance of compliance with their customs, and respect for their persons, Mr. Oldbuck gained more popularity than by all the sums which

sax warp] two dozen

he had yearly distributed in the parish for purpose of private or general charity.

The sad procession now moved slowly forward, preceded by the beadles, or saulies, with their batons – miserable-looking old men, tottering as if on the edge of that grave to which they were marshalling another, and clad, according to Scottish guise, with threadbare black coats, and hunting-caps decorated with rusty crape. Monkbarns would probably have remonstrated against this superfluous expence, had he been consulted; but, in doing so, he would have given more offence than he gained popularity by condescending to perform the office of chief mourner. Of this he was quite aware, and wisely withheld rebuke, where rebuke and advice would have been equally unavailing. In truth, the Scottish peasantry are still infected with that rage for funeral ceremonial, which once distinguished the grandees of the kingdom so much, that a sumptuary law was made by the parliament of Scotland for the purpose of restraining it; and I have known many in the lowest stations, who have denied themselves not merely the comforts, but almost the necessaries of life, in order to save such a sum of money as might enable their surviving friends to bury them like Christians, as they termed it, nor could their faithful executors be prevailed upon though equally necessitous, to turn to the use and maintenance of the living, the money vainly wasted upon the interment of the dead.

The procession to the church-yard, at about half a mile's distance, was made with the mournful solemnity usual on these occasions, – the body was consigned to its parent earth, – and when the labour of the grave-diggers had filled up the trench, and covered it with fresh sod, Mr. Oldbuck, taking his hat off, saluted the assistants, who had stood by in mournful silence, and with that adieu dispersed the mourners.

Sir Walter Scott
The Antiquary (1816)

An Invitation to Dinner

"But why should Mrs. Grant ask Fanny?" said Lady Bertram. "How came she to think of asking Fanny? – Fanny never dines there, you know, in this sort of way. I cannot spare her, and I am sure she does not want to go. . . . Fanny, you do not want to go, do you?"

"If you put such a question to her," cried Edmund, preventing his cousin's speaking, "Fanny will immediately say, no; but I am sure, my dear mother, she would like to go; and I can see no reason why she should not."

"I cannot imagine why Mrs. Grant should think of asking her. . . . She never did before. . . . She used to ask your sisters now and then, but she never asked Fanny."

"If you cannot do without me, ma'am," said Fanny, in a self-denying tone –

"But my mother will have my father with her all the evening."

"To be sure, so I shall."

"Suppose you take my father's opinion, ma'am."

"That's well thought of. So I will, Edmund. I will ask Sir Thomas, as soon as he comes in, whether I can do without her."

"As you please, ma'am, on that head; but I meant my father's opinion as to the *propriety* of the invitation's being accepted or not; and I think he will consider it a right thing by Mrs. Grant, as well as by Fanny, that being the *first* invitation it should be accepted."

"I do not know. We will ask him. But he will be very much surprised that Mrs. Grant should ask Fanny at all."

There was nothing more to be said, or that could be said to any purpose, till Sir Thomas were present; but the subject involving, as it did, her own evening's comfort for the morrow, was so much uppermost in Lady Bertram's mind, that half an hour afterwards, on his looking in for a minute in his way from his plantation to his dressing-room, she called him back again when he had almost closed the door, with "Sir Thomas, stop a moment . . . I have something to say to you."

Her tone of calm languor, for she never took the trouble of raising her voice, was always heard and attended to; and Sir Thomas came back. Her story began; and Fanny immediately slipped out of the room; for to hear herself the subject of any discussion with her uncle, was more than her nerves could bear. She was anxious, she knew . . . more anxious perhaps than she ought to be . . . for what was it after all whether she went or staid? . . . but if her uncle were to be a great while considering and deciding, and with very grave looks, and those grave looks directed to her, and at last decide against her, she might not be able to appear properly submissive and indifferent. Her cause meanwhile went on well. It began on Lady Bertram's part with, "I have something to tell you that will surprise you. Mrs. Grant has asked Fanny to dinner!"

"Well," said Sir Thomas, as if waiting more to accomplish the surprise.

"Edmund wants her to go. But how can I spare her?"

"She will be late," said Sir Thomas, taking out his watch, "but what is your difficulty?"

Edmund found himself obliged to speak and fill up the blanks in his mother's story. He told the whole, and she had only to add, "So strange! for Mrs. Grant never used to ask her."

"But is not it very natural," observed Edmund, "that Mrs. Grant should wish to procure so agreeable a visitor for her sister?"

"Nothing can be more natural," said Sir Thomas, after a short deliberation; "nor, were there no sister in the case, could anything in my opinion be more natural. Mrs. Grant's shewing civility to Miss Price, to Lady Bertram's niece, could never want explanation. The only surprise I can feel is that this should be the *first* time of its being paid. Fanny was perfectly right in giving only a conditional answer. She appears to feel as she ought. But as I conclude that she must wish to go, since all young people like to be together, I can see no reason why she should be denied the indulgence."

"But can I do without her, Sir Thomas?"

"Indeed I think you may."

"She always makes tea, you know, when my sister is not here."

"Your sister perhaps may be prevailed on to spend the day with us, and I shall certainly be at home."

"Very well, then, Fanny may go, Edmund."

The good news soon followed her. Edmund knocked at her door on his way to his own.

"Well, Fanny, it is all happily settled, and without the smallest hesitation on your uncle's side. He had but one opinion. You are to go."

"Thank you, I am *so* glad," was Fanny's instinctive reply; though when she had turned from him and shut the door, she could not help feeling, "And yet, why should I be glad? for am I not certain of seeing or hearing something there to pain me?"

In spite of this conviction, however, she was glad. Simple as such an engagement might appear in other eyes, it had novelty and importance in hers, for excepting the day at Sotherton, she had scarcely ever dined out before; and though now going only half a mile and only to three people, still it was dining out, and all the little interests of preparation were enjoyments in themselves. She had neither sympathy nor assistance from those who ought to have entered into her feelings and directed her taste; for Lady Bertram never thought of being useful to any body, and Mrs. Norris, when she came on the morrow, in consequence of an early call and invitation from Sir Thomas, was in a very ill humour, and seemed intent only on lessening her niece's pleasure, both present and future, as much as possible.

"Upon my word, Fanny, you are in high luck to meet with such attention and indulgence! You ought to be very much obliged to Mrs. Grant for thinking of you, and to your aunt for letting you go, and you ought to look upon it as something extraordinary: for I hope you are aware that there is no real occasion for your going into company in this sort of way, or ever dining out at all; and it is what you must not depend upon ever being repeated. Nor must you be fancying, that the invitation is meant as any particular compliment to *you*; the compliment is intended to your uncle and aunt, and me. Mrs. Grant thinks it a civility due to *us* to take a little notice of you, or else it would never have come into her head, and you may be very certain, that if your cousin Julia had been at home, you would not have been asked at all."

Mrs. Norris had now so ingeniously done away all Mrs. Grant's part of the favour, that Fanny, who found herself expected to speak, could only say that she was very much obliged to her aunt Bertram for sparing her, and that she was endeavouring to put her aunt's evening work in such a state as to prevent her being missed.

"Oh! depend upon it, your aunt can do very well without you, or you would not be allowed to go. *I* shall be here, so you may be quite easy about your aunt. And I hope you will have a very *agreeable* day and find it all mighty *delightful*. But I must observe, that five is the very awkwardest of all possible numbers to sit down to table; and I cannot but be surprised that such an elegant lady as Mrs. Grant should not contrive better! And round their enormous great wide table too, which fills up the room so dreadfully! Had the doctor been contented to take my dining table when I came away, as anybody in their senses would have done, instead of having that absurd new one of his own which is wider, literally wider than the dinner table here – how infinitely better it would have been! and how much more he would have been respected! for people are never respected when they step out of their proper sphere. Remember *that*, Fanny. Five, only five to be sitting round that table! However, you will have dinner enough on it for ten I dare say."

Mrs. Norris fetched breath and went on again.

"The nonsense and folly of people's stepping out of their rank and trying to appear above themselves, makes me think it right to give *you* a hint, Fanny, now that you are going into company without any of us; and I do beseech and intreat you not to be putting yourself forward, and talking and giving your opinion as if you were one of your cousins – as if you were dear Mrs. Rushworth or Julia. *That* will never do, believe me. Remember, where-ever you are, you must be the lowest and last; and though Miss Crawford is in a manner at home, at the Parsonage, you are not to be taking place of her. And as to coming away at night, you are to stay just as long as Edmund chuses. Leave him to settle *that*."

"Yes, ma'am, I should not think of anything else."

"And if it should rain, which I think exceedingly likely, for I never saw it more threatening for a wet evening in my life – you must manage as well as you can, and not be expecting the carriage to be sent for you. I certainly do not go home to-night, and therefore, the carriage will not be out on my account; so you must make up your mind to what may happen, and take your things accordingly."

Her niece thought it perfectly reasonable. She rated her own claims to comfort as low even as Mrs. Norris could; and when Sir Thomas, soon afterwards, just opening the door, said "Fanny, at what time would you have the carriage come round?" she felt a degree of astonishment which made it impossible for her to speak.

"My dear Sir Thomas!" cried Mrs. Norris, red with anger, "Fanny can walk."

"Walk!" repeated Sir Thomas, in a tone of most unanswerable dignity, and coming farther into the room. . . . "My niece walk to a dinner engagement at this time of the year! Will twenty minutes after four suit you?"

"Yes, sir," was Fanny's humble answer, given with the feelings almost of a criminal towards Mrs. Norris; and not bearing to remain with her in what might seem a state of triumph, she followed her uncle out of the room, having staid behind him only long enough to hear these words spoken in angry agitation:

"Quite unnecessary! . . . a great deal too kind! But Edmund goes; . . . true . . . it is upon Edmund's account. I observed he was hoarse on Thursday night."

But this could not impose on Fanny. She felt that the carriage was for herself and herself alone; and her uncle's consideration of her, coming immediately after such representations from her aunt, cost her some tears of gratitude when she was alone.

The coachman drove round to a minute; another minute brought down the gentleman, and as the lady had, with a most scrupulous fear of being late, been many minutes seated in the drawing room, Sir Thomas saw them off in as good time as his own correctly punctual habits required.

Jane Austen
Mansfield Park (1814)

THE RUINS OF ROME

SINCE I last wrote to you, I have seen the ruins of Rome, the Vatican, St. Peter's, and all the miracles of ancient and modern art contained in that majestic city. The impression of it exceeds anything I have ever experienced in my travels. We stayed there only a week, intending to return at the end of February, and devote two or three months to its mines of inexhaustible contemplation, to which period I refer you for a minute account of it. We visited the Forum and the ruins of the Coliseum every day. The Coliseum is unlike any work of human hands I ever saw before. It is of enormous height and circuit, and the arches built of massy stones are piled on one another, and jut into the blue air, shattered into the forms of overhanging rocks. It has been changed by time into the image of an amphitheatre of rocky hills overgrown by the wild olive, the myrtle, and the fig-tree, and threaded by little paths, which wind among its ruined stairs and immeasurable galleries: the copsewood overshadows you as you wander through its labyrinths, and the wild weeds of this climate of flowers bloom under your feet. The arena is covered with grass, and pierces, like the skirts of a natural plain, the chasms of the broken arches around. But a small part of the exterior circumference remains – it is exquisitely light and beautiful; and the effect of the perfection of its architecture, adorned with ranges of Corinthian pilasters, supporting a bold cornice, is such, as to diminish the effect of its greatness. The interior is all ruin. I can scarcely believe that when encrusted with Dorian marble and ornamented by columns of Egyptian granite, its effect could have been so sublime and so impressive as in its present state. It is open to the sky, and it was the clear and sunny weather of the end of November in this climate when we visited it, day after day.

Near it is the arch of Constantine, or rather the arch of Trajan; for the servile and avaricious senate of degraded Rome, ordered that the monument of his predecessor should be demolished in order to dedicate one to the Christian reptile, who had crept among the blood of his murdered family to the supreme power. It is exquisitely beautiful and perfect.

The Forum is a plain in the midst of Rome, a kind of desert full of heaps of stones and pits, and though so near the habitations of men, is the most desolate place you can conceive. The ruins of temples stand in and around it, shattered columns and ranges of others complete, supporting cornices of exquisite workmanship, and vast vaults of shattered domes distinct with regular compartments, once filled with sculptures of ivory or brass. The temples of Jupiter, and Concord, and Peace, and the Sun, and the Moon, and Vesta, are all within a short distance of this spot. Behold the wrecks of what a great nation once dedicated to the abstractions of the mind! Rome is a city, as it were, of the dead, or rather of those who cannot die, and who survive the puny generations which inhabit and pass over the spot which they have made sacred to eternity. In Rome, at least in the first enthusiasm of your recognition of ancient time, you see nothing of the Italians. The nature of the city assists the delusion, for its vast and antique walls describe a circumference of sixteen miles, and thus the population is thinly scattered over this space, nearly as great as London. Wide wild fields are enclosed within it, and there are grassy lanes and copses winding among the ruins, and a great green hill, lonely and bare, which overhangs the Tiber. The gardens of the modern palaces are like wild woods of cedar, and cypress, and pine, and the neglected walks are overgrown with weeds. The English burying-place is a green slope near the walls, under the pyramidal tomb of Cestius, and is, I think, the most beautiful and solemn cemetery I ever beheld. To see the sun shining on its bright grass, fresh, when we first visited it, with the autumnal dews, and hear the whispering of the wind among the leaves of the trees which have overgrown the tomb of Cestius, and the soil which is stirring in the sun-warm earth, and to mark the tombs, mostly of women and young people who were buried there, one might, if one were to die, desire the sleep they seem to sleep. Such is the human mind, and so it peoples with its wishes vacancy and oblivion.

Percy Bysshe Shelley

Letter to Thomas Love Peacock (22 December, 1818) from
Essays, Letters from Abroad, Translations and Fragments,
edited by Mary Shelley (1840)

THREE SISTERS

MISS JACKY, the senior of the trio, was what is reckoned a very sensible woman – which generally means, a very disagreeable, obstinate, illiberal director of all men, women and children – a sort of superintendent of all actions, time, and place – with unquestioned authority to arraign, judge, and condemn, upon the statutes of her own supposed sense. Most country parishes have their sensible woman, who lays down the law on all affairs spiritual and temporal. Miss Jacky stood unrivalled as the sensible woman of Glenfern. She had attained this eminence, partly from having a little more understanding than her sisters, but principally from her dictatorial manner, and the pompous, decisive tone, in which she delivered the most common-place truths. At home, her supremacy in all matters of sense was perfectly established; and thence the infection, like other superstitions, had spread over the whole neighbourhood. As sensible woman, she regulated the family, which she took care to let every body see; she was conductor of her nieces' education, which she took care to let every body hear; she was a sort of post-mistress general – a detector of all abuses and impositions; and deemed it her prerogative to be consulted about all the useful and useless things, which every body else could have done as well. She was liberal of her advice to the poor, always enforcing upon them the iniquity of idleness, but doing nothing for them in the way of employment – strict economy being one of the many points in which she was particularly sensible. The consequence was, while she was lecturing half the poor women in the parish for their idleness, the bread was kept out of their mouths, by the incessant carding of wool and knitting of stockings, and spinning, and reeling, and winding, and pirning, that went on amongst the ladies themselves. And, by the bye, Miss Jacky is not the only sensible woman who thinks she is acting a meritorious part, when she converts what ought to be the portion of the poor into the employment of the affluent.

In short, Miss Jacky was all over sense. A skilful physiognomist would, at a single glance, have detected the sensible woman, in the erect head, the compressed lips, square elbows, and firm judicious step. Even her very garments seemed to partake of the prevailing character of their mistress: her ruff always looked more sensible than any other body's; her shawl sat most sensibly on her shoulders; her walking shoes were acknowledged to be very sensible; and she drew on her gloves with an air of sense, as if the one arm had been Seneca, the other Socrates. From what has been said, it may easily be inferred, that Miss Jacky was, in fact, any thing but a sensible woman; as indeed no woman can be, who bears such visible outward marks of what is in reality the most quiet and unostentatious of all good qualities. But there is a spurious sense, which passes equally well with the multitude: it is easily assumed, and still easier maintained; common truths and a grave dictatorial air being all that is necessary for its support.

Miss Grizzy's character will not admit of so long a commentary as that of her sister: she was merely distinguishable from nothing by her simple good nature, the inextricable entanglement of her thoughts, her love of letter writing, and her friendship with Lady Maclaughlan. Miss Nicky had about as much sense as Miss Jacky; but, as no kingdom can maintain two kings, so no family can admit of two sensible women;

and Nicky was, therefore, obliged to confine hers to the narrowest possible channels of house-keeping, mantua-making, &c., and to sit down for life (or at least till Miss Jacky should be married) with the dubious character of "not wanting for sense either." With all these little peccadilloes, the sisters possessed some good properties: they were well-meaning, kind-hearted, and, upon the whole, good-tempered; they loved one another, revered their brother, doated upon their nephews and nieces, took a lively interest in the poorest of their poor cousins, a hundred degrees removed, and had a firm conviction of the perfectibility of human nature, as exemplified in the persons of all their own friends.

Susan Edmonstone Ferrier

Marriage (1818)

The Monster's Mate is Destroyed

I SAT one evening in my laboratory; the sun had set, and the moon was just rising from the sea; I had not sufficient light for my employment, and I remained idle, in a pause of consideration of whether I should leave my labour for the night, or hasten its conclusion by an unremitting attention to it. As I sat, a train of reflection occurred to me, which led me to consider the effects of what I was now doing. Three years before I was engaged in the same manner, and had created a fiend whose unparalleled barbarity had desolated my heart, and filled it for ever with the bitterest remorse. I was now about to form another being, of whose dispositions I was alike ignorant; she might become ten thousand times more malignant than her mate, and delight, for its own sake, in murder and wretchedness. He had sworn to quit the neighbourhood of man, and hide himself in deserts; but she had not; and she, who in all probability was to become a thinking and reasoning animal, might refuse to comply with a compact made before her creation. They might even hate each other; the creature who already lived loathed his own deformity, and might he not conceive a greater abhorrence for it when it came before his eyes in the female form? She also might turn with disgust from him to the superior beauty of man; she might quit him, and he be again alone, exasperated by the fresh provocation of being deserted by one of his own species.

Even if they were to leave Europe, and inhabit the deserts of the new world, yet one of the first results of those sympathies for which the dæmon thirsted would be children, and a race of devils would be propagated upon the earth, who might make the very existence of the species of man a condition precarious and full of terror. Had I right, for my own benefit, to inflict this curse upon everlasting generations? I had before been moved by the sophisms of the being I had created; I had been struck senseless by his fiendish threats: but now, for the first time, the wickedness of my promise burst upon me; I shuddered to think that future ages might curse me as their pest, whose selfishness had not hesitated to buy its own peace at the price perhaps of the existence of the whole human race.

I trembled, and my heart failed within me; when, on looking up, I saw, by the light of the moon, the dæmon at the casement. A ghastly grin wrinkled his lips as he gazed on me, where I sat fulfilling the task which he had allotted to me. Yes, he had followed me in my travels; he had loitered in forests, hid himself in caves, or taken refuge in wide and desert heaths; and he now came to mark my progress, and claim the fulfilment of my promise.

As I looked on him, his countenance expressed the utmost extent of malice and treachery. I thought with a sensation of madness on my promise of creating another like to him, and trembling with passion, tore to pieces the thing on which I was engaged. The wretch saw me destroy the creature on whose future existence he depended for happiness, and, with a howl of devilish despair and revenge, withdrew.

Mary Shelley
Frankenstein; or, The Modern Prometheus (1818)

DAFT MEG

IN the course of the summer, Mr. Henry Melcomb, who was a nephew to Mr. Cayenne, came down from England to see his uncle. He had just completed his education at the College of Christ Church, in Oxford, and was the most perfect young gentleman that had ever been seen in this part of the country.

In his appearance he was a very paragon, with a fine manly countenance, frank-hearted, blithe, and, in many points of character, very like my old friend the Lord Eglesham, who was shot. Indeed, in some respects, he was even above his lordship, for he had a great turn at ready wit, and could joke and banter in a most agreeable manner. He came very often to the Manse to see me, and took great pleasure in my company, and really used a freedom that was so droll, I could scarcely keep my composity and decorum with him. Among others that shared in his attention, was daft Meg Gaffaw, whom he had forgathered with one day in coming to see me, and after conversing with her for some time, he handed her, as she told me herself, over the kirk-stile, like a lady of high degree, and came with her to the Manse-door linking by the arm.

From the ill-timed daffin of that hour, poor Meg fell deep in love with Mr. Melcomb, and it was just a play-acting to see the arts and antics she put in practice to win his attention. In her garb, she had never any sense of a proper propriety, but went about the country asking for shapings of silks and satins, with which she patched her duds, calling them by the divers names of robes and negligées. All hitherto, however, had been moderation, compared to the daffadile of vanity which she was now seen, when she had searched, as she said, to the bottom of her coffer. I cannot take it upon me to describe her, but she kithed in such a variety of cuffs and ruffles, feathers and flowers, old gumflowers, painted paper knots, ribbans, and furs, and laces, and went about gecking and simpering with an old fan in her hand, that it was not in the power of nature to look at her with sobriety.

Her first appearance in this masquerading, was at the kirk on the Sunday following her adventure with Mr. Melcomb, and it was with a sore difficulty that I could keep my eyes off her, even in prayer; and when the kirk skailed, she walked before him, spreading all her grandeur to catch his eye in such a manner as had not been seen or heard of since the prank that Lady Macadam played Miss Betty Wudrife.

Any other but Mr. Melcomb would have been provoked by the fool's folly, but he humoured her wit, and, to the amazement of the whole people, presented her his hand, and allemanded her along in a manner that should not have been seen in any street out of a king's court, and far less on the Lord's day. But alas! this sport did not last long. Mr. Melcomb had come from England to be married to his cousin, Miss Virginia Cayenne, and poor daft Meg never heard of it till the banns for their purpose of marriage was read out by Mr. Loremore on the Sabbath after. The words were scarcely out of his mouth, when the simple and innocent natural gave a loud shriek, that terrified the whole congregation, and ran out of the kirk demented. There was no more finery for poor Meg; but she went and sat opposite to the windows of Mr. Cayenne's house, where Mr. Melcomb was, with clasped hands and beseeching eyes, like a monumental statue in alabaster, and no entreaty could drive her away. Mr. Melcomb sent her money, and the bride many a fine thing, but Meg flung them from her, and clasped her hands again, and still sat.

Mr. Cayenne would have let loose the house-dog on her, but was not permitted.

In the evening it began to rain, and they thought that and the coming darkness would drive her away, but when the servants looked out before barring the doors, there she was in the same posture. I was to perform the marriage ceremony at seven o'clock in the morning, for the young pair were to go that night to Edinburgh; and when I went, there was Meg sitting looking at the windows with her hands clasped. When she saw me she gave a shrill cry, and took me by the hand, and wised me to go back, crying out in a heart-breaking voice, "O, sir! No yet – no yet! He'll maybe draw back, and think of a far truer bride." I was wae for her, and very angry with the servants for laughing at the fond folly of the ill-less thing.

When the marriage was over, and the carriage at the door, the bridegroom handed in the bride. Poor Meg saw this, and jumping up from where she sat, was at his side like a spirit, as he was stepping in, and taking him by the hand, she looked in his face so piteously, that every heart was sorrowful, for she could say nothing. When he pulled away his hand, and the door was shut, she stood as if she had been charmed to the spot, and saw the chaise drive away. All that were about the door then spoke to her, but she heard us not. At last she gave a deep sigh, and the water coming into her eye, she said, "The worm —the worm is my bonny bridegroom, and Jenny with the many-feet my bridal maid. The milldam water's the wine o' the wedding, and the clay and the clod shall be my bedding. A lang night is meet for a bridal, but none shall be langer than mine." In saying which words, she fled from among us, with heels like the wind. The servants pursued, but o'er long before they could stop her, she was past redemption in the deepest plumb of the cotton-mill dam.

John Galt

Annals of the Parish ; or the Chronicle of Dalmailing (1821)

PRISONERS OF THE INQUISITION

"It was on the night of the 29th November 17—, that this extraordinary circumstance took place – extraordinary from the well-known precautions adopted by the vigilance of the holy office against such an accident, and also from the very small quantity of fuel consumed within its walls. On the first intimation that the fire was spreading rapidly, and threatened danger, the prisoners were ordered to be brought from their cells, and guarded in a court of the prison. I must acknowledge we were treated with great humanity and consideration. We were conducted deliberately from our cells, placed each of us between two guards, who did us no violence, nor used harsh language, but assured us, from time to time, that if the danger became imminent, we would be permitted every fair opportunity to effect our escape. It was a subject worthy of the pencil of Salvator Rosa, or of Murillo, to sketch us as we stood. Our dismal garbs and squalid looks, contrasted with the equally dark, but imposing and authoritative looks of the guards and officials, all displayed by the light of torches, which burned, or appeared to burn, fainter and fainter, as the flames rose and roared in triumph above the towers of the Inquisition. The heavens were all on fire – and the torches, held no longer in firm hands, gave a tremulous and pallid light. It seemed to me like a wildly painted picture of the last day. God appeared descending in the light that enveloped the skies – and we stood pale and shuddering in the light below.

"Among the groupe of prisoners, there were fathers and sons, who perhaps had been inmates of adjacent cells for years, without being conscious of each other's vicinity or existence – but they did not dare to recognize each other. Was not this like the day of judgement, where similar mortal relations may meet under different classes of the sheep and goats, without presuming to acknowledge the strayed one amid the flock of a different shepherd? There were also parents and children who *did* recognize and stretch out their wasted arms to each other, though feeling they must never meet, – some of them condemned to the flames, some to imprisonment, and some to the official duties of the Inquisition, as a mitigation of their sentence, – and was not this like the day of judgement, where parent and child may be allotted different destinations, and the arms that would attest the last proof of mortal affection, are expanded in vain over the gulph of eternity. Behind and around us stood the officials and guards of the Inquisition, all watching and intent on the progress of the flames, but fearless of the result with regard to themselves. Such may be the feeling of those spirits who watch the doom of the Almighty, and know the destination of those they are appointed to watch. And is not this like the day of judgement? Far, far, above us, the flames burst out in volumes, in solid masses of fire, spiring up to the burning heavens. The towers of the Inquisition shrunk into cinders – that tremendous monument of the power, and crime, and gloom of the human mind, was wasting like a scroll in the fire. Will it not be thus also at the day of judgement?"

Charles Robert Maturin
Melmoth the Wanderer (1820)

AN ANTIPATHY TO SCOTCHMEN

I HAVE been trying all my life to like Scotchmen, and am obliged to desist from the experiment in despair. They cannot like me – and in truth, I never knew one of that nation who attempted to do it. There is something more plain and ingenuous in their mode of proceeding. We know one another at first sight. There is an order of imperfect intellects (under which mine must be content to rank) which in its constitution is essentially anti-Caledonian. The owners of the sort of faculties I allude to have minds rather suggestive than comprehensive. They have no pretences to much clearness or precision in their ideas, or in their manner of expressing them. Their intellectual wardrobe (to confess fairly) has few whole pieces in it. They are content with fragments and scattered pieces of Truth. She presents no full front to them – a feature or side-face at the most. Hints and glimpses, germs and crude essays at a system, is the utmost they pretend to. They beat up a little game peradventure – and leave it to knottier heads, more robust constitutions, to run it down. The light that lights them is not steady and polar, but mutable and shifting; waxing, and again waning. Their conversation is accordingly. They will throw out a random word in or out of season, and be content to let it pass for what it is worth. They cannot speak always as if they were upon their oath—but must be understood, speaking or writing, with some abatement. They seldom wait to mature a proposition, but e'en bring it to market in the green ear. They delight to impart their defective discoveries as they arise, without waiting for their full development. They are no systematizers, and would but err more by attempting it. Their minds, as I said before, are suggestive merely. The brain of a true Caledonian (if I am not mistaken) is constituted upon quite a different plan. His Minerva is born in panoply. You are never admitted to see his ideas in their growth – if, indeed, they do grow, and are not rather put together upon principles of clock-work. You never catch his mind in an undress. He never hints or suggests anything, but unlades his stock of ideas in perfect order and completeness. He has no falterings of self-suspicion. Surmises, guesses, suppositions, half-intuitions, demi-consciousnesses, misgivings, partial illuminations, "dim instincts," embryo conceptions, and every stage that stops short of absolute certainty and conviction – his intellectual faculty seems a stranger to. He brings his total

wealth into company, and gravely unpacks it. His riches are
always about him. He never stoops to catch a glittering something in your presence, to share it with you before he quite
knows whether it be true touch or not. You cannot cry *halves*
to anything that he finds. He does not find, but bring. You
never witness his first apprehension of a thing. His understanding is always at its meridian – you never see the first
dawn, the early streaks. The twilight of dubiety never falls
upon him. Is he orthodox – he has no doubts. Is he an infidel
– he has none either. Between the affirmative and the negative
there is no border-line with him. You cannot hover with him
upon the confines of truth, or wander in the maze of a probable argument. He always keeps the path. You cannot make
excursions with him – for he sets you right. His taste never
fluctuates. His morality never abates. He cannot compromise,
or understand middle actions. There can be but a right and a
wrong. His conversation is as a book. His affirmations have
the sanctity of an oath. You must speak upon the square with
him. He stops a metaphor like a suspected person in an enemy's
country. "A healthy book!" – said one of his countrymen to
me, who had ventured to give that appellation to John
Buncle, – "did I catch rightly what you said? I have heard of
a man in health, and of a healthy state of body, but I do not
see how that epithet can be properly applied to a book."
Above all, you must beware of indirect expressions before a
Caledonian. Clap an extinguisher upon your irony, if you are
unhappily blest with a vein of it. Remember you are upon
your oath. – I have a print of a graceful female after Leonardo
da Vinci, which I was showing off to Mr. ——. After he had
examined it minutely, I ventured to ask him how he liked
MY BEAUTY (a foolish name it goes by among my friends) –
when he very gravely assured me, that "he had considerable
respect for my character and talents" (so he was pleased to
say), "but had not given himself much thought about the

degree of my personal pretensions." The misconception staggered me, but did not seem much to disconcert him. – Persons of this nation are particularly fond of affirming a truth – which nobody doubts. They do not so properly affirm, as annunciate it. They do indeed appear to have such a love of truth – as if, like virtue, it were valuable for itself – that all truth becomes equally valuable, whether the proposition that contains it be new or old, disputed, or such as is impossible to become a subject of disputation. I was present not long since at a party of North Britons where a son of Burns was expected; and happened to drop a silly expression (in my south British way), that I wished it were the father instead of the son – when four of them started up at once to inform me, that "that was impossible, because he was dead." An impracticable wish, it seems, was more than they could conceive. Swift has hit off this part of their character, namely their love of truth, in his biting way, but with an illiberality that necessarily confines the passage to the margin. The tediousness of the Scotch is certainly proverbial. I wonder if they ever tire one another! – In my early life I had a passionate fondness for the poetry of Burns. I have sometimes foolishly hoped to ingratiate myself with his countrymen by expressing it. But I have always found that a true Scot resents your admiration of his compatriot, even more than he would your contempt of him. The latter he imputes to your "imperfect acquaintance with many of the words which he uses;" and the same objection makes it a presumption in you to suppose that you can admire him. I have a great mind to give up Burns. There is certainly a bragging spirit of generosity, a swaggering assertion of independence, and *all that*, in his writings. Thomson they seem to have forgotten. Smollett they have neither forgotten nor forgiven, for his delineation of Rory and his companion, upon their first introduction to our metropolis. – Speak of Smollett as a great genius, and they will retort upon you Hume's History compared with *his* Continuation of it. What if the historian had continued Humphrey Clinker?

Charles Lamb

'Jews, Quakers, Scotchmen, and Other Imperfect Sympathies' from *The London Magazine* (August, 1821)

OPIUM DREAMS

UNDER the connecting feeling of tropical heat and vertical sun-lights, I brought together all creatures, birds, beasts, reptiles, all trees and plants, usages and appearances, that are found in all tropical regions, and assembled them together in China or Indostan. From kindred feelings, I soon brought Egypt and all her gods under the same law. I was stared at, hooted at, grinned at, chattered at, by monkeys, by paroquets, by cockatoos. I ran into pagodas: and was fixed, for centuries, at the summit, or in secret rooms; I was the idol; I was the priest; I was worshipped; I was sacrificed. I fled from the wrath of Brama through all the forests of Asia: Vishnu hated me: Seeva laid wait for me. I came suddenly upon Isis and Osiris: I had done a deed, they said, which the ibis and the crocodile trembled at. I was buried, for a thousand years, in stone coffins, with mummies and sphynxes, in narrow chambers at the heart of eternal pyramids. I was kissed, with cancerous kisses, by crocodiles; and laid, confounded with all unutterable slimy things, amongst reeds and Nilotic mud.

I thus give the reader some slight abstraction of my oriental dreams, which always filled me with such amazement at the monstrous scenery, that horror seemed absorbed, for a while, in sheer astonishment. Sooner or later, came a reflux of feeling that swallowed up the astonishment, and left me, not so much in terror, as in hatred and abomination of what I saw. Over every form, and threat, and punishment, and dim sightless incarceration, brooded a sense of eternity and infinity that drove me into an oppression as of madness. Into these dreams only, it was, with one or two slight exceptions, that any circumstances of physical horror entered. All before had been moral and spiritual terrors. But here the main agents were ugly birds, or snakes, or crocodiles; especially the last. The cursed crocodile became to me the object of more horror than almost all the rest. I was compelled to live with him; and (as was always the case almost in my dreams) for centuries. I escaped sometimes, and found myself in Chinese houses, with cane tables, &c. All the feet of the tables, sophas, &c. soon became instinct with life: the abominable head of the crocodile, and his leering eyes, looked out at me, multiplied into a thousand repetitions: and I stood loathing and fascinated. And so very often did this hideous reptile haunt my dreams, that many times the very same dream was broken up in the very same way: I heard gentle voices speaking to me (I hear every thing when I am sleeping); and instantly I awoke: it was broad noon; and my children were standing, hand in hand, at my bed-side; come to show me their coloured shoes, or new frocks or to let me see them dressed for going out. I protest that so awful was the transition from the damned crocodile, and the other unutterable monsters and abortions of my dreams, to the sight of innocent *human* natures and of infancy, that, in the mighty and sudden revulsion of mind, I wept, and could not forbear it, as I kissed their faces.

*

As a final specimen, I cite one of a different character, from 1820.

The dream commenced with a music which now I often heard in dreams – a music of preparation and of awakening suspense; a music like the opening of the Coronation Anthem, and which, like *that*, gave the feeling of a vast march – of infinite cavalcades filing off – and the tread of innumerable armies. The morning was come of a mighty day – a day of crisis and of final hope for human nature, then suffering some mysterious eclipse, and labouring in some dread extremity. Somewhere, I knew not where – somehow, I knew not how – by some beings, I knew not whom – a battle, a strife, an agony, was conducting, – was evolving like a great drama, or piece of music; with which my sympathy was the more insupportable from my confusion as to its place, its cause, its nature, and its possible issue. I, as is usual in dreams (where, of necessity, we make ourselves central to every movement), had the power, and yet had not the power, to decide it. I had the power, if I could raise myself, to will it; and yet again, had not the power, for the weight of twenty Atlantics was upon me, or the oppression of inexpiable guilt. "Deeper than ever plummet sounded," I lay inactive. Then, like a chorus, the passion deepened. Some greater interest was at stake; some mightier cause than ever yet the sword had pleaded, or trumpet had proclaimed. Then came sudden alarms: hurryings to and fro: trepidations of innumerable fugitives, I knew not whether from the good cause or the bad: darkness and lights: tempests and human faces; and at last, with the sense that all was lost, female forms, and the features that were worth all the world to me, and but a moment allowed, – and clasped hands, and heart-breaking partings, and then – everlasting farewells! and with a sigh, such as the caves of hell sighed when the incestuous mother uttered the abhorred name of death, the sound was reverberated – everlasting farewells! and again, and yet again reverberated – everlasting farewells!

And I awoke in struggles, and cried aloud – "I will sleep no more!"

Thomas De Quincey

'Confessions of an English Opium-Eater' from
The London Magazine (October, 1821)

A LETTER TO THE ANTIPODES

AND first, for news. In them the most desirable circumstance, I suppose, is that they shall be true. But what security can I have that what I now send you for truth shall not before you get it unaccountably turn into a lie? For instance, our mutual friend P. is at this present writing – *my Now* – in good health, and enjoys a fair share of worldly reputation. You are glad to hear it. This is natural and friendly. But at this present reading – *your Now* – he may possibly be in the Bench, or going to be hanged, which in reason ought to abate something of your transport (*i.e.*, at hearing he was well, &c.), or at least considerably to modify it. I am going to the play this evening, to have a laugh with Joey Munden. You have no theatre, I think you told me, in your land of d—d realities. You naturally lick your lips, and envy me my felicity. Think but a moment, and you will correct the hateful emotion. Why, is it Sunday morning with you, and 1823? This confusion of tenses, this grand solecism of *two presents*, is in a degree common to all postage. But if I sent you word to Bath or the Devizes, that I was expecting the aforesaid treat this evening, though at the moment you received the intelligence my full feast of fun would be over, yet there would be for a day or two after, as you would well know, a smack, a relish left upon my mental palate, which would give rational encouragement to you to foster a portion at least of the disagreeable passion, which it was in part my intention to produce. But ten months hence your envy or your sympathy would be as useless as a passion spent upon the dead. Not only does truth, in these long intervals, unessence herself, but (what is harder) one cannot venture a crude fiction for the fear that it may ripen into a truth upon the voyage. What a wild improbable banter I put upon you some three years since – of Will Weatherall having married a servant-maid! I remember gravely consulting you how we were to receive her – for Will's wife was in no case to be rejected; and your no less serious replication in the matter; how tenderly you advised an abstemious introduction of literary topics before the lady, with a caution not to be too forward in bringing on the carpet matters more within the sphere of her intelligence; your deliberate judgment, or rather wise suspension of sentence, how far jacks, and spits, and mops, could with propriety be introduced as subjects; whether the conscious avoiding of all such matters in discourse would not have a worse look than the taking of them casually in our way; in what manner we should carry ourselves to our maid Becky, Mrs. William Weatherall being by; whether we should show more delicacy, and a truer sense of respect for Will's wife, by treating Becky with our customary chiding before her, or by an unusual deferential civility paid to Becky as to a person of great worth, but thrown by the caprice of fate into a humble station. There were difficulties, I remember, on both sides, which you did me the favour to state with the precision of a lawyer, united to the tenderness of a friend. I laughed in my sleeve at your solemn pleadings, when, lo! while I was valuing myself upon this flam put upon you in New South Wales, the devil in England, jealous possibly of any lie-children not his own, or working after my copy, has actually instigated our friend (not three days since) to the commission of a matrimony, which I had only conjured up for your diversion. William Weatherall has married Mrs. Cotterel's maid. But to take it in its truest sense, you will see, my dear F., that news from me must become history to you; which I neither profess to write, nor indeed care much for reading. No person, under a diviner, can with any prospect of veracity conduct a correspondence at such an arm's length. Two prophets, indeed, might thus interchange intelligence with effect; the epoch of the writer (Habakkuk) falling in with the true present time of the receiver (Daniel); but then we are no prophets.

Charles Lamb

'Distant Correspondents' from *The London Magazine* (March, 1822)

ONE OF THE ELECT

LIKE the sinful king of Israel, I had been walking softly before the Lord for a season. I had been humbled for my transgressions, and, as far as I recollect, sorry on account of their numbers and heinousness. My reverend father had been, moreover, examining me every day regarding the state of my soul, and my answers sometimes appeared to give him satisfaction, and sometimes not. As for my mother, she would harp on the subject of my faith for ever; yet, though I knew her to be a Christian, I confess that I always despised her motley instructions, nor had I any great regard for her person. If this was a crime in me, I never could help it. I confess it freely, and believe it was a judgment from heaven inflicted on her for some sin of former days, and that I had no power to have acted otherwise towards her than I did.

In this frame of mind was I, when my reverend father one morning arose from his seat, and, meeting me as I entered the room, he embraced me, and welcomed me into the community of the just upon earth. I was struck speechless, and could make no answer save my looks of surprise. My mother also came to me, kissed, and wept over me; and after showering unnumbered blessings on my head, she also welcomed me into the society of *the just made perfect*. Then each of them took me by a hand, and my reverend father explained to me how he had wrestled with God, as the patriarch of old had done, not for a night, but for days and years, and that in bitterness and anguish of spirit, on my account; but that *he* had at last prevailed, and had now gained the long and earnestly desired assurance of my acceptance with the Almighty, in and through the merits and sufferings of his Son: that I was now a justified person, adopted among the number of God's children – my name written in the Lamb's book of life, and that no bypast transgression, nor any future act of my own, or of other men, could be instrumental in altering the decree. "All the powers of darkness," added he, "shall never be able to pluck you again out of your Redeemer's hand. And now, my son, be strong and stedfast in the truth. Set your face against sin, and sinful men, and resist even to blood, as many of the faithful of this land have done, and your reward shall be double. I am assured of your acceptance by the word and spirit of him who cannot err, and your sanctification and repentance unto life will follow in due course. Rejoice and be thankful, for you are plucked as a brand out of the burning, and now your redemption is sealed and sure."

I wept for joy to be thus assured of my freedom from all sin, and of the impossibility of my ever again falling away from my new state. I bounded away into the fields and the woods, to pour out my spirit in prayer before the Almighty for his kindness to me: my whole frame seemed to be renewed; every nerve was buoyant with new life; I felt as if I could have flown in the air, or leaped over the tops of the trees. An exaltation of spirit lifted me, as it were, far above the earth, and the sinful creatures crawling on its surface; and I deemed myself as an eagle among the children of men, soaring on high, and looking down with pity and contempt on the grovelling creatures below.

James Hogg
*The Private Memoirs and Confessions
of a Justified Sinner* (1824)

AN OLD BACHELOR

MR SIDNEY was, as might be conjectured, an epicure; he was also an old bachelor, a clergyman, and senior fellow of — College, a post which he had long filled, being, although only a second son, so well provided for that he could afford to reject living after living in expectation of one favourite rectory, to which he had taken an early fancy from the pleasantness of the situation and the imputed salubrity of the air. Of the latter quality, indeed, he used to give an instance, which, however satisfactory as confirming his prepossession, could hardly have been quite agreeable, as preventing him from gratifying it; – namely, the extraordinary and provoking longevity of the incumbent, who at upwards of ninety gave no sign of decay, and bade fair to emulate the age of old Parr.

Whilst waiting for the expected living, Mr. Sidney, who disliked a college residence, built himself a very pretty house in our neighbourhood, which he called his home; and where he lived, as much as a love of Bath and Brighton and London and lords would let him. He counted many noble families amongst his near connexions, and passed a good deal of his time at their country seats – a life for which he was by character and habit peculiarly fitted.

In person he was a tall stout gentlemanly man, "about fifty, or by'r lady inclining to threescore," with fine features, a composed gravity of countenance and demeanour, a bald head most accurately powdered, and a very graceful bow – quite the pattern of an elderly man of fashion. His conversation was in excellent keeping with the calm imperturbability of his countenance and the sedate gravity of his manner, – smooth, dull, common-place, exceedingly safe, and somewhat imposing. He spoke so little, that people really fell into the mistake of imagining that he thought; and the tone of decision with which he would advance some second-hand opinion, was well calculated to confirm the mistake. Gravity was certainly his chief characteristic, and yet it was not a clerical gravity either. He had none of the generic marks of his profession. Although perfectly decorous in life and word and thought, no stranger ever took Mr. Sidney for a clergyman. He never did any duty any where, that ever I heard of, except the agreeable duty of saying grace before dinner; and even that was often performed by some lay host, in pure forgetfulness of his guest's ordination. Indeed, but for the direction of his letters, and an eye to —— Rectory, I am persuaded that the circumstance might have slipped out of his own recollection.

His quality of old bachelor was more perceptible. There lurked under all his polish, well covered but not concealed, the quiet selfishness, the little whims, the precise habits, the primness and priggishness of that disconsolate condition. His man Andrews, for instance, valet, groom, and body-servant abroad; butler, cook, caterer, and major domo at home; tall, portly, powdered and black-coated as his master, and like him in all things but the knowing pig-tail which stuck out horizontally above his shirt-collar, giving a ludicrous dignity to his appearance; – Andrews, who, constant as the dial pointed nine, carried up his chocolate and shaving water, and regular as "the chimes at midnight," prepared his white-wine whey; who never forgot his gouty shoe in travelling, (once for two days he had a slight touch of that gentlemanly disorder,) and never gave him the newspaper unaired; – to whom could this jewel of a valet, this matchless piece of clock-work belong, but an old bachelor? And his little dog Viper, unparagoned of terriers, black, sleek, sharp, and shrewish; who would beg and sneeze and fetch and carry like a Christian; eat olives and sweetmeats and mustard, drink coffee and wine and liqueurs; – who but an old bachelor could have taught Viper his multifarious accomplishments?

Mary Russell Mitford

Our Village: Sketches of Rural Character and Scenery (1824)

THE PERQUISITES OF OFFICE

HE said, 'Do not suppose that the salary which the Shah gives his servants is a matter of much consideration with them: no, the value of their places depends upon the range of extortion which circumstances may afford, and upon their ingenuity in taking advantage of it. As, for instance, take our chief: his salary is 1000 tomauns per annum, which may or may not be regularly paid; that signifies little to him. He spends at least five or six times that sum; and how is he to get it, if it flows not from the contributions of those who come under his cognizance? A khan has incurred the Shah's displeasure; he is to be beaten and fined: the chief executioner beats and mulcts in the inverse proportion of the present which the sufferer makes him. A rebel's eyes are to be put out; it depends upon what he receives, whether the punishment is done rudely with a dagger, or neatly with a penknife. He is sent on an expedition at the head of an army; wherever he goes presents are sent him from the towns and villages on his road to induce him not to quarter his troops upon them; and he uses his discretion, according to the value of what he receives, in choosing his halting stations. Most of those in high offices, even the viziers, make him annual gifts, in case the day of the Shah's displeasure should come, and then they would hope to be dealt with gently by him. In short, wherever a stick is to be brandished, wherever punishment is to be inflicted, there the chief executioner levies his dues; and they descend in a gradual measure from him to the lowest of his officers. Before I was a naib, and when I was called upon to lay the bastinado on some wretched culprit, many is the time that my compassion has been moved by a direct appeal to my purse; and then, instead of beating the sufferer's feet, I struck the *felek* upon which they rested. It was but last year that the principal secretary of state incurred the wrath of the Shah. He was ordered to receive the bastinado, and, by way of distinction, a small carpet was spread for him to lie upon: I and another were the operators, whilst two more held the felek. When we were taking the shawl and cap from his head, his girdle and outer coat (which became our lawful perquisites), he whispered to us, low enough not to be heard by the Shah (for this was all done in his presence), "By the mothers that bore you, do not beat me much! I'll give you each ten tomauns if you will not strike me." His heels were tripped up, his feet placed in the noose, whilst his back reposed on the carpet; and then we set to work. For our own sakes, we were obliged to start fair, and we laid on until he roared sufficiently; and then, having ably made him increase his offer until he had bid up to any price we wished, we gradually ceased beating his feet, and only broke our sticks over the felek. Much ingenuity was displayed on both sides, in order that the Shah might not discover that there was any understanding between us. His bidding was interwoven with his groans, something after this manner; – "*Ahi amān! amān!* For pity's sake, by the soul of the Prophet! twelve tomauns. – By the love of your fathers and mothers! fifteen tomauns. By the king's beard! twenty tomauns. – By all the Imâms! by all the prophets! thirty, forty, fifty, sixty, hundred, thousand, – anything you want." When it was over, we soon found that his generosity had diminished quite as rapidly as it had before increased, and we were satisfied to receive what he first offered to us, which he was obliged to give, fearing if a similar misfortune again overtook him, we should then show him no mercy.'

James Justinian Morier
The Adventures of Hajji Baba, of Ispahan (1824)

KING JAMES THE FIRST

JAMES, though an able man, was a weak monarch. His quickness of apprehension and soundness of judgment were marred by his credulity and partialities, his childish fears and habit of vacillation. Eminently qualified to advise as a counsellor, he wanted the spirit and resolution to act as a sovereign. His discourse teemed with maxims of political wisdom, his conduct frequently bore the impress of political folly. If in the language of his flatterers he was the British Solomon, in the opinion of less interested observers he merited the appellation given to him by the duke of Sully, that of "wisest fool in Europe."

The anomalies of his character may be traced to that love of personal ease which seems to have formed his ruling passion. To this we see him continually sacrificing his duties and his interests, seeking in his earlier years to shun by every expedient the tedium of public business, and shifting at a later period the burthen of government from himself to the shoulders of his favourites. It taught him to practise in pursuit of his ends duplicity and cunning, to break his word with as much facility as he gave it, to swear and forswear as best suited his convenience. It plunged him into debt that he might spare himself the pain of refusing importunate suitors, and induced him to sanction measures which he condemned, that he might escape from the contradiction of his son and his favourite. To forget his cares in the hurry of the chase, or the exercise of the golf, in carousing at table, or laughing at the buffoonery of those around him, seem to have constituted the chief pleasures of his life.

His conversation was eloquent but pedantic, interspersed with numerous oaths, and often disgraced by profane allusions. Though he was no admirer of female beauty, he is charged with encouraging the immoralities of Somerset and Buckingham: and the caresses which he heaped on his favourites, joined to the indelicacy of his familiar correspondence, have induced some writers to hint a suspicion of more degrading habits. But so odious a charge requires more substantial proof than an obscure allusion in a petition, or the dark insinuations of a malicious libeller.

From his preceptor, Buchanan, James had imbibed the maxim that "a sovereign ought to be the most learned clerk in his dominions." Of his intellectual acquirements he has left us abundant evidence: but his literary pride and self-sufficiency, his habit of interrogating others that he might discover the extent of their reading, the ostentatious display which he continually made of his own learning, though they won the flattery of his attendants and courtiers, provoked the contempt and derision of real scholars. Theology he considered as the first of sciences on account of its object, and of the highest importance to himself in quality of head of the church and defender of the faith. But though he was always orthodox, his belief was not exempt from change. For many years his opinions retained a deep tinge of calvinism; this was imperceptibly cleared away by the conversation of Laud and Montague, and other high churchmen; and before the close of his reign he had adopted the milder, but contrary doctrines of Arminius. To the last he employed himself in theological pursuits: and to revise works of religious institution, to give directions to preachers, to confute the heresies of foreign divines, were objects which occupied the attention, and divided the cares of the sovereign of three kingdoms.

Besides divinity, there was another science with which he was equally conversant, that of demonology. With great parade of learning, he demonstrated the existence of witches and the mischiefs of witchcraft, against the objections of Scot and Wierus; he even discovered a satisfactory solution of that obscure but interesting question, "why the devil did worke more with auncient women than others." But ancient women had no reason to congratulate themselves on the sagacity of their sovereign. Witchcraft, at his solicitation, was made a capital offence, and from the commencement of his reign there scarcely passed a year, in which some aged female or other was not condemned to expiate on the gallows her imaginary communications with the evil spirit.

Had the lot of James been cast in private life, he would have made a respectable country gentleman: the elevation of the throne exposed his foibles to the gaze of the public, and that at a time, when the growing spirit of freedom and the more general diffusion of knowledge, had rendered men less willing to admit the pretensions, and more eager to censure the defects of their superiors. With all his learning and eloquence, he failed to acquire the love or the esteem of his subjects; and, though he deserved not the reproaches cast on his memory by the revolutionary writers of the next and succeeding reigns, posterity has agreed to consider him as a weak and prodigal king, a vain and loquacious pedant.

John Lingard
A History of England ..., Vol. VI (1825)

CROMWELL'S PRETENSIONS TO THE THRONE

CROMWELL, like so many other usurpers, felt his position too precarious, or his vanity ungratified, without the name which mankind have agreed to worship. He had, as evidently appears from the conversations recorded by Whitelock, long since aspired to this titular, as well as to the real, pre-eminence; and the banished king's friends had contemplated the probability of his obtaining it with dismay. Affectionate towards his family, he wished to assure the stability of his son's succession, and perhaps to please the vanity of his daughters. It was indeed a very reasonable object with one who had already advanced so far. His assumption of the crown was desirable to many different classes; to the lawyers, who, besides their regard for the established constitution, knew that an ancient statute would protect those who served a de facto king in case of a restoration of the exiled family; to the nobility, who perceived that their legislative right must immediately revive; to the clergy, who judged the regular ministry more likely to be secure under a monarchy; to the people, who hoped for any settlement that would put an end to perpetual changes; to all of every rank and profession, who dreaded the continuance of military despotism, and demanded only the just rights and privileges of their country. A king of England could succeed only to a bounded prerogative, and must govern by the known laws; a protector, as the nation had well felt, with less nominal authority, had all the sword could confer. And, though there might be little chance that Oliver would abate one jot of a despotism, for which not the times of the Tudors could furnish a precedent, yet his life was far worn, and under a successor it was to be expected that future parliaments might assert again all those liberties for which they had contended against Charles. A few of the royalists might perhaps fancy that the restoration of the royal title would lead to that of the lawful heir; but a greater number were content to abandon a nearly desperate cause, if they could but see the more valuable object of their concern, the form itself of polity, re-established. There can be, as it appears to me, little room for doubt, that if Cromwell had overcome the resistance of his generals, he would have transmitted the sceptre to his descendants with the acquiescence and tacit approbation of the kingdom. Had we been living ever since under the rule of his dynasty, what tone would our historians have taken as to his character and that of the house of Stuart?

Henry Hallam
The Constitutional History of England from the Accession of Henry VII to the Death of George II (1827)

CRUSADER AND SARACEN

As the Knight of the Couchant Leopard continued to fix his eyes attentively on the yet distant cluster of palm-trees, it seemed to him as if some object was moving among them and beside them. The distant form separated itself from the trees, which partly hid its motions, and advanced towards the knight with a speed which soon showed a mounted horseman, whom his turban, long spear, and green caftan floating in the wind, on his nearer approach, showed to be a Saracen cavalier. "In the desert," saith an Eastern proverb, "no man meets a friend." The crusader was totally indifferent whether the infidel, who now approached on his gallant barb, as if borne on the wings of an eagle, came as friend or foe – perhaps, as a vowed champion of the Cross, he might rather have preferred the latter. He disengaged his lance from his saddle, seized it with the right hand, placed it in rest with its point half elevated, gathered up the reins in the left, waked his horse's mettle with the spur, and prepared to encounter the stranger, with the calm self-confidence belonging to the victor in many contests.

The Saracen came on at the speedy gallop of an Arab horseman, managing his steed more by his limbs, and the inflection of his body, than by any use of the reins, which hung loose in his left hand; so that he was enabled to wield the light round buckler of the skin of the rhinoceros, ornamented with silver loops, which he wore on his arm, swinging it as if he meant to oppose its slender circle to the formidable thrust of the western lance. His own spear was not couched or levelled like that of his antagonist, but grasped by the middle with his right hand, and brandished at arm's length above his head. As the cavalier approached his enemy at full career, he seemed to expect that the Knight of the Leopard should put his horse to the gallop to encounter him. But the Christian knight, well acquainted with the customs of Eastern warriors, did not mean to exhaust his good horse by any unnecessary exertion; and, on the contrary, made a dead halt, confident that, if his enemy advanced to the actual shock, his own weight, and that of his powerful charger, would give him sufficient advantage, without the additional momentum of rapid motion. Equally sensible and apprehensive of such a probable result, the Saracen cavalier, when he had approached towards the Christian within twice the length of his lance, wheeled his steed to the left with inimitable dexterity, and rode twice round his antagonist, who, turning without quitting his ground, and presenting his front constantly to his enemy, frustrated his attempts to attack him on an unguarded point; so that the Saracen, wheeling his horse, was fain to retreat to the distance of an hundred yards. A second time, like a hawk attacking a heron, the Moor renewed the charge, and a second time was fain to retreat without coming to a close struggle. A third time he approached in the same manner, when the Christian knight, desirous to terminate this illusory warfare, in which he might at length have been worn out by the activity of his foeman, suddenly seized the mace which hung at his saddle-bow, and, with a strong hand and unerring aim, hurled it against the head of the Emir, for such and not less his enemy appeared. The Saracen was just aware of the formidable missile in time to interpose his light buckler betwixt the mace and his head; but the violence of the blow forced the buckler down on his turban, and though that defence also contributed to deaden its violence, the Saracen was beaten from his horse. Ere the Christian could avail himself of this mishap, his nimble foeman sprung from the ground, and, calling on his steed, which instantly returned to his side, he leaped into his seat without touching the stirrup, and regained all the advantage of which the Knight of the Leopard hoped to deprive him. But the latter had in the meanwhile recovered his mace, and the Eastern cavalier, who remembered the strength and dexterity with which he had aimed it, seemed to keep cautiously out of reach of that weapon, of which he had so lately felt the force, while he showed his purpose of waging a distant warfare with missile weapons of his own. Planting his long spear in the sand at a distance from the scene of combat, he strung with great address a short bow, which he carried at his back, and putting his horse to the gallop, once more described two or three circles of a wider extent than formerly, in the course of which he discharged six arrows at the Christian with such unerring skill, that the goodness of his harness alone saved him from being wounded in as many places. The seventh shaft apparently found a less perfect part of the armour, and the Christian dropped heavily from his horse. But what was the surprise of the Saracen, when, dismounting to examine the condition of his prostrate enemy, he found himself suddenly within the grasp of the European, who had had recourse to this artifice to bring his enemy within his reach! Even in this deadly grapple, the Saracen was saved by his agility and presence of mind. He unloosed the sword-belt, in which the Knight of the Leopard had fixed his hold, and thus eluding his fatal grasp, mounted his horse, which seemed to watch his motions with the intelligence of a human being, and again rode off. But in the last encounter the Saracen had lost his sword and his quiver of arrows, both of which were attached to the girdle, which he was obliged to abandon. He had also lost his turban in the struggle. These disadvantages seemed to incline the Moslem to a truce: he approached the Christian with his right hand extended, but no longer in a menacing attitude.

"There is truce betwixt our nations," he said, in the lingua franca commonly used for the purpose of communication with the crusaders; "wherefore should there be war betwixt thee and me? – Let there be peace betwixt us."

"I am well contented," answered he of the Couchant Leopard; "but what security dost thou offer that thou wilt observe the truce?"

"The word of a follower of the Prophet was never broken," answered the Emir. "It is thou, brave Nazarene, from whom I should demand security, did I not know that treason seldom dwells with courage."

The crusader felt, that the confidence of the Moslem made him ashamed of his own doubts.

"By the cross of my sword," he said, laying his hand on the weapon as he spoke, "I will be true companion to thee, Saracen, while our fortune wills that we remain in company together."

"By Mohammed, Prophet of God, and by Allah, God of the Prophet," replied his late foeman, "there is not treachery in my heart towards thee. And now wend we to yonder fountain, for the hour of rest is at hand, and the stream had hardly touched my lip when I was called to battle by thy approach."

The Knight of the Couchant Leopard yielded a ready and courteous assent; and the late foes, without an angry look or gesture of doubt, rode side by side to the little cluster of palm-trees.

Sir Walter Scott
The Talisman from *Tales of the Crusaders* (1825)

The Cotingas

Next to the humming-birds, the Cotingas display the gayest plumage. They are of the order of passer, and you number five species betwixt the seacoast and the rock Saba. Perhaps the scarlet Cotinga is the richest of the five, and is one of those birds which are found in the deepest recesses of the forest. His crown is flaming red; to this abruptly succeeds a dark shining brown, reaching half way down the back: the remainder of the back, the rump, and tail, the extremity of which is edged with black, are a lively red; the belly is a somewhat lighter red; the breast reddish black; the wings brown. He has no song, is solitary, and utters a monotonous whistle which sounds like "quet." He is fond of the seeds of the Hitia-tree, and those of the Siloabali and bastard-Siloabali trees, which ripen in December, and continue on the trees for above two months. He is found throughout the year in Demerara; still nothing is known of his incubation. The Indians all agree in telling you that they have never seen his nest.

The purple-breasted Cotinga has the throat and breast of a deep purple, the wings and tail black, and all the rest of the body a most lovely shining blue.

The purple-throated Cotinga has black wings and tail, and every other part a light and glossy blue, save the throat, which is purple.

The Pompadour Cotinga is entirely purple, except his wings, which are white, their four first feathers tipped with brown. The great coverts of the wings are stiff, narrow, and pointed, being shaped quite different from those of any other bird. When you are betwixt this bird and the sun, in his flight, he appears uncommonly brilliant. He makes a hoarse noise, which sounds like "Wallababa." Hence his name amongst the Indians.

... The fifth species is the celebrated Campanero of the Spaniards, called Dara by the Indians, and bell-bird by the English. He is about the size of the Jay. His plumage is white as snow. On his forehead rises a spiral tube nearly three inches long. It is jet black, dotted all over with small white feathers. It has a communication with the palate, and when filled with air, looks like a spire; when empty, it becomes pendulous. His note is loud and clear, like the sound of a bell, and may be heard at the distance of three miles. In the midst of these extensive wilds, generally on the dried top of an aged Mora, almost out of gun reach, you will see the Campanero. No sound or song from any of the winged inhabitants of the forest, not even the clearly pronounced "Whip-poor-Will," from the goatsucker, cause such astonishment as the toll of the Campanero.

With many of the feathered race, he pays the common tribute of a morning and evening song; and even when the meridian sun has shut in silence the mouths of almost the whole of animated nature, the Campanero still cheers the forest. You hear his toll, and then a pause for a minute, then another toll, and then a pause again, and then a toll, and again a pause. Then he is silent for six or eight minutes, and then another toll, and so on. Acteon would stop in mid chase, Maria would defer her evening song, and Orpheus himself would drop his lute to listen to him; so sweet, so novel and romantic is the toll of the pretty snow-white Campanero. He is never seen to feed with the other Cotingas, nor is it known in what part of Guiana he makes his nest.

Charles Waterton
Wanderings in South America ... (1825)

A Rebel Army

The title of Army, as the term is generally used, could not properly be given to the mass of armed men who crowded the hill of Ballyorvil, preparing for the attack of Enniscorthy. As Sir William joined them, their leaders were employed, by entreaties, by threats, by curses, by shoutings, and by main force, in arranging the unruly throng into some disposition for march and battle. Of their leaders, the generality belonged to the middle class of farmers, and had been dubbed, or had dubbed themselves, with the military titles of General, Colonel, or Captain, according as the esteem or consideration in which they were held operated upon the opinions of the multitude. By force of the predominance which superior intellect, or courage, or daring, never fails to afford, bold spirits had already raised themselves above their compeers; and men whose former characters had stood well for bravery and sagacity, here found their claims admitted and rewarded. But as these various leaders, of few degrees in grade – for no one would answer to a less sounding title than that of Captain – endeavoured, as has been mentioned, to raise their tones of command above the general clamour of voices, in which the shrill screams of women and children took no inconsiderable part; as they shouted, and pulled, and dragged those whom they considered under their command to the positions they decreed should be taken up: it was easy to perceive that their martial titles were little more than nominal; that the insubordinate throng might follow their leader in conflict, or gain spirit from the boldness of his example, but would allow him, meantime, no more superiority, and pay him no more deference, than is conceded by a mob to its ringleader.

To the front of what may be called the centre of this self-willed force, were collected all such as bore fire-arms; and they might amount to eight hundred men. Some shouldered the muskets they had wrested from the soldiers on Owlard hill, and also wore the cross-belts and pouches of that ill-fated detachment; others bore muskets, too, found in the first village they had, as Mr. Rourke described, conquered on their roundabout and wavering march; others clutched guns of every kind and calibre, plundered from houses, or drawn from places of long concealment to grace this anticipated day. But, distinguished amongst "the gunsmen," as they were termed, stood the hardy inhabitants of the eastern sea-coast beyond the town of Wexford, carrying very long fire-locks, used by them in shooting water-fowl. This little band was famed as the best marksmen of the force; its sharp-shooter's company, as it were, of a very unusual kind: and, indeed, the men were well used to the enormous guns they bore; and quite as proud of the consideration they justly enjoyed amongst a throng, of whom the greater number did not know how to charge their pieces. They were particularized by the title of Shelmaliers, the name of the barony whence the first of such valued "guns" came to join the insurgents; and when afterwards reinforced by all who grew expert in the use of the trigger, they became still more distinguished for their real good services during the memorable campaign. At their sides hung portions of cows' horn, to hold their powder and ball; and these were other marks of superiority; for, excepting the few hundreds who ostentatiously displayed the pouches of the military they had slain, the greater number of the "gunsmen" carried their scanty supplies of ammunition in morsels of paper, or in old rags, thrust inconveniently into the depths of their pockets.

Behind the "gunsmen" arose a wood of long pikes, roughly fashioned from the anvil, without polished surface from which to reflect the sunbeams, or to cast the glitter of chivalry around the infliction of death. Black and rude, they seemed, indeed, fit instruments of that species of warfare – civil strife – in which chivalrous feeling, as well as chivalrous display, seldom finds a place. At each wing, a dense mass of men, bearing the same savage weapon, supported the centre.

Michael Banim
The Croppy; a Tale of 1798 (1828)

MR CROTCHET DEFENDS HIS
STATUES OF VENUS

MR CROTCHET

SIR, ancient sculpture is the true school of modesty. But where the Greeks had modesty, we have cant; where they had poetry, we have cant; where they had patriotism, we have cant; where they had any thing that exalts, delights, or adorns humanity, we have nothing but cant, cant, cant. And, sir, to show my contempt for cant in all its shapes, I have adorned my house with the Greek Venus, in all her shapes, and am ready to fight her battle, against all the societies that ever were instituted for the suppression of truth and beauty.

THE REV. DR FOLLIOTT

My dear sir, I am afraid you are growing warm. Pray be cool. Nothing contributes so much to good digestion as to be perfectly cool after dinner.

MR CROTCHET

Sir, the Lacedaemonian virgins wrestled naked with young men; and they grew up, as the wise Lycurgus had foreseen, into the most modest of women, and the most exemplary of wives and mothers.

THE REV. DR FOLLIOTT

Very likely, sir; but the Athenian virgins did no such thing, and they grew up into wives who stayed at home, – stayed at home, sir, and looked after the husband's dinner, – his dinner, sir, you will please to observe.

MR CROTCHET

And what was the consequence of that, sir? that they were such very insipid persons that the husband would not go home to eat his dinner, but preferred the company of some Aspasia, or Lais.

THE REV. DR FOLLIOTT

Two very different persons, sir, give me leave to remark.

MR CROTCHET

Very likely, sir; but both too good to be married in Athens.

THE REV. DR FOLLIOTT

Sir, Lais was a Corinthian.

MR CROTCHET

'Od's vengeance, sir, some Aspasia and any other Athenian name of the same sort of person you like –

THE REV. DR FOLLIOTT

I do not like the sort of person at all: the sort of person I like, as I have already implied, is a modest woman, who stays at home and looks after her husband's dinner.

MR CROTCHET

Well, sir, that was not the taste of the Athenians. They preferred the society of women who would not have made any scruple about sitting as models to Praxiteles; as you know, sir, very modest women in Italy did to Canova: one of whom, an Italian countess, being asked by an English lady, "how she could bear it?" answered, "Very well; there was a good fire in the room."

THE REV. DR FOLLIOTT

Sir, the English lady should have asked how the Italian lady's husband could bear it. The phials of my wrath would overflow if poor dear Mrs. Folliott — sir, in return for your story, I will tell you a story of my ancestor, Gilbert Folliott. The devil haunted him, as he did Saint Francis, in the likeness of a beautiful damsel; but all he could get from the exemplary Gilbert was an admonition to wear a stomacher and longer petticoats.

MR CROTCHET

Sir, your story makes for my side of the question. It proves that the devil, in the likeness of a fair damsel, with short petticoats and no stomacher, was almost too much for Gilbert Folliott. The force of the spell was in the drapery.

THE REV. DR FOLLIOTT

Bless my soul, sir!

MR CROTCHET

Give me leave, sir. Diderot —

THE REV. DR FOLLIOTT

Who was he, sir?

MR CROTCHET

Who was he, sir? the sublime philosopher, the father of the encyclopaedia, of all the encyclopaedias that have ever been printed.

THE REV. DR FOLLIOTT

Bless me, sir, a terrible progeny! they belong to the tribe of *Incubi*.

MR CROTCHET

The great philosopher, Diderot, –

THE REV. DR FOLLIOTT

Sir, Diderot is not a man after my heart. Keep to the Greeks, if you please; albeit this Sleeping Venus is not an antique.

MR CROTCHET

Well, sir, the Greeks: why do we call the Elgin marbles inestimable? Simply because they are true to nature. And why are they so superior in that point to all modern works, with all our greater knowledge of anatomy? Why, sir, but because the Greeks, having no cant, had better opportunities of studying models?

THE REV. DR FOLLIOTT

Sir, I deny our greater knowledge of anatomy. But I shall take the liberty to employ, on this occasion, the *argumentum ad hominem*. Would you have allowed Miss Crotchet to sit for a model to Canova?

Yes, sir.

"God bless my soul, sir!" exclaimed the Reverend Doctor Folliott, throwing himself back into a chair, and flinging up his heels, with the premeditated design of giving emphasis to his exclamation: but by miscalculating his *impetus*, he overbalanced his chair, and laid himself on the carpet in a right angle, of which his back was the base.

Thomas Love Peacock

Crotchet Castle (1831)

Boccaccio's Dream of Fiammetta

Here in this chamber she appeared to me more visibly in a dream.

"Thy prayers have been heard, O Giovanni," said she.

I sprang to embrace her.

"Do not spill the water! Ah! you have spilt a part of it."

I then observed in her hand a crystal vase. A few drops were sparkling on the sides and running down the rim; a few more were trickling from the base and from the hand that held it.

"I must go down to the brook," said she, "and fill it again as it was filled before."

What a moment of agony was this to me! Could I be certain how long might be her absence? She went: I was following: she made a sign for me to turn back: I disobeyed her only an instant: yet my sense of disobedience, increasing my feebleness and confusion, made me lose sight of her. In the next moment she was again at my side, with the cup quite full. I stood motionless: I feared my breath might shake the water over. I looked her in the face for her commands . . and to see it . . to see it so calm, so beneficent, so beautiful. I was forgetting what I had prayed for, when she lowered her head, tasted of the cup, and gave it me. I drank; and suddenly sprang forth before me, many groves and palaces and gardens, and their statues and their avenues, and their labyrinths of alaternus and bay, and alcoves of citron, and watchful loopholes in the retirements of impenetrable pomegranate. Farther off, just below where the fountain slipt away from its marble hall and guardian gods, arose, from their beds of moss and drosera and darkest grass, the sisterhood of oleanders, fond of tantalizing with their bosomed flowers and their moist and pouting blossoms the little shy rivulet, and of covering its face with all the colours of the dawn. My dream expanded and moved forward. I trod again the dust of Posilipo, soft as the feathers in the wings of Sleep: I emerged on Baia; I crossed her innumerable arches; I loitered in the breezy sunshine of her mole; I trusted the faithful seclusion of her caverns, the keepers of so many secrets; and I reposed on the buoyancy of her tepid sea. Then Naples, and her theatres and her churches, and grottoes and dells and forts and promontories, rushed forward in confusion, now among soft whispers, now among sweetest sounds, and subsided, and sank, and disappeared. Yet a memory seemed to come fresh from every one: each had time enough for its tale, for its pleasure, for its reflection, for its pang. As I mounted with silent steps the narrow staircase of the old palace, how distinctly did I feel against the palm of my hand the coldness of that smooth stone-work, and the greater of the cramps of iron in it!

"Ah me! is this forgetting?" cried I anxiously to Fiammetta.

"We must recall these scenes before us," she replied: "such is the punishment of them. Let us hope and believe that the apparition, and the compunction which must follow it, will be accepted as the full penalty, and that both will pass away almost together."

I feared to lose anything attendant on her presence: I feared to approach her forehead with my lips: I feared to touch the lily on its long wavy leaf in her hair, which filled my whole heart with fragrance. Venerating, adoring, I bowed my head at last to kiss her snow-white robe, and trembled at my presumption. And yet the effulgence of her countenance vivified while it chastened me. I loved her . . I must not say *more* than ever . . *better* than ever; it was Fiammetta who had inhabited the skies. As my hand opened toward hers,

"Beware!" said she, faintly smiling; "beware, Giovanni! Take only the crystal: take it, and drink again."

"Must all be then forgotten?" said I sorrowfully.

"Remember your prayer, and mine, Giovanni! Shall both have been granted . . O how much worse than in vain?"

Walter Savage Landor
Pentameron and Pentalogia (1837)

A SAMPLE OF CAPTAIN KEARNEY

CAPTAIN KEARNEY certainly dealt in the marvellous to admiration, and really told his stories with such earnestness, that I actually believe that he thought he was telling the truth. Never was there such an instance of confirmed habit. Telling a story of a cutting-out expedition, he said, "The French captain would have fallen by my hand, but just as I levelled my musket, a ball came, and cut off the cock of the lock, as clean as if it was done with a knife – a very remarkable instance," observed he.

"Not equal to what occurred in a ship I was in," replied the first lieutenant, "when the second lieutenant was grazed by a grape shot, which cut off one of his whiskers, and turning round his head to ascertain what was the matter, another grape shot came and took off the other. Now that's what I call a *close shave*."

"Yes," replied Captain Kearney, "very close, indeed, if it were true; but you'll excuse me, Mr. Phillott, but you sometimes tell strange stories. I do not mind it myself, but the example is not good to my young relation here, Mr. Simple."

"Captain Kearney," replied the first lieutenant, laughing very immoderately, "do you know what the pot called the kettle?"

"No sir, I do not," retorted the captain, with offended dignity. "Mr. Simple, will you take a glass of wine?"

I thought that this little *brouillerie* would have checked the captain; it did so, but only for a few minutes, when he again commenced. The first lieutenant observed that it would be necessary to let water into the ship every morning, and pump it out, to avoid the smell of the bilge water. "There are worse smells than bilge water," replied the captain. "What do you think of a whole ship's company being nearly poisoned with otto of roses? Yet that occurred to me when in the Mediterranean. I was off Smyrna, cruising for a French ship, that was to sail to France, with a pasha on board, as an ambassador. I knew she would be a good prize, and was looking sharp out, when one morning we discovered her on the lee bow. We made all sail, but she walked away from us, bearing away gradually till we were both before the wind, and at night we lost sight of her. As I knew that she was bound to Marseilles, I made all sail to fall in with her again. The wind was light and variable; but five days afterwards, as I lay in my cot, just before daylight, I smelt a very strong smell, blowing in at the weather port, and coming down the skylight which was open; and after sniffing at it two or three times, I knew it to be otto of roses. I sent for the officer of the watch, and asked him if there was any thing in sight. He replied 'that there was not;' and I ordered him to sweep the horizon with his glass, and look well out to windward. As the wind freshened, the smell became more powerful. I ordered him to get the royal yards across, and all ready to make sail, for I knew that the Turk must be near us. At daylight, there he was, just three miles a-head in the wind's eye. But although he beat us going free, he was no match for us on a wind, and before noon we had possession of him and all his harem. By-the-bye, I could tell you a good story about the ladies. She was a very valuable prize, and among other things, she had a *puncheon* of otto of roses on board –"

"Whew!" cried the first lieutenant. "What! a whole puncheon?"

"Yes," replied the captain, "a Turkish puncheon – not quite so large, perhaps, as ours on board; their weights and measures are different. I took out most of the valuables into the brig I commanded – about 20,000 sequins – carpets – and among the rest, this cask of otto of roses, which we had smelt three miles off. We had it safe on board, when the mate of the hold, not slinging it properly, it fell into the spirit-room with a run, and was stove to pieces. Never was such a scene; my first lieutenant and several men on deck fainted; and the men in the hold were brought up lifeless: it was some time before they were recovered. We let the water into the brig, and pumped it out, but nothing would take away the smell, which was so overpowering, that before I could get to Malta I had forty men on the sick list. When I arrived there I turned the mate out of the service for his carelessness. It was not until after having smoked the brig, and finding that of little use, after having sunk her for three weeks, that the smell was at all bearable; but even then, it could never be eradicated, and the admiral sent the brig home, and she was sold out of the service. They could do nothing with her at the dock-yards. She was broken up, and bought by the people at Brighton and Tunbridge Wells, who used her timbers for turning fancy articles, which, smelling as they did, so strongly of otto of roses, proved very profitable. Were you ever at Brighton, Mr. Simple?"

"Never, sir."

Just at this moment, the officer of the watch came down to say that there was a very large shark under the counter, and wished to know if the captain had any objection to the officers attempting to catch it?

"By no means," replied Captain Kearney; "I hate sharks as I do the devil. I nearly lost 14,000*l.* by one, when I was in the Mediterranean."

"May I inquire how, Captain Kearney?" said the first lieutenant, with a demure face; "I'm very anxious to know."

"Why the story is simply this," replied the captain. . . . .

Frederick Marryat

Peter Simple (1834)

IV

THE CRITICISM OF THE ARTS

Some Principles of Landscape Gardening

THE road through the park. . . . should be spacious, or moderate, like the house it approaches. Let it wind: but let it not take any deviation, which is not well accounted for. To have the convenience of winding along a valley, or passing a commodious bridge, or avoiding a wood, or a piece of water, any traveller would naturally wish to deviate a little; and obstacles of this kind, if necessary, must be interposed. Mr. Brown[1] was often very happy in creating these artificial obstructions.

From every part of the approach, and from the ridings, and favourite walks about the park, let all the boundaries be secreted. A view of paling, tho in some cases it may be picturesque, is in general disgusting.

If there be a *natural* river, or a real ruin in the scene, it may be a happy circumstance: let the best use be made of it: but I should be cautious in advising the *creation* of either. At least, I have rarely seen either ruins, or rivers well manufactured. Mr. Brown, I think, has failed more in river-making than in any of his attempts. An artificial lake has sometimes a good effect; but neither propriety, nor beauty can arise from it, unless the heads and extremities of it are perfectly well managed; and concealed: and after all, the success is hazardous. You must always suppose it a portion of a larger piece of water; and it is not easy to carry on the imposition. If the

1. 'Capability' Brown (1715–83), the landscape gardener.

house be magnificent, it seldom receives much benefit from
an artificial production of this kind. Grandeur is rarely
produced.

. . . The most natural inhabitants of parks are fallow deer; and
very beautiful they are: but flocks of sheep, and herds of
cattle are more useful; and, in my opinion, more beautiful.
Sheep particularly are very ornamental in a park. Their colour
is just that dingy hue, which contrasts with the verdure of the
ground; and the flakiness of their wool is rich, and picturesque.
I should wish them however to wear their natural livery; and
not to be patched with letters, and daubed over with red-
ochre. To see the side of a hill spread with groups of sheep –
or to see them through openings among the boles of trees,
at a little distance, with a gleam of light falling upon them,
is very picturesque.

As the garden, or *pleasure-ground*, as it is commonly called,
approaches nearer to the house, than the park, it takes of
course a higher polish. Here the lawns are shorn, instead of
being grazed. The roughness of the road is changed into an
elegant gravel walk; and knots of flowers, and flowering
shrubs are introduced, yet blended with clumps of forest-
trees, which connect it with the park. Single trees also
take their station here with great propriety. The spreading
oak, or elm, are no disgrace to the most ornamental scene.
It is the property of these noble plants to harmonize with
every species of landscape. They equally become the forest,
and the lawn: only here they should be beautiful in their
kind; and luxuriant in their growth. Neither the scathed,
nor the unbalanced oak would suit a polished situation.

Here too, if the situation suits it, the elegant temple may
find a place. But it is an expensive, a hazardous, and often a
useless decoration. If more than one however be introduced
in the same view, they croud the scene, unless it be very extensive. More than two should in no case be admitted. In the

most polished landscape, unless nature, and simplicity lead the way, the whole will be deformed.

William Gilpin
*Remarks on Forest Scenery, and Other
Woodland Views*... (1791)

THE PICTURESQUE AND THE BEAUTIFUL

GOTHIC architecture is generally considered as more picturesque, though less beautiful, than Grecian; and, upon the same principle that a ruin is more so than a new edifice. The first thing that strikes the eye in approaching any building is the general outline against the sky (or whatever it may be opposed to) and the effect of the openings: in Grecian buildings the general lines of the roof are strait, and even when varied and adorned by a dome or a pediment, the whole has a character of symmetry and regularity.

In Gothic buildings, the outline of the summit presents such a variety of forms, of turrets and pinnacles, some open, some fretted and variously enriched, that even where there is an exact correspondence of parts, it is often disguised by an appearance of splendid confusion and irregularity. In the doors and windows of Gothic churches, the pointed arch has as much variety as any regular figure can well have, the eye too is not so strongly conducted from the top of the one to that of the other, as by the parallel lines of the Grecian; and every person must be struck with the extreme richness and intricacy of some of the principal windows of our cathedrals and ruined abbeys. In these last is displayed the triumph of the picturesque; and its charms to a painter's eye are often so great as to rival those of beauty itself.

Some people may, perhaps, be unwilling to allow, that in ruins of Grecian and Gothic architecture any considerable part of the spectator's pleasure arises from the picturesque circumstances, and may chuse to attribute the whole to what may justly claim a great share in that pleasure, the elegance or grandeur of their forms, the veneration of high antiquity, or the solemnity of religious awe; in a word, to the mixture of the two other characters: but were this true, yet there are many buildings, highly interesting to all who have united the study of art with that of nature, in which beauty and grandeur are equally out of the question; such as hovels, cottages, mills, ragged insides of old barns and stables, &c. whenever they have any marked and peculiar effect of form, tint, or light and shadow. In mills particularly, such is the extreme intricacy of the wheels and the wood work; such the singular variety of forms, and of lights and shadows, of mosses and weather stains from the constant moisture, of plants springing from the rough joints of the stones; such the assemblage of every thing which most conduces to picturesqueness, that even without the addition of water, an old mill has the greatest charm for a painter.

It is owing to the same causes that a building with scaffolding has often a more picturesque appearance than the building itself when the scaffolding is taken away – that old mossy rough hewn park pales of unequal heights are an ornament to landscape, especially when they are partially concealed by thickets; while a neat post and rail, regularly continued round a field, and seen without any interruption, is one of the most unpicturesque, as being one of the most uniform of all boundaries.

But among all the objects of nature, there is none in which roughness and smoothness more strongly mark the distinction between the two characters, than in water. A calm clear lake, with the reflections of all that surround it, seen under the influence of a setting sun, at the close of an evening clear and serene as its own surface, is, perhaps, of all scenes, the most congenial to our ideas of beauty in its strictest and in its most general sense.

Nay, though the scenery around should be the most wild and picturesque (I might almost say the most savage), every thing is so softened and melted together by the reflection of such a mirror, that the prevailing idea, even then, might possibly be that of beauty, as long as the water itself was chiefly regarded. On the other hand, all water whose surface is broken, and whose motion is abrupt and irregular, as universally accords with our ideas of the picturesque; and whenever the word is mentioned, rapid and stony torrents and cataracts, and the waves dashing against rocks, are among the first images that present themselves to our imagination. The two characters also approach and balance each other, as roughness or smoothness, as gentle undulation or abruptness prevail.

Among trees, it is not the smooth young beech, or the fresh and tender ash, but the rugged old oak, or knotty wych elm, that are picturesque; nor is it necessary they should be of great bulk; it is sufficient if they are rough, mossy, with a character of age, and with sudden variations in their forms. The limbs of huge trees, shattered by lightning or tempestuous winds, are in the highest degree picturesque; but whatever is caused by those dreaded powers of destruction must always have a tincture of the sublime.

Sir Uvedale Price

An Essay on the Picturesque, as compared with the
Sublime and the Beautiful (1794)

A Complaint to a Publisher

(c. 1784)

I DID not write the line that has been tampered with hastily, or without due attention to the construction of it; and what appeared to me its only merit is, in its present state, entirely annihilated.

I know that the ears of modern verse-writers are delicate to an excess, and their readers are as troubled with the squeamishness as themselves. So that if a line do not run as smooth as quicksilver, they are offended. A critic of the present day serves a poem as a cook does a dead turkey, when she fastens the legs of it to a post and draws out all the sinews. For this we may thank Pope; but unless we could imitate him in the closeness and compactness of his expression, as well as in the smoothness of his numbers, we had better drop the imitation, which serves no other purpose than to emasculate and weaken all we write. Give me a manly rough line, with a deal of meaning in it, rather than a whole poem full of musical periods, that have nothing but their oily smoothness to recommend them.

I have said thus much, as I hinted in the beginning, because I have just finished a much longer poem than the last, which our common friend will receive by the same messenger that has the charge of this letter. In that poem there are many lines which an ear so nice as the gentleman's who made the above-mentioned alteration would undoubtedly condemn; and yet (if I may be permitted to say it) they cannot be made smoother without being the worse for it. There is a roughness on a plum which nobody that understands fruit would rub off, though the plum would be much more polished without it. But, lest I tire you, I will only add that I wish you to guard me from all such meddling; assuring you that I always write as smoothly as I can; but that I never did, never will, sacrifice the spirit or sense of a passage to the sound of it.

William Cowper

Letter to Joseph Johnson (n.d.) from *The Correspondence of William Cowper*, edited by Thomas Wright (1904)

THE LANGUAGE OF POETRY

IN poetry, in which every line, every phrase, may pass the ordeal of deliberation and deliberate choice, it is possible, and barely possible, to attain that ultimatum which I have ventured to propose as the infallible test of a blameless style; namely: its *untranslatableness* in words of the same language without injury to the meaning. Be it observed, however, that I include in the *meaning* of a word not only its correspondent object, but likewise all the associations which it recalls. For language is framed to convey not the object alone, but likewise the character, mood and intentions of the person who is representing it. In poetry it *is* practicable to preserve the diction uncorrupted by the affectations and misappropriations, which promiscuous authorship, and reading not promiscuous only because it is disproportionately most conversant with the compositions of the day, have rendered general. Yet even to the poet, composing in his own province, it is an arduous work: and as the result and pledge of a watchful good sense, of fine and luminous distinction, and of complete self-possession, may justly claim all the honour which belongs to an attainment equally difficult and valuable, and the more valuable for being rare. It is at *all* times the proper food of the understanding; but in an age of corrupt eloquence it is both food and antidote.

In prose I doubt whether it be even possible to preserve our style wholly unalloyed by the vicious phraseology which meets us every where, from the sermon to the newspaper, from the harangue of the legislator to the speech from the convivial chair, announcing a *toast* or sentiment. Our chains rattle, even while we are complaining of them.

Samuel Taylor Coleridge
Biographia Literaria ... (1817)

POETIC DICTION

HAVING dwelt thus long on the subjects and aim of these Poems, I shall request the Reader's permission to apprize him of a few circumstances relating to their *style*, in order, among other reasons, that I may not be censured for having performed what I never attempted. The Reader will find that personifications of abstract ideas rarely occur in these volumes; and, I hope, are utterly rejected as an ordinary device to elevate the style, and raise it above prose. I have proposed to myself to imitate, and, as far as is possible, to adopt the very language of men; and assuredly such personifications do not make any regular or natural part of that language. They are, indeed, a figure of speech occasionally prompted by passion, and I have made use of them as such; but I have endeavoured utterly to reject them as a mechanical device of style, or as a family language which Writers in metre seem to lay claim to by prescription. I have wished to keep my Reader in the company of flesh and blood, persuaded that by so doing I shall interest him. I am, however, well aware that others who pursue a different track may interest him likewise; I do not interfere with their claim, I only wish to prefer a different claim of my own. There will also be found in these volumes little of what is usually called poetic diction; I have taken as much pains to avoid it as others ordinarily take to produce it; this I have done for the reason already alleged, to bring my language near to the language of men, and further, because the pleasure which I have proposed to myself to impart is of a kind very different from that which is supposed by many persons to be the proper object of poetry. I do not know how without being culpably particular I can give my Reader a more exact notion of the style in which I wished these poems to be written than by informing him that I have at all times endeavoured to look steadily at my subject, consequently, I hope that there is in these Poems little falsehood of description, and that my ideas are expressed in language fitted to their respective importance. Something I must have gained by this practice, as it is friendly to one property of all good poetry, namely, good sense; but it has necessarily cut me off from a large portion of phrases and figures of speech which from father to son have long been regarded as the common inheritance of Poets. I have also thought it expedient to restrict myself still further, having abstained from the use of many expressions in themselves proper and beautiful, but which have been foolishly repeated by bad Poets, till such feelings of disgust are connected with them as it is scarcely possible by any art of association to overpower.

William Wordsworth

Preface to *Lyrical Ballads* (1800). Text from revised edition of 1802

A RHAPSODY ON POETRY

POETRY is indeed something divine. It is at once the centre and circumference of knowledge; it is that which comprehends all science, and that to which all science must be referred. It is the root and blossom of all other systems of thought; it is that from which all spring, and that which adorns all; and that which, if blighted, denies the fruit and the seed, and withholds from the barren world the nourishment and the succession of the scions of the tree of life. It is the perfect and consummate surface and bloom of all things; it is as the odour and the colour of the rose to the texture of the elements which compose it, as the form and splendour of unfaded beauty to the secrets of anatomy and corruption. What were virtue, love, patriotism, friendship, – what were the scenery of this beautiful universe which we inhabit; what were our consolations on this side of the grave – and what were our aspirations beyond it, if poetry did not ascend to bring light and fire from those eternal regions where the owl-winged faculty of calculation dare not ever soar? Poetry is not like reasoning, a power to be exerted according to the determination of the will. A man cannot say, "I will compose poetry." The greatest poet even cannot say it; for the mind in creation is as a fading coal, which some invisible influence, like an inconstant wind, awakens to transitory brightness; this power arises from within, like the colour of a flower which fades and changes as it is developed, and the conscious portions of our natures are unprophetic either of its approach or its departure. Could this influence be durable in its original purity and force, it is impossible to predict the greatness of the results; but when composition begins, inspiration is already on the decline, and the most glorious poetry that has ever been communicated to the world is probably a feeble shadow of the original conceptions of the poet.

Percy Bysshe Shelley

A Defence of Poetry from *Essays, Letters from Abroad, Translations and Fragments*, edited by Mary Shelley (1840). Written 1821

SCIENCE AND POETRY

THE Man of Science seeks truth as a remote and unknown benefactor; he cherishes and loves it in his solitude: the Poet, singing a song in which all human beings join with him, rejoices in the presence of truth as our visible friend and hourly companion. Poetry is the breath and finer spirit of all knowledge; it is the impassioned expression which is in the countenance of all Science. Emphatically may it be said of the Poet, as Shakespeare hath said of man, "that he looks before and after." He is the rock of defence of human nature; an upholder and preserver, carrying every where with him relationship and love. In spite of difference of soil and climate, of language and manners, of laws and customs, in spite of things silently gone out of mind and things violently destroyed, the Poet binds together by passion and knowledge the vast empire of human society, as it is spread over the whole earth, and over all time. The objects of the Poet's thoughts are every where; though the eyes and senses of man are, it is true, his favourite guides, yet he will follow wheresoever he can find an atmosphere of sensation in which to move his wings. Poetry is the first and last of all knowledge – it is as immortal as the heart of man. If the labours of men of Science should ever create any material revolution, direct or indirect, in our condition, and in the impressions which we habitually receive, the Poet will sleep then no more than at present, but he will be ready to follow the steps of the man of Science, not only in those general indirect effects, but he will be at his side, carrying sensation into the midst of the objects of the Science itself. The remotest discoveries of the Chemist, the Botanist, or Mineralogist, will be as proper objects of the Poet's art as any upon which it can be employed, if the time should ever come when these things shall be familiar to us, and the relations under which they are contemplated by the followers of these respective Sciences shall be manifestly and palpably material to us as enjoying and suffering beings.

William Wordsworth
Preface to *Lyrical Ballads* (1800). Text from
revised edition of 1802

THE ORIGIN OF 'LYRICAL BALLADS'

DURING the first year that Mr. Wordsworth and I were neighbours, our conversations turned frequently on the two cardinal points of poetry, the power of exciting the sympathy of the reader by a faithful adherence to the truth of nature, and the power of giving the interest of novelty by the modifying colours of imagination. The sudden charm, which accidents of light and shade, which moon-light or sun-set diffused over a known and familiar landscape, appeared to represent the practicability of combining both. These are the poetry of nature. The thought suggested itself (to which of us I do not recollect) that a series of poems might be composed of two sorts. In the one, the incidents and agents were to be, in part at least, supernatural; and the excellence aimed at was to consist in the interesting of the affections by the dramatic truth of such emotions, as would naturally accompany such situations, supposing them real. And real in *this* sense they have been to every human being who, from whatever source of delusion, has at any time believed himself under supernatural agency. For the second class, subjects were to be chosen from ordinary life; the characters and incidents were to be such as will be found in every village and its vicinity, where there is a meditative and feeling mind to seek after them, or to notice them, when they present themselves.

In this idea originated the plan of the "Lyrical Ballads"; in which it was agreed, that my endeavours should be directed to persons and characters supernatural, or at least romantic; yet so as to transfer from our inward nature a human interest and a semblance of truth sufficient to procure for these shadows of imagination that willing suspension of disbelief for the moment, which constitutes poetic faith. Mr. Wordsworth, on the other hand, was to propose to himself as his object, to give the charm of novelty to things of every day, and to excite a feeling analogous to the supernatural, by awakening the mind's attention from the lethargy of custom, and directing it to the loveliness and the wonders of the world before us; an inexhaustible treasure, but for which in consequence of the film of familiarity and selfish solicitude we have eyes, yet see not, ears that hear not, and hearts that neither feel nor understand.

With this view I wrote the "Ancient Mariner," and was preparing among other poems, the "Dark Ladie," and the "Christabel," in which I should have more nearly realized my ideal, than I had done in my first attempt. But Mr. Wordsworth's industry had proved so much more successful, and the number of his poems so much greater, that my compositions, instead of forming a balance, appeared rather an interpolation of heterogeneous matter. Mr. Wordsworth added two or three poems written in his own character, in the impassioned, lofty, and sustained diction, which is characteristic of his genius. In this form the "Lyrical Ballads" were published; and were presented by him, as an *experiment*, whether subjects, which from their nature rejected the usual ornaments and extra-colloquial style of poems in general, might not be so managed in the language of ordinary life as to produce the pleasureable interest, which it is the peculiar business of poetry to impart.

Samuel Taylor Coleridge
Biographia Literaria ... (1817)

THE LAKE POETS

MR WORDSWORTH is at the head of that which has been denominated the Lake school of poetry; a school which, with all my respect for it, I do not think sacred from criticism or exempt from faults, of some of which faults I shall speak with becoming frankness; for I do not see that the liberty of the press ought to be shackled, or freedom of speech curtailed, to screen either its revolutionary or renegado extravagances. This school of poetry had its origin in the French revolution, or rather in those sentiments and opinions which produced that revolution; and which sentiments and opinions were indirectly imported into this country in translations from the German about that period. Our poetical literature had, towards the close of the last century, degenerated into the most trite, insipid, and mechanical of all things, in the hands of the followers of Pope and the old French school of poetry. It wanted something to stir it up, and it found that something in the principles and events of the French revolution. From the impulse it thus received, it rose at once from the most servile imitation and tamest common-place, to the utmost pitch of singularity and paradox. The change in the belles-lettres was as complete, and to many persons as startling, as the change in politics, with which it went hand in hand. There was a mighty ferment in the heads of statesmen and poets, kings and people. According to the prevailing notions, all was to be natural and new. Nothing that was established was to be tolerated. All the common-place figures of poetry, tropes, allegories, personifications, with the whole heathen mythology, were instantly discarded; a classical allusion was considered as a piece of antiquated foppery; capital letters were no more allowed in print, than letters-patent of nobility were permitted in real life; kings and queens were dethroned from their rank and station in legitimate tragedy or epic poetry, as they were decapitated elsewhere; rhyme was looked upon as a relic of the feudal system, and regular metre was abolished along with regular government. Authority and fashion, elegance or arrangement, were hooted out of countenance, as pedantry and prejudice. Every one did that which was good in his own eyes. The object was to reduce all things to an absolute level; and a singularly affected and outrageous simplicity prevailed in dress and manners, in style and sentiment. A striking effect produced where it was least expected, something new and original, no matter whether good, bad, or indifferent, whether mean or lofty, extravagant or childish, was all that was aimed at, or considered as compatible with sound philosophy and an age of reason. The licentiousness grew extreme: Coryate's Crudities were nothing to it. The world was to be turned topsy-turvy; and poetry, by the good will of our Adam-wits, was to share its fate and begin *de novo*. It was a time of promise, a renewal of the world and of letters; and the Deucalions, who were to perform this feat of re-generation, were the present poet-laureat and the authors of the Lyrical Ballads. The Germans, who made heroes of robbers, and honest women of cast-off mistresses, had already exhausted the extravagant and marvellous in sentiment and situation: our native writers adopted a wonderful simplicity of style and matter. The paradox they set out with was, that all things are by nature equally fit subjects for poetry; or that if there is any preference to be given, those that are the meanest and most unpromising are the best, as they leave the greatest scope for the unbounded stores of thought and fancy in the writer's own mind.

William Hazlitt
Lectures on the English Poets (1818)

'CHILDE HAROLD', 'LALLA ROOKH' AND POETRY IN GENERAL

THE other day I wrote to convey my proposition with regard to the fourth and concluding Canto.[1] I have gone over and extended it to one hundred and fifty stanzas, which is almost as long as the two first were originally, and longer by itself than any of the smaller poems except 'The Corsair'. Mr. Hob-house has made some very valuable and accurate notes of considerable length, and you may be sure I will do for the text all that I can to finish with decency. I look upon 'Childe

1. Of *Childe Harold*.

Harold' as my best; and as I begun, I think of concluding with it. But I make no resolutions on that head, as I broke my former intention with regard to 'The Corsair'. However, I fear that I shall never do better; and yet, not being thirty years of age, for some moons to come, one ought to be progressive as far as Intellect goes for many a good year. But I have had a devilish deal of wear and tear of mind and body in my time, besides having published too often and much already. God grant me some judgement to do what may be most fitting in that and everything else, for I doubt my own exceedingly.

I have read 'Lalla Rookh', but not with sufficient attention yet, for I ride about, and lounge, and ponder, and – two or three other things; so that my reading is very desultory, and not so attentive as it used to be. I am very glad to hear of its popularity, for Moore is a very noble fellow in all respects, and will enjoy it without any of the bad feeling which success – good or evil – sometimes engenders in the men of rhyme. Of the Poem itself, I will tell you my opinion when I have mastered it: I say of the *Poem*, for I don't like the *prose* at all at all; and in the meantime, the 'Fire worshippers' is the best, and the 'Veiled Prophet' the worst, of the volume.

With regard to poetry in general, I am convinced, the more I think of it, that he and *all* of us – Scott, Southey, Wordsworth, Moore, Campbell, I, – are all in the wrong, one as much as another; that we are upon a wrong revolutionary poetical system, or systems, not worth a damn in itself, and from which none but Rogers and Crabbe are free; and that the present and next generations will finally be of this opinion. I am the more confirmed in this by having lately gone over some of our classics, particularly *Pope*, whom I tried in this way – I took Moore's poems and my own and some others, and went over them side by side with Pope's, and I was really astonished (I ought not to have been so) and mortified at the ineffable distance in point of sense, learning, effect, and even *imagination*, passion, and *invention*, between the little Queen Anne's man, and us of the Lower Empire. Depend upon it, it is all Horace then, and Claudian now, among us; and if I had to begin again, I would mould myself accordingly.

George Gordon, Lord Byron

Letter to John Murray (15 September, 1817) from
T. Moore's *Letters and Journals of Lord Byron: with
Notices of his Life* (1830)

ON THE REVIEWS OF 'ENDYMION'

I CANNOT but feel indebted to those Gentlemen who have taken my part – As for the rest, I begin to get a little acquainted with my own strength and weakness. – Praise or blame has but a momentary effect on the man whose love of beauty in the abstract makes him a severe critic on his own Works. My own domestic criticism has given me pain without comparison beyond what Blackwood or the Quarterly could possibly inflict, and also when I feel I am right, no external praise can give me such a glow as my own solitary reperception & ratification of what is fine. J. S. is perfectly right in regard to the slip-shod Endymion. That it is so is no fault of mine. – No! – though it may sound a little paradoxical. It is as good as I had power to make it – by myself. Had I been nervous about its being a perfect piece, & with that view asked advice, & trembled over every page, it would not have been written; for it is not in my nature to fumble – I will write independantly. – I have written independently *without Judgment.* – I may write independently, & *with Judgment* hereafter. The Genius of Poetry must work out its own salvation in a man: It cannot be matured by law and precept, but by sensation & watchfulness in itself. That which is creative must

249

create itself – In Endymion, I leaped headlong into the Sea, and thereby have become better acquainted with the Soundings, the quicksands, & the rocks, than if I had stayed upon the green shore, and piped a silly pipe, and took tea & comfortable advice. – I was never afraid of failure; for I would sooner fail than not be among the greatest.

John Keats

Letter to James Augustus Hessey (9 October, 1818) from
The Letters of John Keats, edited by M. B. Forman (1935)

BLAKE

BLAKE is a real name, I assure you, and a most extraordinary man, if he be still living. He is the Robert Blake,[1] whose wild designs accompany a splendid folio edition of the "Night Thoughts," which you may have seen, in one of which he pictures the parting of soul and body by a solid mass of human form floating off, God knows how, from a lumpish mass (fac Simile to itself) left behind on the dying bed. He paints in water colours marvellous strange pictures, visions of his brain, which he asserts that he has seen. They have great merit. He has *seen* the old Welsh bards on Snowdon – he has seen the Beautifullest, the Strongest, and the Ugliest Man, left alone from the Massacre of the Britons by the Romans, and has painted them from memory (I have seen his paintings), and asserts them to be as good as the figures of Raphael and Angelo, but not better, as they had precisely the same retro-visions and prophetic visions with themself (himself). The painters in oil (which he will have it that neither of them practised) he affirms to have been the ruin of art, and affirms that all the while he was engaged in his Water paintings,

1. The mistake over William Blake's name is significant of his obscurity in his lifetime.

Titian was disturbing him, Titian the Ill Genius of Oil Painting. His Pictures – one in particular the Canterbury Pilgrims (far above Stothard's) – have great merit, but hard, dry, yet with grace. He has written a Catalogue of them, with a most spirited criticism on Chaucer, but mystical and full of Vision. His poems have been sold hitherto only in Manuscript. I never read them, but a friend at my desire procured the Sweep Song. There is one to a tiger, which I have heard recited, beginning

> "Tiger Tiger, burning bright,
> Thro' the desarts of the night"

which is glorious, but alas! I have not the book; for the man is flown, whither I know not – to Hades or a Mad House. But I must look on him as one of the most extraordinary persons of the age.

Charles Lamb

Letter to Bernard Barton (15 May, 1824) from *The Letters of Charles Lamb*, edited by A. Ainger (1878)

NEXT TO SHAKESPEARE

Porson – You poets are still rather too fond of the unsubstantial. Some will have nothing else than what they call pure imagination. Now air-plants ought not to fill the whole conservatory; other plants, I would modestly suggest, are worth cultivating, which send their roots pretty deep into the ground. I hate both poetry and wine without body. Look at Shakespeare, Bacon, and Milton; were these your pure-imagination-men? The least of them, whichever it was, carried a jewel of poetry about him, worth all his tribe that came after. Did the two of them who wrote in verse build upon nothing? Did their predecessors? And, pray, whose daughter was the

Muse they invoked? Why, Memory's. They stood among substantial men, and sang upon recorded actions. The plain of Scamander, the promontory of Sigaeum, the palaces of Tros and Dardanus, the citadel in which the Fates sang mournfully under the image of Minerva, seem fitter places for the Muses to alight on, than artificial rockwork or than faeryrings. But your great favourite, I hear, is Spenser, who shines in allegory, and who, like an aerolith, is dull and heavy when he descends to the ground.

Southey – He continues a great favourite with me still, although he must always lose a little as our youth declines. Spenser's is a spacious but somewhat low chamber, hung with rich tapestry, on which the figures are mostly disproportioned, but some of the faces are lively and beautiful; the furniture is part creaking and worm-eaten, part fragrant with cedar and sandal-wood and aromatic gums and balsams; every table and mantelpiece and cabinet is covered with gorgeous vases, and birds, and dragons, and houses in the air.

Porson – There is scarcely a poet of the same eminence, whom I have found it so delightful to read *in*, or so tedious to read *through*. Give me Chaucer in preference. He slaps us on the shoulder, and makes us spring up while the dew is on the grass, and while the long shadows play about it in all quarters. We feel strong with the freshness round us, and we return with a keener appetite, having such a companion in our walk. Among the English poets, both on this side and the other side of Milton, I place him next to Shakespeare; but the word *next*, must have nothing to do with the word *near*. I said before, that I do not estimate so highly as many do the mushrooms that sprang up in a ring under the great oak of Arden.

Walter Savage Landor
'Imaginary Conversation: Southey and Porson' from
Blackwood's Magazine (December, 1842)

Pseudo-Elizabethan Drama

When we look candidly and calmly to the works of our early dramatists, it is impossible, we think, to dispute, that after criticism has done its worst on them – after all deductions for impossible plots and fantastical characters, unaccountable forms of speech, and occasional extravagance, indelicacy, and horrors – there is a facility and richness about them, both of thought and of diction – a force of invention, and a depth of sagacity – an originality of conception, and a play of fancy – a nakedness and energy of passion, and, above all, a copiousness of imagery, and a sweetness and flexibility of verse, which is altogether unrivalled, in earlier or in later times; – and places them, in our estimation, in the very highest and foremost place among ancient or modern poets.

It is in these particulars that the inferiority of their recent imitators is most apparent – in the want of ease and variety – originality and grace. There is, in all their attempts, whatever may be their other merits or defects, an air of anxiety and labour – and indications, by far too visible, at once of timidity and ambition. This may arise, in part, from the fact of their being, too obviously and consciously, imitators. They do not aspire so much to rival the genius of their originals, as to copy their manner. They do not write as *they* would have written in the present day, but as they imagine they themselves would have written two hundred years ago. They revive the antique phraseology, repeat the venerable oaths, and emulate the quaint familiarities of that classical period – and wonder that they are not mistaken for new incarnations of its departed poets! One great cause why they are not, is, that they speak an unnatural dialect, and are constrained by a masquerade habit; in neither of which it is possible to display that freedom, and those delicate traits of character, which are the life of the drama, and were among the chief merits of those who once

253

exalted it so highly. Another bad effect of imitation, and especially of the imitation of unequal and irregular models in a critical age, is, that nothing is thought fit to be copied but the exquisite and shining passages; – from which it results, in the *first* place, that all our rivalry is reserved for occasions in which its success is most hopeless; and, in the *second* place, that instances, even of occasional success, want their proper grace and effect, by being deprived of the relief, shading, and preparation, which they would naturally have received in a less fastidious composition; and, instead of the warm and native and ever-varying graces of a spontaneous effusion, the work acquires the false and feeble brilliancy of a prize essay in a foreign tongue – a collection of splendid patches of different texture and pattern.

Francis, Lord Jeffrey
Review of Byron's *Sardanapalus, The Two Foscari* and *Cain* from the *Edinburgh Review* (February, 1822)

THE CHARACTER OF IAGO

THE character of Iago, in fact, belongs to a class of characters common to SHAKESPEAR, and at the same time peculiar to him, namely, that of great intellectual activity, accompanied with a total want of moral principle, and therefore displaying itself at the constant expence of others, making use of reason as a pander to will – employing its ingenuity and its resources to palliate its own crimes and aggravate the faults of others, and seeking to confound the practical distinctions of right and wrong, by referring them to some overstrained standard of speculative refinement.

Some persons more nice than wise, have thought the whole of the character of Iago unnatural. SHAKESPEAR, who was quite as good a philosopher as he was a poet, thought otherwise. He knew that the love of power, which is another name for the love of mischief, was natural to man. He would know this as well or better than if it had been demonstrated to him by a logical diagram, merely from seeing children paddle in the dirt, or kill flies for sport. We might ask those who think the character of Iago not natural, why they go to see it performed – but from the interest it excites, the sharper edge which it sets on their curiosity and imagination? Why do we go to see tragedies in general? Why do we always read the accounts in the newspapers of dreadful fires and shocking murders, but for the same reason? Why do so many persons frequent executions and trials; or why do the lower classes almost universally take delight in barbarous sports and cruelty to animals, but because there is a natural tendency in the mind to strong excitement, a desire to have its faculties roused and stimulated to the utmost? Whenever this principle is not under the restraint of humanity or the sense of moral obligation, there are no excesses to which it will not of itself give rise, without the assistance of any other motive, either of passion or self-interest. Iago is only an extreme instance of the kind; that is, of diseased intellectual activity, with an almost perfect indifference to moral good or evil, or rather with a preference of the latter, because it falls more in with his favourite propensity, gives greater zest to his thoughts and scope to his actions. Be it observed, too, (for the sake of those who are for squaring all human actions by the maxims of Rochefoucault), that he is quite or nearly as indifferent to his own fate as to that of others: that he runs all risks for a trifling and doubtful advantage; and is himself the dupe and victim of his ruling passion – an incorrigible love of mischief – and insatiable craving after action of the most difficult and dangerous kind. Our Ancient is a philosopher, who fancies that a lie that kills, has more point in it than an alliteration or an antithesis; who thinks a fatal experiment on the peace of a family a better thing than watching the palpitations in the heart of a flea in an air-pump; who plots the ruin of his friends as an exercise for his understanding, and stabs men in the dark to prevent *ennui*.

William Hazlitt
A View of the English Stage (1818)

Two Notes on 'The Tempest'

Shakespeare's Heroines

In the second scene, Prospero's speeches, till the entrance of Ariel, contain the finest example I remember of retrospective narration for the purpose of exciting immediate interest, and putting the audience in possession of all the information necessary for the understanding of the plot. Observe, too, the perfect probability of the moment chosen by Prospero (the very Shakspeare himself, as it were, of the tempest) to open out the truth to his daughter, his own romantic bearing, and how completely any thing that might have been disagreeable to us in the magician, is reconciled and shaded in the humanity and natural feelings of the father. In the very first speech of Miranda the simplicity and tenderness of her character are at once laid open; – it would have been lost in direct contact with the agitation of the first scene. The opinion once prevailed, but, happily, is now abandoned, that Fletcher alone wrote for women; – the truth is, that with very few, and those partial, exceptions, the female characters in the plays of Beaumont and Fletcher are, when of the light kind, not decent; when heroic, complete viragos. But in Shakspeare all the elements of womanhood are holy, and there is the sweet, yet dignified feeling of all that *continuates* society, as sense of ancestry and of sex, with a purity unassailable by sophistry, because it rests not in the analytic processes, but in that sane equipoise of the faculties, during which the feelings are representative of all past experience, – not of the individual only, but of all those by whom she has been educated, and their predecessors even up to the first mother that lived. Shakspeare saw that the want of prominence, which Pope notices for sarcasm, was the blessed beauty of the woman's character, and knew that it arose not from any deficiency, but from the more exquisite harmony of all the parts of the moral being constituting one living total of head and heart. He has drawn it, indeed, in all its distinctive energies of faith, patience, constancy, fortitude, – shown in all of them as following the heart, which gives its results by a nice tact and happy intuition, without the intervention of the discursive faculty, – sees all things in and by the light of the affections, and errs, if it ever err, in the exaggerations of love alone. In all the Shakspearian women there is essentially the same foundation and principle; the distinct individuality and variety are merely the result of the modification of circumstances, whether in Miranda the maiden, in Imogen the wife, or in Katharine the queen.

Shakespeare's Political Views

In this play . . . are also shown the springs of the vulgar in politics, – of that kind of politics which is inwoven with human nature. In his treatment of this subject, wherever it occurs, Shakspeare is quite peculiar. In other writers we find the particular opinions of the individual; in Massinger it is rank republicanism; in Beaumont and Fletcher even *jure divino* principles are carried to excess; – but Shakspeare never promulgates any party tenets. He is always the philosopher and the moralist, but at the same time with a profound veneration for all the established institutions of society, and for those classes which form the permanent elements of the state – especially never introducing a professional character, as such, otherwise than as respectable. If he must have any name, he should be styled a philosophical aristocrat, delighting in those hereditary institutions which have a tendency to bind one age to another, and in that distinction of ranks, of which, although few may be in possession, all enjoy the advantages. Hence, again, you will observe the good nature with which he seems always to make sport with the passions and follies of a mob, as with an irrational animal. He is never angry with it, but hugely content with holding up its absurdities to its face; and sometimes you may trace a tone of almost affectionate superiority, something like that in which a father speaks of the rogueries of a child. See the good-humoured way in which he describes Stephano passing from the most licentious freedom to absolute despotism over Trinculo and Caliban. The truth is, Shakspeare's characters are all *genera* intensely individualized; the results of meditation, of which observation supplied the drapery and the colours necessary to combine them with each other. He had virtually surveyed all the great component powers and impulses of human nature, – had seen that their different combinations and subordinations were in fact the individualizers of men, and showed how their harmony was produced by reciprocal disproportions of excess or deficiency. The language in which these truths are expressed was not drawn from any set fashion, but from the profoundest depths of his moral being, and is therefore for all ages.

Samuel Taylor Coleridge
Literary Remains, Vol. II (1836)

THE INFANCY OF OPERA

DURING the infancy of the opera, says Rousseau, its inventors trying to elude the most natural effects arising from the union of poetry and Music by their imitations of human life, transported the scene into heaven and hell; and being unable to express the language and passions of men, chose rather to make divinities and demons sing than heroes and shepherds. Hence magic and every thing marvellous became the most essential parts of the Lyric theatre; and content with superiority in this particular, they never enquired into its propriety. To support such fantastic illusions, it was necessary to exhaust all that human invention could furnish most seducing among a people whose taste for pleasure and the fine arts was indulged by every possible degree of refinement. Theatres were erected throughout Italy which equalled in magnitude the palaces of kings, and in elegance the monuments of antiquity with which that country abounded. It was there, in order to ornament these theatres, that the art of perspective and decoration was invented. Artists of all kinds strained every nerve to display their talents. Machines the most ingenious, flights the most daring, with tempests, thunder, lightning, and all the delusions of the magic wand, were practised to fascinate the eye, while innumerable voices and instruments astonished the ear.

But with so many means of surprise, the action always remained cold, and the situations uninteresting; as there was no plot or intrigue but what was easily solved by the assistance of some divinity, the spectator, who knew the poet's power of extricating his heroes and heroines from all kinds of difficulty and danger, reposed such entire confidence in him as to remain tranquil during the most perilous situations. Hence, though the apparatus was great, the effect was small, as the imitations were always clumsy and imperfect; for actions out of nature interest us but little, and the senses are never much affected by illusions in which the heart has nothing to do; so that, upon the whole, it is hardly possible to fatigue an assembly at a greater expence.

This spectacle, imperfect as it was, remained long the admiration of the public, who knew no better. They felicitated themselves on the discovery of so admirable a species of representation, in which a new principle was added to those of Aristotle; for wonder is here added to terror and pity. They did not see that this apparent fertility was in reality but a sign of indigence, like the flowers blended with the corn, which render the fields so gay before harvest. It was for want of a power to move and affect, that they wished to surprise; and this pretended admiration was in fact so childish, that they ought to have blushed at it. A false air of magnificence, Fairyism, and inchantment, imposed on the public, and inclined them to speak with enthusiasm and respect of a theatre which was a disgrace to reason and good taste.

Though the authors of the first operas had hardly any other idea than to dazzle the eyes and stun the ears, it was hardly possible for the musician not to endeavour, sometimes, to express the sentiments interspersed through the poem. The songs of nymphs, the hymns of priests, the din of war, and infernal screams, did not so entirely occupy these coarse dramas, but that he sometimes discovered those interesting moments of situation when the audience was disposed to give way to feeling. And it was soon found, that independent of musical declamation or recitative, a peculiar movement, harmony, or melody, on some occasions, was necessary; and that Music, though it had hitherto only affected the sense, was capable of reaching the heart. Melody, which at first was only separated from poetry through necessity, availing itself of its independence, aimed at beauties that were purely musical; harmony, discovered or perfected, furnished new resources of pathos and expression; and measure, freed from the slavery of syllables, and restraint of poetical rhythm, acquired a species of accent and cadence peculiar to itself.

Charles Burney

A General History of Music, from the Earliest Ages to the Present Period, Vol. IV (1789)

MRS SIDDONS

IT is out of our power to compare her with former celebrated and rival actresses whom we have never seen; but if any of them excelled her in certain characters, the public must form to itself a nobler idea of a stage than any which it is accustomed to entertain. Her *Queen Katharine, Constance,* and *Lady Macbeth* were almost perfect pieces of acting – the first perhaps completely perfect, though of a less striking nature than the others. The sleep-walking scene in the last has been much and deservedly admired; the deathlike stare of her countenance, while the body was in motion, was sublime; and the anxious whispering with which she made her exit, as if beckoning her husband to bed, took the audience along with her into the silent and dreaming horror of her retirement; but we know not whether in attempting a natural monotony of gesture she did not throw too great an air of indolence over the scene in general, and whether in particular the dribbling and domestic familiarity with which she poured the water on her hands and slid them over each other, was not even unnatural in a person so situated: we are aware that in every species of passion a sublime effect is producible by the occasional mixture of every-day action with strong feeling; but in the instance before us the character is one of violence; and after a general wash of the hands, the poet seems to have marked out the single and decided action with which *Lady Macbeth* aims continually at the "damned *spot.*" Her finest passages in this character appear to have been those of the scene before the murder and the dismissal of the guests, the latter of which she performed with a finished royalty. The performance of *Constance* was unexceptionable; and here her lofty indignation came into play with all its nobleness in the scene with the Cardinal; her performance of this part also, the violence of which is such a provocation to the noise of inferior actresses, set a fine example of majestic excess, and was even clamorous without losing its dignity. But it was in *Queen Katharine* that this dignity was seen in all its perfection; never was lofty grief so equally kept up, never a good conscience so nobly prepared, never a dying hour so royal and so considerate to the last. That was a beautiful touch with which she used to have her chair and cushions changed, during the wearisome pain of her resting body! And her cheek too against the pillow! We could almost as soon forget the grand and melancholy composure of its parting despair as the gentler meekness of that of *Clarissa Harlowe* with the dying tinge in it – that dying cheek, virgin in spite of the despoiler. In considering these performances of her loftier tragedy, it will be found, we think, that, although there was no passion in the range of that loftiness which Mrs. Siddons could not finely portray, the predominant feature of her excellence, and that which gave a cast to its whole aspect, was a certain regality and conscious dignity, which exalted her powers in proportion to the rank and supposed consequence of her characters. What she failed in particularly was the meekness or humility opposed to this general feature, including every species of gentler tenderness, especially that of love. Her *Belvidera*, for instance, was excellent where she had to complain of wrong or to resent injustice, but little less than distasteful in the amatory part of it. This deficiency she partook with her brother John: but while she resembled him in this respect, as well as in the singular advantages of his person and the dignity of his aspect, she was in everything else as much his superior as nature is to art, or as a fine, unaffected, and deep-toned picture is to one full of hard outlines, stiff attitudes, and coldness of colour.

James Henry Leigh Hunt

The Examiner (5 July, 1812) from *Leigh Hunt's Dramatic Criticism*, edited by L. H. and C. W. Houtchens (1950)

The Scope of
Fiction and Drama Compared

OUR impression is that a careful examination of all that has been produced in either department, would terminate in perfect proof that there is no element of dramatic composition which may not be successfully employed in the romantic; but that the drama, being essentially a much more limited representation of life than the romance, many sources of interest are open to the latter from which the former is completely debarred. Indeed while it is easy to see that the drama takes in that only which may be embodied in the shape of action, and the dialogue of action, it seems to us to be altogether out of the question to limit in any manner whatever the dominion of the sister art. We may tell what has been done in it by the masters with whose works we are acquainted; but we have no belief that there is any element of interest in human life itself, which might not be brought into the service of the romance. And it is in this very width of range, this unrivalled and unlimited capacity, this perfect power of adaptation, that we recognize one main source of the modern superiority of the modern form over the antique. The older the world grows, we have no doubt the imagination of mankind will get more and more cold, or at least more and more fastidious; and as nature is the end of art as well as the beginning, we should not be surprized if, the habits of reflection widening along with those of reading, and gaining necessarily new strength and refinement with every step of extension, the result should be hereafter a triumph of the romantic form infinitely more striking even than has as yet been exhibited. In a word, we think that, as to materials, the empire of romance includes that of the drama, and includes therein perhaps its finest province; but that as to *art*, the department which has the more limited range of material is immeasurably the more difficult of the two. To a certain extent, perhaps, their relative situation may be compared to that in which sculpture and painting stand to each other. In one point of view, at least, painting includes the sister art – it includes all the dominion of *form*, although it cannot present form with the same bold and perfect projection of effect. In like manner, the romance includes action, and all the dialogue of action; and if it does not present these embodied in actual human organs, what it loses in that curtailment is more than made up for in the expanse of peculiar and unpartaken empire all around. The sculptor carves his group, and his art is at an end. The painter finishes his also, and if we cannot go round and round it, nor see it stand out from the canvass as if it were hewn from the rock, we have, to make us amends, tints and demi-tints, a fore-ground and a back-ground, and all the magic of the *chiaroscuro*.

John Gibson Lockhart
Review of Scott's *Lives of the Novelists* from the
Quarterly Review (September, 1826)

MRS RADCLIFFE'S ROMANCES

THE species of romance which Mrs. Radcliffe introduced bears nearly the same relation to the novel that the modern anomaly entitled a Melo-drame does to the proper drama. It does not appeal to the judgment by deep delineations of human feeling, or stir the passions by scenes of deep pathos, or awaken the fancy by tracing out, with spirit and vivacity, the lighter traces of life and manners, or excite mirth by strong representations of the ludicrous or humorous. In other words, it attains its interest neither by the path of comedy nor of tragedy; and yet it has, notwithstanding, a deep, decided, and powerful effect, gained by means independent of both –

by an appeal, in one word, to the passion of fear, whether excited by natural dangers, or by the suggestions of superstition. The force, therefore, of the production, lies in the delineation of external incident, while the characters of the agents, like the figures in many landscapes, are entirely subordinate to the scenes in which they are placed; and are only distinguished by such outlines as make them seem appropriate to the rocks and trees, which have been the artist's principal objects. The persons introduced, – and here also the correspondence holds betwixt the melodrame and such romances as *The Mysteries of Udolpho*, – bear the features, not of individuals, but of the class to which they belong. A dark and tyrannical count; an aged crone of a housekeeper, the depositary of many a family legend; a garrulous waiting-maid; a gay and light-hearted valet; a villain or two of all work; and a heroine, fulfilled with all perfections, and subjected to all manner of hazards, form the stock-in-trade of a romancer or a melo-dramatist; and if these personages be dressed in the proper costume, and converse in language sufficiently appropriate to their stations and qualities, it is not expected that the audience shall shake their sides at the humour of the dialogue, or weep over its pathos.

*

The materials of these celebrated romances, and the means employed in conducting the narrative, are all selected with a view to the author's primary object, of moving the reader by ideas of impending danger, hidden guilt, supernatural visitings, – by all that is terrible, in short, combined with much that is wonderful. For this purpose, her scenery is generally as gloomy as her tale, and her personages are those at whose frown that gloom grows darker. She has uniformly selected the south of Europe for her place of action, whose passions, like the weeds of the climate, are supposed to attain portentous growth under the fostering sun; which abounds with ruined monuments of antiquity, as well as the more massive remnants of the middle ages, and where feudal tyranny and catholic superstition still continue to exercise their sway over the slave and bigot, and to indulge to the haughty lord, or more haughty priest, that sort of despotic power, the exercise of which seldom fails to deprave the heart, and disorder the judgment. These circumstances are skilfully selected, to give probability to events which could not, without great violation of truth, be represented as having taken place in England. Yet, even with the allowances which we make for foreign minds and manners, the unterminating succession of misfortunes which press upon the heroine, strikes us as unnatural. She is continually struggling with the tide of adversity, and hurried downwards by its torrent; and if any more gay description is occasionally introduced, it is only as a contrast, not a relief, to the melancholy and gloomy tenor of the narrative.

In working upon the sensations of natural and superstitious fear, Mrs. Radcliffe has made much use of obscurity and suspense, the most fertile source, perhaps, of sublime emotion; for there are few dangers that do not become familiar to the firm mind, if they are presented to consideration as certainties, and in all their open and declared character, whilst, on the other hand, the bravest have shrunk from the dark and the doubtful. To break off the narrative, when it seemed at the point of becoming most interesting – to extinguish a lamp just when a parchment containing some hideous secret ought to have been read, to exhibit shadowy forms and half-heard sounds of woe, were resources which Mrs. Radcliffe has employed with more effect than any other writer of romance.

Sir Walter Scott

Prefatory Memoir to the novels of Mrs Ann Radcliffe in
Ballantyne's Novelist's Library, Vol. X (1824)

Sir Walter Scott

THE old world is to him a crowded map; the new one a dull, hateful blank. He dotes on all well-authenticated superstitions; he shudders at the shadow of innovation. His retentiveness of memory, his accumulated weight of interested prejudice or romantic association have overlaid his other faculties. The cells of his memory are vast, various, full even to bursting with life and motion; his speculative understanding is empty, flaccid, poor and dead. His mind receives and treasures up every thing brought to it by tradition or custom – it does not project itself beyond this into the world unknown, but mechanically shrinks back as from the edge of a precipice. The land of pure reason is to his apprehension like *Van Dieman's Land*; – barren, miserable, distant, a place of exile, the dreary abode of savages, convicts, and adventurers. Sir Walter would make a bad hand of a description of the *Millennium*, unless he could lay the scene in Scotland five hundred years ago, and then he would want facts and worm-eaten parchments to support his drooping style. Our historical novelist firmly thinks that nothing *is* but what *has been* – that the moral world stands still, as the material one was supposed to do of old – and that we can never get beyond the point where we actually are without utter destruction, though every thing changes and will change from what it was three hundred years ago to what it is now, – from what it is now to all that the bigoted admirer of the good old times most dreads and hates!

It is long since we read, and long since we thought of our author's poetry. It would probably have gone out of date with the immediate occasion, even if he himself had not contrived to banish it from our recollection. It is not to be denied that it had great merit, both of an obvious and intrinsic kind. It abounded in vivid descriptions, in spirited action, in smooth and flowing versification. But it wanted character. It was "poetry of no mark or likelihood." It slid out of the mind as soon as read, like a river; and would have been forgotten, but that the public curiosity was fed with ever new supplies from the same teeming liquid source. It is not every man that can write six quarto volumes in verse, that are caught up with avidity, even by fastidious judges. But what a difference between *their* popularity and that of the Scotch Novels! It is true, the public read and admired the *Lay of the last Minstrel*, *Marmion*, and so on, and each individual was contented to read and admire because the public did so: but with regard to the prose-works of the same (supposed) author, it is quite *another-guess* sort of thing. Here every one stands forward to applaud on his own ground, would be thought to go before the public opinion, is eager to extol his favourite characters louder, to understand them better than every body else, and has his own scale of comparative excellence for each work, supported by nothing but his own enthusiastic and fearless convictions. It must be amusing to the *Author of Waverley* to hear his readers and admirers (and are not these the same thing?) quarrelling which of his novels is the best, opposing character to character, quoting passage against passage, striving to surpass each other in the extravagance of their encomiums, and yet unable to settle the precedence, or to do the author's writings justice – so various, so equal, so transcendent are their merits!

William Hazlitt

The Spirit of the Age (1825). Text from the
revised second edition of the same year

JANE AUSTEN TO THE PRINCE REGENT'S LIBRARIAN

Dec. 11 (1815)

Dear Sir,

My "Emma" is now so near publication that I feel it right to assure you of my not having forgotten your kind recommendation of an early copy for Carlton House, and that I have Mr. Murray's promise of its being sent to His Royal Highness, under cover to you, three days previous to the work being really out. I must make use of this opportunity to thank you, dear Sir, for the very high praise you bestow on my other novels. I am too vain to wish to convince you that you have praised them beyond their merits. My greatest anxiety at present is that this fourth work should not disgrace what was good in the others. But on this point I will do myself the justice to declare that, whatever may be my wishes for its success, I am strongly haunted with the idea that to those readers who have preferred "Pride and Prejudice" it will appear inferior in wit, and to those who have preferred "Mansfield Park" inferior in good sense. Such as it is, however, I hope you will do me the favour of accepting a copy. Mr. Murray will have directions for sending one. I am quite honoured by your thinking me capable of drawing such a clergyman as you gave the sketch of in your note of Nov. 16th. But I assure you I am *not*. The comic part of the character I might be equal to, but not the good, the enthusiastic, the literary. Such a man's conversation must at times be on subjects of science and philosophy, of which I know nothing; or at least be occasionally abundant in quotations and allusions which a woman who, like me, knows only her own mother tongue, and has read little in that, would be totally without the power of giving. A classical education, or at any rate a very extensive acquaintance with English literature, ancient and modern, appears to me quite indispensable for the person who would do any justice

to your clergyman; and I think I may boast myself to be, with
all possible vanity, the most unlearned and uninformed female
who ever dared to be an authoress.

Believe me, dear Sir,

Your obliged and faithful hum^{bl} Ser^t.

Jane Austen

Text from James Edward Austen-Leigh's
Memoir of Jane Austen (1870)

Mr Cobbett's Opinions

MIGHT say that Mr. Cobbett is a very honest man, with a
total want of principle; and I might explain this paradox thus,
I mean that he is, I think, in downright earnest in what he says,
in the part he takes at the time; but in taking that part, he is
led entirely by headstrong obstinacy, caprice, novelty, pique
or personal motive of some sort, and not by a steadfast regard
for truth or habitual anxiety for what is right uppermost in
his mind. He is not a fee'd, time-serving, shuffling advocate
(no man could write as he does who did not believe himself
sincere) – but his understanding is the dupe and slave of his
momentary, violent, and irritable humours. He does not
adopt an opinion "deliberately or for money"; yet his conscience is at the mercy of the first provocation he receives, of
the first whim he takes in his head; he sees things through the
medium of heat and passion, not with reference to any general
principles, and his whole system of thinking is deranged by
the first object that strikes his fancy or sours his temper. – One
cause of this phenomenon is perhaps his want of a regular
education. He is a self-taught man, and has the faults as well as
excellences of that class of persons in their most striking and
glaring excess. It must be acknowledged that the Editor of
the Political Register (the *two-penny trash*, as it was called, till

a Bill passed the House to raise the price to sixpence) is not "the gentleman and scholar:" though he has qualities that, with a little better management, would be worth (to the public) both those titles. For want of knowing what has been discovered before him, he has not certain general landmarks to refer to, or a general standard of thought to apply to individual cases. He relies on his own acuteness and the immediate evidence, without being acquainted with the comparative anatomy or philosophical structure of opinion. He does not view things on a large scale or at the horizon (dim and airy enough perhaps); but as they affect himself, – close, palpable, tangible. Whatever he finds out is his own, and he only knows what he finds out. He is in the constant hurry and fever of gestation: his brain teems incessantly with some fresh project. Every new light is the birth of a new system, the dawn of a new world to him. He is continually outstripping and over-reaching himself. The last opinion is the only true one. He is wiser to-day than he was yesterday. Why should he not be wiser to-morrow than he was to-day? – Men of a learned education are not so sharp-witted as clever men without it; but they know the balance of the human intellect better: if they are more stupid, they are more steady; and are less liable to be led astray by their own sagacity and the overweening petulance of hard-earned and late-acquired wisdom. They do not fall in love with every meretricious extravagance at first sight, or mistake an old battered hypothesis for a vestal, because they are new to the ways of this old world. They do not seize upon it as a prize, but are safe from gross imposition by being as wise and no wiser than those who went before them.

Paine said on some occasion, "What I have written, I have written" – as rendering any farther declaration of his principles unnecessary. Not so Mr. Cobbett. What he has written is no rule to him what he is to write. He learns something every day, and every week he takes the field to maintain the opinions of the last six days against friend or foe. I doubt whether this outrageous inconsistency, this headstrong fickleness, this understood want of all rule and method, does not enable him to go on with the spirit, vigour, and variety that he does. He is not pledged to repeat himself. Every new Register is a kind of new Prospectus. He blesses himself from all ties and shackles on his understanding; he has no mortgages on his brain; his notions are free and unincumbered. If he was put in trammels, he might become a vile hack like so many more. But he gives himself "ample scope and verge enough." He takes both sides of a question, and maintains one as sturdily as the other. If nobody else can argue against him, he is a very good match for himself. He writes better in favour of reform than any body else; he used to write better against it. Wherever he is, there is the tug of war, the weight of the argument, the strength of abuse. He is not like a man in danger of being *bedrid* in his faculties – he tosses and tumbles about his unwieldy bulk, and when he is tired of lying on one side, relieves himself by turning on the other. His shifting his point of view from time to time not merely adds variety and greater comforts to his topics (so that the Political Register is an armoury and magazine for all the materials and weapons of political warfare), but it gives a greater zest and liveliness to his manner of treating them. Mr. Cobbett takes nothing for granted, as what he has proved before; he does not write a book of reference. We see his ideas in their first concoction, fermenting and overflowing with the ebullitions of a lively conception. We look on at the actual process, and are put in immediate possession of the grounds and materials on which he forms his sanguine, unsettled conclusions.

William Hazlitt

The Spirit of the Age (1825). Text from the
revised second edition of the same year

The Pictures at Petworth

I AM much interested with your account of the pictures at Petworth. I remember most of Turner's early works; amongst them was one of singular intricacy and beauty; it was a canal with numerous boats making thousands of beautiful shapes, and I think the most complete work of genius I ever saw. The Claude I well know; grand and solemn, but cold, dull and heavy; a picture of his old age. Claude's exhilaration and light departed from him when he was between fifty and sixty, and he then became a professor of the 'higher walks of art,' and fell in a great degree into the manner of the painters around him; so difficult it is to be natural, so easy to be superior in our own opinion. When we have the pleasure of being together at the National Gallery, I think I shall not find it difficult to illustrate these remarks, as Carr has sent a large picture of the latter description. Hobbema, if he misses colour, is very disagreeable, as he has neither shapes nor composition. Your mention of a solemn twilight by Gainsborough has awakened all my sympathy; do pray make me a sketch of it of some kind or other, if it is only a slight splash.

As to meeting you in these grand scenes, dear Leslie, remember the Great were not made for me, nor I for the Great; things are better as they are. My limited and abstracted art is to be found under every hedge and in every lane, and therefore nobody thinks it worth picking up; but I have my admirers, each of whom I consider an host.

John Constable

Letter to C. R. Leslie (14 January, 1832) from *Memoirs of the Life of John Constable* by C. R. Leslie (1843)

BIOGRAPHICAL NOTES

Austen, Jane (1775–1817). The outstanding novelist and satirist of the period. During the course of her uneventful provincial life she wrote, apart from juvenilia and fragments, *Sense and Sensibility* (1811), *Pride and Prejudice* (1813), *Mansfield Park* (1814), *Emma* (1816), *Persuasion* (1818), and *Northanger Abbey* (1818). There is an edition of her *Letters* by R. W. Chapman (revised 1952).

Bage, Robert (1728–1801). Paper-manufacturer and self-educated author; *Hermsprong* (1796), the last and best of his six novels, is the story of a 'natural man' without morals or religion.

Banim, Michael (1796–1874). Irish novelist; collaborated with his brother John (1798–1842) in writing some of the *Tales by the O'Hara Family* (1825). *The Croppy* (1828), which he acknowledged to be one of the novels which he wrote alone, paints a sombre picture of the rising of 1798.

Beckford, William (1759–1844). Travelled extensively in Europe, but from 1796 lived in seclusion at Fonthill Abbey, on the Gothic elaboration of which he spent a fortune. Best known for his extravagant oriental tale *Vathek* (English version, 1786). There is a modern edition of his *Travel Diaries* by G. Chapman (1928).

Bentham, Jeremy (1748–1832). Writer on jurisprudence. Principally remembered for his thoroughgoing application of the criterion of 'utility' to ethics and politics. His works include *A Fragment on Government* (1776) and *An Introduction to the Principles of Morals and Legislation* (1789). There is an engaging description of him in Hazlitt's *Spirit of the Age*.

Blake, William (1757–1827). Poet, painter and engraver; an isolated artist and visionary of genius, who thought in paradoxes and invented private mythologies. His few prose works include *The Marriage of Heaven and Hell* (*c.* 1790) and comments on Chaucer's pilgrims in *A Descriptive Catalogue of Pictures* (1809).

Brougham, Henry Peter, Baron Brougham and Vaux (1778–1868). Barrister, M.P., and law-reformer. His defence of Queen Caroline against charges of adultery made him a popular idol (1820). One of the founders of London University and Mechanics' Institutes. Published his very miscellaneous *Collected Works* (1855–61).

Burke, Edmund (1729–97). Statesman and orator. M.P. 1765–94. Held only minor office in short-lived administrations, but his eloquence, knowledge of politics, and passionate sympathies made him an outstanding figure. His works include *A Philosophical Enquiry into our Ideas of the Sublime and Beautiful* (1757), *Thoughts on the Cause of the Present Discontents* (1770), *Conciliation with the Colonies* (1775), and *Reflections on the Revolution in France* (1790).

Burney, Charles (1726–1814). Organist; friend of Burke, Johnson, Reynolds and Garrick. Travelled in Europe to collect material for his *History of Music* (1776–89) and published accounts of his tours.

Burney, Frances (1752–1840). Novelist daughter of Charles Burney. Held a tedious appointment at Court, from which she had difficulty in escaping, and eventually married General d'Arblay, a French refugee. *Evelina* (1778), which was deservedly successful, was followed by three further novels which declined progressively into unreadability. Her *Diary and Letters* were published 1842–46 and her *Early Diary* in 1889.

Burns, Robert (1759–96). Became an Edinburgh celebrity on the appearance of his first volume of poems (1786). Took an exciseman's place in 1789 to eke out his earnings as a farmer. His letters are disappointing: some have only a biographical interest, others are literary in the same way as his inferior poems. The standard edition is that by J. De L. Ferguson (1931).

Byng, John, fifth Viscount Torrington (1742–1813). Professional soldier and afterwards an official in the Inland Revenue. *The Torrington Diaries* (1934–8) are pleasant accounts of his tours in England and Wales.

Byron, George Gordon, sixth Baron Byron (1788–1824). Narrative poet, satirist and verse dramatist. His letters resemble his poetry in their harmless vanity and self-dramatisation; there are many lively passages, especially those describing his amours in Venice. The standard edition is that of R. E. Prothero (1898–1901).

Chalmers, Thomas (1780–1847). Scottish theologian; celebrated preacher and founder of the Free Church. Author of numerous works on natural theology and social economy.

Cobbett, William (1763–1835). Political journalist and farmer; cross-grained, over-emphatic and voluminous writer, but capable of a fine simplicity, especially in autobiographical passages. *Advice to Young Men* (1829) and *Rural Rides* (collected in 1830 from his *Political Register*) are accessible and well worth reading.

Coleridge, Samuel Taylor (1772–1834). Poet, critic, essayist, dramatist, translator, journalist, lecturer, theologian, metaphysician and talker; the key figure of English Romanticism. Prose works published during his lifetime include *Biographia Literaria* (1817), *The Friend* (1818), and *Aids to Reflection* (1825). Several volumes of prose remains have been published since his death and there are more to come; the general reader may find a selection such as that in Stephen Potter's verse and prose anthology (1933) the easiest approach to a daunting mass of material.

Colman, George, 'the Younger' (1762–1836). A prolific manufacturer of comedies who succeeded his father as manager of the Haymarket Theatre. His best known plays are *The Iron Chest* (first produced 1796), *The Heir at Law* (1797), and *John Bull* (1803). As official Examiner of Plays (from 1824) he was surprisingly puritanical.

Constable, John (1776–1837). Son of a Suffolk miller. His genius as a landscape painter met with little contemporary recognition. There is a good biography by C. R. Leslie (1843), which includes a number of his letters.

Cowper, William (1731–1800). Distinguished minor poet; was called to the bar but lived in retirement in the country because of recurring fits of insanity. His letters (of which there are several one-volume selections) resemble his poetry in their simplicity and in their occasional firm expression of his beliefs.

Creevey, Thomas (1768–1838). Barrister; Whig M.P. for two pocket boroughs in succession. High spirited gossip and popular guest of the great. *The Creevey Papers* (1903) consist of selections from his correspondence and diaries.

Darwin, Erasmus (1731–1802). Physician and naturalist; one of the most attractive personalities of the period. In *The Loves of the Plants* (1789) and *The Economy of Vegetation* (1791) he put Linnaean botany into fantastic verse with long and curious footnotes. In *Zoonomia* (1794–6), his principal prose work, he anticipated Lamarck's views on evolution.

Davy, Sir Humphry (1778–1829). Scientist who made important discoveries in chemistry and electricity, and a fashionable lecturer. Friend of Scott and Coleridge and had himself some literary ability. His works include *Elements of Chemical Philosophy* (1812), *Elements of Agricultural Chemistry* (1813) and *Salmonia, or Days of Fly-fishing* (1828).

De Quincey, Thomas (1785–1859). Essayist, critic and self-conscious stylist. Most of his works first published in periodicals; *Confessions of an English Opium Eater* (1821–22), *On the Knocking at the Gate in Macbeth* (1823) and *Recollections of the Lakes and the Lake Poets* (1834–39) are among the best known. (See Biographical Note, Vol V.)

Edgeworth, Maria (1767–1849). Irish novelist whose good-humoured and lively stories have an unobtrusive didactic purpose, as their titles often imply. *Castle Rackrent* (1800), *The Absentee* (1812) and *Ormond* (1817) can be recommended.

Erskine, Thomas, first Baron Erskine (1750–1823). Barrister who made an unrivalled reputation by his defence of Admiral Keppel and Lord George Gordon. His Radical sympathies induced him to defend Thomas Hardy and others in the treason trials of 1794, with equal success. His *Speeches* were published in 1810.

Farington, Joseph (1747–1821). Landscape painter and Royal Academy politician. His awkwardly written but valuable diary was found in a garret in 1921.

Ferrier, Susan Edmonstone (1782–1854). Author of *Marriage* (1818), *The Inheritance* (1824) and *Destiny* (1831); specialised in comic characterisation of Scottish gentry.

Fox, Charles James (1749–1806). Whig statesman; formidable opponent of North's government during the American War of Independence and later of Pitt's. Burke called him 'the greatest debater the world ever saw'. Only a few of his *Speeches in the House of Commons* (1815) are given in direct speech.

Galt, John (1779–1839). Author of many miscellaneous works but only his entertaining (and in parts sentimental) novels about Scottish provincial families are now read: *The Ayrshire Legatees* (1820), *Annals of the Parish* (1821) and *The Entail* (1823).

Gilpin, William (1724–1804). Hampshire vicar who published accounts of a series of tours made in search of 'picturesque beauty'. They include *Observations on the River Wye* (1782), *The Mountains and Lakes of Cumberland and Westmoreland* (1786) and *The Highlands of Scotland* (1789).

Godwin, William (1756–1836). Dissenting minister who turned atheist and idealistic Radical. *An Enquiry concerning Political Justice* (1793) was as effective at the intellectual level as Paine's *Rights of Man* at the popular. Other works include the doctrinaire novel *The Adventures of Caleb Williams* (1794) and *Memoirs* (1798) of his wife, Mary Wollstonecraft.

Greville, Charles Cavendish Fulke (1794–1865). Clerk to the Council 1821–59, a post which gave him facilities for studying Court life and politicians of both parties. *The Greville Memoirs* were published in three instalments, in 1874, 1885, and 1887.

Hallam, Henry (1777–1859). Whig historian. Occasional contributor to the *Edinburgh Review*. Wrote *A View of the State of Europe during the Middle Ages* (1818), *A Constitutional History of England* (1827), etc. Had nearly all the historian's virtues, but his prose is featureless.

Haydon, Benjamin Robert (1786–1846). Historical and religious painter who had much more enthusiasm than talent. One of the first to recognize the value of the Elgin marbles. His naïve *Autobiography and Journals* (1853) contain some vivid descriptions.

Hazlitt, William (1778–1830). Essayist, critic and lecturer. A member of the Wordsworth-Coleridge-Lamb group, but quarrelled with them all at various times. His most valuable work, *The Spirit of the Age* (1825), consists of portraits of contemporaries. Other works include *The Characters of Shakespeare's Plays* (1817), *Lectures on the English Poets* (1818) and *Table Talk* (1821–2).

Heber, Reginald (1783–1826). Bishop of Calcutta. Best known for his hymns 'From Greenland's Icy Mountains' and 'Holy, holy, holy'. *A Narrative of a Journey through the Upper Provinces of India* (1828) is a pleasant travel book.

Hogg, James (1770–1835). Scottish peasant-poet; wrote a number of prose tales, the best known of which, *The Private Memoirs and Confessions of a Justified Sinner* (1824) is a technically ambitious attempt at showing that a conviction of salvation may be the beginning of damnation.

Holcroft, Thomas (1745–1809). Dramatist, novelist and actor, friend of Paine and Godwin; tried for high treason in 1794. *The Road to Ruin* (1792) was his most successful play. His *Memoirs* (1816) contain some good passages, especially the account of his life as a Newmarket stable-boy.

Hunt, James Henry Leigh (1784–1859). Lightweight essayist, critic and poet who became a celebrity when he was imprisoned for a libel on the Prince Regent; friend of Keats and Shelley. His essays are best read in a modern selection.

Jeffrey, Francis, Lord Jeffrey (1773–1850). Scottish barrister and judge. Editor of the *Edinburgh Review*, 1803–29. As a reviewer he was free from malice but suspicious of innovations. Published his *Contributions to the Edinburgh Review* in 1844.

Keats, John (1795–1821). Published three volumes of poetry (1817, 1818, and 1820) in which he made astonishing progress towards maturity. His spontaneous and self-revealing letters are among the best in the language. The standard edition is by M. B. Forman (1931, fourth edition 1952).

Lackington, James (1746–1815). London bookseller whose shop was known as 'The Temple of the Muses'. He was inordinately proud of his business success. Published his *Memoirs* (1791) and *Confessions* (1804).

Lamb, Charles (1775–1834). Essayist and critic and, with the exception of Dr Johnson, the best known 'personality' in English literature. His works include *Tales from Shakespeare* (with Mary Lamb, 1807), *Specimens of the English Dramatic Poets contemporary with Shakespeare* (1808) and *Essays of Elia* (collected from the *London Magazine* in two volumes, 1823 and 1833). There is a modern edition of his letters by E. V. Lucas.

Lancaster, Joseph (1778–1838). Quaker educationalist; founder of the monitorial or mutual system which he described in *Improvements in Education* (1803).

Landor, Walter Savage (1775–1864). Wrote narrative poetry and verse drama but is remembered now for a few lyrics and *Imaginary Conversations* (published at various dates from 1824 onwards).

His resolute cultivation of the classical virtues made his prose artificial.

Lewis, Matthew Gregory (1775–1818). 'Good-hearted, lachrymose, clever little Mat,' friend of the Prince Regent, Scott and Byron. His terror novels, which include *The Monk* (1795), are much inferior to *The Journal of a West India Proprietor* (1834). He died of yellow fever contracted in Jamaica.

Lingard, John (1771–1851). Catholic priest; author of *The Antiquities of the Anglo-Saxon Church* (1806) and a judicious and soberly written *History of England* to 1688 (1819–30) which annoyed extreme Protestant and Catholic critics.

Lockhart, John Gibson (1794–1854). A savage reviewer for *Blackwood's Magazine* and afterwards editor of the *Quarterly Review*. His works include *Peter's Letters to his Kinsfolk* (a series of lively sketches of Edinburgh and Glasgow society, 1819), *Some Passages in the Life of Adam Blair* (a novel, 1822), and a fine life of his father-in-law, Sir Walter Scott (1837–8).

Macdonald, John (? – ?). A gentleman's servant who travelled with his employers in India, Spain and France; he seems to have deserved his nickname of 'Beau Macdonald'. There is a modern edition by J. Beresford of his *Travels in Various Parts*.

Mackintosh, Sir James (1765–1832). While a law student published *Vindiciae Gallicae* (1791) in reply to Burke's *Reflections on the French Revolution*, but was shortly converted to the latter's views. Knighted 1804 and held judicial appointments in India.

Malthus, Thomas Robert (1766–1834). Clergyman and political economist. His *Essay on the Principle of Population* (1798) aroused a storm of protest and provoked a score of replies. The revised second edition (1803) is inferior in style.

Marryat, Frederick (1792–1848). Naval officer turned novelist in the Smollett tradition; created some odd characters and wrote excellent descriptions of fighting at sea. *Peter Simple* (1834), *Jacob Faithful* (1834) and *Mr. Midshipman Easy* (1836) are among the best of his stories.

Maturin, Charles Robert (1782–1824). Dublin clergyman who wrote terror novels which equal those of Mrs Radcliffe and M. G. Lewis in extravagance but have an occasional gloomy power beyond the range of either. Only *Melmoth the Wanderer* (1820) is now read.

Mill, James (1773–1836). Political philosopher and economist; associate of Bentham and influential in the diffusion of utilitarian ideas. His *History of British India* (1818) earned him a high position with the East India Company. Other works include *Elements of Political Economy* (1821) and *An Analysis of the Phenomena of the Human Mind* (1829).

Mitford, Mary Russell (1787–1855). Wrote much miscellaneous work now forgotten. The sketches which were collected as *Our Village* (1824–32) were copied, she said, from 'nature and Miss Austen'.

Moore, Sir John (1761–1809). Commander-in-chief in the Peninsula; conducted the famous retreat to Coruña, where he was killed. His intelligence, sense of justice and professional zeal are apparent in his well-written *Diary* (1904).

Moore, Thomas (1779–1852). Dublin-born poet, biographer and musician. His superficial verse was very popular with his contemporaries. Published lives of Sheridan (1825), Byron (1830), and Lord Edward Fitzgerald (1831). His *Memoirs* (1853–6) are crowded with the names of celebrities and accounts of dinner parties.

Morier, James Justinian (1780?–1849). Diplomat and novelist; wrote informative travel books about Persia and the Near East and several novels. *The Adventures of Hajji Baba, of Ispahan* (1824) is the best of the latter; it was an amusing corrective to Romantic fancies about the East.

Paine, Thomas (1737–1809). Son of a Norfolk stay-maker; led an eventful life which included helping on the American side in the War of Independence and residence in France where he was elected to the National Convention and narrowly escaped the guillotine. *Rights of Man* (1791–92) and *The Age of Reason* (1793–1807) are able popularisations of current radicalism and deism respectively.

Paley, William (1743–1805). Lucid exponent of Anglican theology who was rewarded with ample preferment. *Principles of Moral and Political Philosophy* (1785) is the text-book of theological utilitarianism. In *Natural Theology* (1802) he found proof of the existence of God in the design apparent in nature and denied evolutionary adaptation.

Park, Mungo (1771–1806). Surgeon; published an account of his attempt to trace the course of the Niger in *Travels in the Interior of Africa* (1799). His second attempt to trace the river to its mouth, which was not then identified, resulted in his death. His *Journal* of this expedition appeared in 1815.

Peacock, Thomas Love (1785–1866). Novelist and minor poet; a classicist who ridiculed contemporary personalities and ideas, though not without Romantic notions of his own. His elegantly written novels consist of high-spirited discussions in a slight comic plot. They include *Headlong Hall* (1816), *Nightmare Abbey* (1818), and *Crotchet Castle* (1831).

Price, Sir Uvedale (1747–1829). Hereford landowner; his *Essay on the Picturesque, as Compared with the Sublime and the Beautiful* (1794), encouraged the fashionable cult of the picturesque.

Priestley, Joseph (1733–1804). Remembered as a pioneer in the chemistry of gases and one of the discoverers of oxygen; by profession a Unitarian minister and was engaged in sharp theological controversies. His collected *Theological and Miscellaneous Works* were published 1817–32.

Radcliffe, Ann (1764–1823). Popular writer of terror novels who had a good eye for wild scenery and ruins. Her works include *The Romance of the Forest* (1791), *The Mysteries of Udolpho* (1794), and *The Italian* (1797).

Robinson, Henry Crabb (1775–1867). Foreign correspondent of *The Times* and afterwards a barrister. Retired from practice with a competence in 1828. His *Diary, Reminiscences and Correspondence* (1869) is a well-written and useful source of information about his many literary friends.

Scott, Sir Walter (1771–1832). Edinburgh advocate; made a reputation as a narrative poet with *The Lay of the Last Minstrel* (1805), etc. and started on a new career as a novelist with *Waverley* (1814). The stories set in the recent Scottish past, notably *Guy Mannering* (1815), *The Antiquary* (1816), *Old Mortality* (1816) and *The Heart of Midlothian* (1818), are generally thought to be the most successful. *The Lives of the Novelists* (his prefaces to Ballantyne's Novelist's Library, collected in 1827) contains some good criticism.

Shelley, Mary Wollstonecraft (1797–1851). Daughter of William

Godwin and Mary Wollstonecraft and second wife of P. B. Shelley. Her only well-known work, *Frankenstein* (1818), is basically a terror novel, but its speculative and scientific curiosity is her own contribution.

Shelley, Percy Bysshe (1792–1822). Second-generation Romantic poet; wrote no extensive prose work. *Essays, Letters from Abroad, Translations and Fragments* (1840), includes *A Defence of Poetry* (1821) and his enthusiastic letters to T. L. Peacock describing Switzerland and Italy. The Godwinian notes to *Queen Mab* (1813) express his early left-wing views on marriage and religion.

Sheridan, Richard Brinsley (1751–1816). Dramatist and parliamentary orator; friend of C. J. Fox and the Prince Regent. *The Rivals* (first performed 1775), *The School for Scandal* (1777) and *The Critic* (1779) are among the very few good plays written in English between 1700 and 1900. His most celebrated speech was his indictment of Warren Hastings.

Smith, Sydney (1771–1845). Clergyman, wit, and co-founder of the *Edinburgh Review*. There are endless contemporary references to his drollery and he also had a reputation as preacher and reformer. His *Works* (1839) include contributions to the *Edinburgh Review*, *Peter Plymley's Letters* (first published 1807) and speeches in favour of the Reform Bill.

Southey, Robert (1774–1843). Miscellaneous prose writer and minor Lake Poet; led an uneventful life as overworked literary factotum, and produced a mass of historical and other works. His clear and unpretentious style can be seen at its best in *Letters from England* (1807), the *Life of Nelson* (1813) and the *Life of Wesley* (1820).

Stewart, Dugald (1753–1828). Professor of moral philosophy at Edinburgh; had a gift for clear exposition as lecturer and writer. His works include *Elements of the Philosophy of the Human Mind* (1792–1827) and *Outlines of Moral Philosophy* (1793).

Waterton, Charles (1782–1865). Eccentric Yorkshire squire and naturalist; travelled extensively in North and South America. *Wanderings in South America* (1825) contains the famous account of his ride on an alligator.

Wellesley, Arthur, first Duke of Wellington (1769–1852). Successful soldier and administrator in India; expelled French from Spain.

Turned to politics after the defeat of Napoleon and was twice Prime Minister. His *Dispatches* were published 1834-8.

Wilson, Harriette (1786-1846). Daughter of a Mayfair shopkeeper and mistress of Lord Craven, the Marquis of Lorne and several others. Thirty editions of her *Memoirs* were sold within a year of publication in 1825.

Windham, William (1750-1810). Statesman and friend of Johnson and Burke; Secretary-at-war under Pitt, 1794-1801. His denunciation of the Treaty of Amiens lost him the seat for Norwich which he had held for eighteen years. His *Speeches in Parliament* were published in 1812 and his *Diary* in 1866.

Wollstonecraft, Mary (1759-97). Schoolmistress, governess and publisher's assistant; was in Paris during the Terror. Lived with and eventually married William Godwin and died in giving birth to their daughter Mary. *A Vindication of the Rights of Woman* (1792) is her most important work.

Woodforde, James (1740-1803). Fellow of New College; held livings in Somerset and Norfolk. His *Diary* (1924-31) gives a vivid picture of life at Oxford and in the country.

Wordsworth, Dorothy (1771-1855). Sister and constant companion of William Wordsworth. He repeatedly acknowledged how much he owed as poet to her encouragement and to her sharp eye for beauty in common things. Her *Journals* should be read in the modern edition by E. de Selincourt (1941).

Wordsworth, William (1770-1850). The most important Romantic poet. Wrote carefully considered critical prose seen at its best in the revolutionary preface to *Lyrical Ballads* (1800). His tract on the Convention of Cintra (1809) and *Guide to the Lakes* (first published separately 1822) can also be recommended. There is a modern edition of his letters by E. de Selincourt (1935-9).

Young, Arthur (1741-1820). Agricultural theorist, unsuccessful farmer and an acute observer of society. Published several volumes of travel journals, of which the best known are the *Tour in Ireland* (1780) and *Travels in France* (1792).

INDEX OF AUTHORS

ACKNOWLEDGEMENTS

FOR permission to quote from their publications we are indebted to:

The Clarendon Press, publishers of *The Letters of Robert Burns* edited by J. De L. Ferguson; the Columbia University Press, publishers of *Leigh Hunt's Dramatic Criticism* edited by L. H. and C. W. Houtchens; Messrs Eyre & Spottiswoode (Publishers), Limited, publishers of *The Torrington Diaries* edited by C. B. Andrews; Messrs Hodder & Stoughton, Limited, publishers of *The Correspondence of William Cowper* edited by T. Wright; Messrs Hutchinson & Company (Publishers), Limited, publishers of *The Farington Diary* edited by J. Grieg; Messrs John Murray (Publishers), Limited, publishers of *The Creevey Papers* edited by Sir H. Maxwell; the Oxford University Press, publishers of *The Letters of John Keats* edited by M. B. Forman and of James Woodforde's *The Diary of a Country Parson* edited by J. Beresford.

SHELLEY

EDITED BY ISABEL QUIGLY

If it was Byron who caught his contemporaries' imagination as the epitome of the romantic poet, it is Shelley who, gradually through the years since their deaths, has come to assume that position for posterity. In Shelley we can find the full flavour and personality of his age – that stimulating period for English poetry during which the romantic movement received its first impetus. Because throughout his short and troubled life Shelley was almost continuously in the position of rebel and even outcast, we tend to think of his poetry, too, as iconoclastic and revolutionary; but in fact he was born into an already well-established romantic climate, and wrote in an atmosphere to some extent sympathetic to his genius and literary method. It is as a lyric poet that Shelley is remembered, a man who had supremely the gift of song. (D 29)

KEATS

EDITED BY J. E. MORPURGO

In his introduction to the Penguin *Keats* the Editor writes of the poet that 'all that matters of his work was produced in four years; in the first of those years he was struggling with his own technical and intellectual inexperience; for the last he was racing with death.'

Yet Keats stands among the very few who have understood and created the full measure of poetry, and almost everything of his mature achievement is printed in this volume, together with much of his early work. In his lifetime Keats met with much criticism but with some 'good success among literary people'. Since his death he has been granted the place that is his by right among the great of English literature. (D 23)

TWO BOOKS ABOUT BYRON

Peter Quennell has written two books on Byron, giving an accurate and striking portrait of our most romantic literary figure, depicted against the intellectual, social, and political background of the nineteenth century.

Byron: The Years of Fame

This book describes the period of Byron's life that began in 1811 with his return from the tour of the Near East and ended five years later when he left England for the last time. During this period *Childe Harold* appeared, ran through seven editions in five weeks, and Byron suddenly found himself famous and became the darling of society. But lameness, financial difficulties, and debauchery led to a storm of public hostility that drove him out of England. (982)

Byron in Italy

The story of strange adventures is continued. Its background is Switzerland and Italy during a period when Europe was war-weary but still beset by fears of revolution. Byron himself represented the spirit of change – wandering with his fantastic household through Italy and dabbling in the activities of the Italian Liberals. When he first left England he had been resigned to making a life of amusement, but a succession of disreputable love-affairs was replaced by a calm domestic relationship with the Countess Guiccioli. His decision to leave Italy for Greece was made in no light-hearted mood. He expected – perhaps he hoped – to meet his death there. (1057)